FASCIST
MODERNISM

FASCIST MODERNISM

Aesthetics, Politics, and the Avant-Garde

ANDREW HEWITT

Stanford University Press *Stanford, California*

Stanford University Press
Stanford, California
© 1993 by the Board of Trustees of the
Leland Stanford Junior University

Printed in the United States of America

CIP data are at the end of the book

For Tony
—and the boys!

Acknowledgments

I t is tempting, upon the publication of a first work, to assay the impossible: to thank everyone whose influence has in any way shaped one's thinking and development. I shall resist the temptation, for those people are too numerous. I trust that they shall take pleasure in the publication of this work, and hope they might find their thanks in its appearance.

To those who played a more direct role in the shaping of this book, however, I express my particular gratitude. Specifically, I would like to thank my colleagues and mentors at Cornell University, Jonathan Culler, Peter Hohendahl, and Sander Gilman. Though they will not recognize this book from the work I undertook with them during my time at Cornell, they should know that the interests informing it took shape during study with them. And for their continued interest and solicitude—above and beyond the call of duty!—I particularly thank Jonathan and Peter.

To my departmental colleagues at SUNY Buffalo—Rodolphe Gasché, Carol Jacobs, and Henry Sussman—I also owe a debt of gratitude for creating an atmosphere in which it would be impossible *not* to produce one's very best.

And to Matias—for your diligence—thanks.

Contents

FASCIST
MODERNISM

Introduction:
Why Fascist Modernism?

T he aim of this study is to understand just what in fascism proved so attractive and exciting to large sections of a literary generation—a generation broadly coextensive with the historical avant-garde. Rather than reading the political exploits of Ezra Pound, Gottfried Benn, or Filippo Tommaso Marinetti as unfortunate aberrations of purely biographical interest, I wish to examine the points of contiguity between a "progressive" aesthetic practice and a "reactionary" political ideology. In other words, while working with the "aestheticization" model, I hope to be a little more specific about the type of aesthetic that could result in this particular political position. Rather than simply hypostatizing or dehistoricizing the category of the aesthetic, I will seek to trace both the institutional and discursive developments that made an expansive aestheticization possible, and the specific aesthetic concerns of those who subsequently embraced various forms of fascism.

It is not and cannot be a question of stigmatizing "aesthetics" or championing "politics." Consequently, generalizable theses regarding the development of the aesthetic as an autonomous discourse had to be supplemented by substantive textual references.

This supplement seeks to render more concrete the ideological maneuvers all too often masked by the hypostatized entities of Art and Politics. By limiting my textual analyses to a closer consideration of Marinetti and his aesthetico-political context, I seek to overcome certain taxonomic difficulties. Clearly, any analysis of Fascist Modernism suggests two prior projects: an analysis of fascism and an analysis of modernism. In fact, the reference to modernism in my title is somewhat misleading, since I will insist—along with Peter Bürger, though I differ from him in my reasons for drawing the distinction[1]—on the necessity of differentiating between modernism and the avant-garde. It is as an exemplar of the avant-garde rather than of modernism that I will treat Marinetti. Consequently, I will be dealing with modernity only at a moment of rupture—the avant-garde—and reconstituting the concept of modernism largely from the perspective of the avant-garde. In speaking of Fascist Modernism, then, I aim to suggest that this ideological rupture made practicable a fascistic ideology consistent with an avant-garde aesthetic. I am not suggesting that the avant-garde and fascism were in any sense identical, nor (unlike Lukács) that they are related causally. The relationship is that of two contemporaneous responses to objective developments in the self-consciousness of modernity.

I will conclude by suggesting that the condition of what is rather loosely termed "postmodernity" is an attempt to revisit that rupture, to reassess issues that the theoretical reification of the avant-garde and the defeat of fascism had apparently laid to rest. It is no coincidence that thinkers such as Jean-François Lyotard should busy themselves at one and the same time with the possibilities of both an avant-garde aesthetic practice and a postfascist pragmatics,[2] or that Lyotard's essay "The Sublime and the Avant-Garde," for example, should veer abruptly into a consideration of the fascist spectacle. Without seeking to add fuel to the fire of the postmodernism debate, I read the terms of that debate very much within the parameters of both fascism and the avant-garde. Not only do these two historical phenomena provide a frame of reference for understanding postmodernism, but the debate itself replicates the ambiguous gestures of self-distantiation from modernism so familiar from both fascist politics and avant-garde aesthetics. Here, I seek only to lay bare the violence that the *postmodern* celebration of heterogeneity does to the concept of modernity. As Fredric Jameson has pointed out, in recent years the failure to define the postmodern as anything other than a heterogeneity defying definition has led theory toward a contrastive and overly homogenized model of modernity.[3] This study of Fascist Modernism seeks to undo that reification of modernity. What, then, will a study of Fascist Modernism tell us? Will we learn something about fascism by way of modernism, or something about modernism by way of fascism? It would be tempting to answer that both eventualities are equally possible and equally impossible— tempting but disingenuous. From an earlier stage of my research, I have at least learned something of the limitations that the study of Fascist Modernism imposes. Starting from a comparison of the works of Marinetti and the German Expressionist and subsequent Nazi Hanns Johst[4] I soon became uncomfortable with the idea of establishing a taxonomy of fascism on the basis of literary and cultural texts alone. More specifically, I became wary of any presumption that such a study might lead to the construction of a transhistorical or even transnational phenomenology of fascism. In short, while the paradigm within which I continue to work in my analysis of fascism—Walter Benjamin's analysis of the "aestheticization of political life"[5]—necessitates a close scrutiny of a certain aesthetic and aestheticizing ideology, any application of Benjamin's model without continued interreference to social and economic determinants must itself fall prey to a form of aestheticization. To analyze fascism as aestheticization smacks, in turn, of aestheticization, and the attempt to establish a universalizable model on the basis of literary production alone risks replicating at the level of theory the practice of aestheticization itself.

The concentration on Marinetti in this work, then, reflects that unease with any attempt to make global claims about fascism on the basis of a literary and cultural analysis. At the same time, however, it would be equally wrong to reify modernism by attempting to isolate elements within it which could be said to be "intrinsically" fascistic. Even if this were the objective, the argument might soon settle into the stale debate of pro- and anti-modernism, of so-called rationalism and irrationalism, politics and aesthetics. What I seek to trace in this work is a process of accommodation. If we accept that attempts to identify fascism with modernism, or to differentiate them in a radical sense, lead only to an oversimplification of both, then what we must attempt to uncover are the strategies by which modernists could make a home or niche for themselves within fascism. Throughout the work, I hypostatize and capitalize "Fascist Modernism" to mark it as a phenomenon produced as the result of a double reification.

To insist upon a margin of relativity in dealing with specific cultural artifacts and ideological structures is not, however, to reduce the question of Fascist Modernism to a disappointing noncommittal on the critic's part. Primarily, what an analysis of Fascist Modernism promises is a radically modified and expanded view of the ideological positions that both fascism and modernism can cover. My reading of Marinetti, for example, attempts to recapture the excitement that was fascism—not in order to reevaluate or revalorize the phenomenon, but in order to comprehend the sources of its energy. We must first desist from painting fascism as stasis, standardization, and regimentation if we are to unsettle our sense of having done with fascism. If anything, the experience of Marinetti's feverish, fervent protofascism should serve to remind us that our own repudiation of fascism (if I may assume this) is itself often grounded in a specifically modernist *aesthetic* judgment. If the rejection of fascism can only be legitimated by the consistent denigration of an ahistorically reified fascist aesthetic, if the project of cultural experimentation can be sustained only by a consistent expunging of figures such as Marinetti from the pages of literary history and critical theory, then I would contend that we are still far from having done with fascism. We merely replicate a form of aestheticization by grounding our political ethics on a judgment of aesthetic value: fascists were not only evil, it would seem—they also had no taste.

It is not, then, a question of recuperating fascism in the name of Marinetti's avant-garde project. Nor, on the other hand, can it be a question of consigning the fascist—Marinetti—to the regions of historical unreadability. In broader terms, we cannot conclude that the entire project of the avant-garde is necessarily fascistic, or that fascism is in some sense intrinsically avant-garde. The only way around the paradoxes of Fascist Modernism is to reevaluate and reconsider those loaded terms "fascism" and "modernism," "aesthetics" and "politics." The convergence of an avant-garde aesthetic and a fascist politics leads us to question the common terms within which political and aesthetic judgments are made.

Since the terms "avant-garde" and "fascist" are generally used with regard to the aesthetic and the political, respectively, we shall also theorize the ideological deformations that take place when material is translated from one discourse into another. As an institutional and discursive framework for the analysis of aestheticization in the genre-mixing writings of Marinetti, this is what I attempt in chapter 2, a prolonged excursus on aesthetic autonomy. It is not enough simply to insist that aesthetics and politics are indistinguishable; we must theorize the ways in which the political valency of the aesthetic is constituted precisely by virtue of its tendential exclusion from the realm of bourgeois politics. In other words, we must examine the extent to which the discursive organization of the bourgeois public sphere facilitates the coexistence of reactionary and progressive ideologies by distributing them across distinct fields of enunciation (namely, aesthetics and politics). If fascism is to be the aestheticization of political life, and if (as Bürger argues) the avant-garde is to be the reconciliation of art and life, then by what ideological process have these two apparently discrete spheres of art and life been constructed? Art and life must be examined not as given entities, but as discourses constituted precisely *in* the process of differentiation from each other. In examining Fascist Modernism we must examine the construction of the aesthetic as a category in order to understand the ideological labor performed by that category in the public sphere.

If such is to be our project, then the study of Fascist Mod-

ernism presents particular possibilities and particular problems. Stated plainly, the problem would consist in the attempt of the avant-garde to rearticulate the relationships pertaining between distinct discursive subsystems. Bürger has encapsulated—and, I think, oversimplified—the project of the avant-garde as an attempt to reconcile art and life. If we can accept, in the broadest of terms, this characterization of the avant-garde project, then the reconciliation of art and life threatens the division of aesthetics and politics and makes possible a greater flow of ideological material from one sphere into another. Although Bürger himself studiously avoids any confrontation with Fascist Modernists such as Marinetti, his model clearly provides for their emergence.

In Bürger's genealogy, the Aestheticists and Symbolists, isolated from the political realm, experience the aesthetic as an alternative; an alternative, that is, to the mundane concern with politics. Subsequently, however, this alternative begins to present itself as a *political* alternative, and a politics emerges that draws its strength directly from a lack of concern for traditional political pragmatics. The avant-garde—as that moment that seeks to reconcile art and life—would therefore necessarily run the risk of an aestheticization of politics, necessarily confront fascism as a political and aesthetic option. As I aim to demonstrate by a consideration of the politics of spectacle in the final chapter, however, this particular conjunction of aesthetics and politics is intrinsic (rather than inimical) to the very organization of the bourgeois public sphere. Fascist Modernism would merely offer the clearest articulation of that fact.

Thinking the avant-garde as a rupture with (or within) modernism serves also to illuminate some of the methodological principles used in this book. More specifically, the ambiguous status of socioeconomic determinants in my own analysis reflects what I take to be one of the fundamental ideological ruptures marking the emergence of Fascist Modernism. Bürger will write—with specific reference to the development of artistic technique—of the phenomenon of "full unfolding" (P. Bürger, *Theory*, p. 17), whereby the conditions of possibility of a specific historically constituted discourse become simultaneously present and possible. Thus, for example, what had been taken to be historically determined artistic techniques become available synchronously: Gothic, Romantic, Classical, and so on lose their value as historical periodizations and function (in the avant-garde) as alternative constructive possibilities in the present. In the course of this work I will problematize such an understanding of history, which though not teleological nevertheless articulates a systemic movement toward historical plenitude and presence. Nevertheless, I feel that it is within just such an ideology that the avant-garde sought to think its own relation to history. As the moment of full unfolding, the avant-garde, no less than fascism, could think itself as both the completion and the liquidation of historical sequentiality. If a modernist history promises such plenitude, it must nevertheless within its own progressive logic defer that moment. In making good on that promise, Fascist Modernism both realizes and de-realizes the modernist logic of history.

Realization would here mean the realization of a metaphysics of presence, which had served a merely ideological and legitimating function within the historical logic of full unfolding. Once reached, the goal (of full unfolding), which had served merely to demarcate the trajectory of progress, disorients and disempowers a progressive political project. This clearly poses problems of aesthetic and political legitimation in a postprogressive (postmodern?) age, and these problems will serve to frame my analysis. At the same time, however, the logic of full unfolding serves to de-realize precisely because it liquidates the historical present within the transcendental presence of History itself. The present becomes no more than one among many historical and stylistic possibilities, and thereby loses its determinant power. Bürger will analyze this phenomenon in terms of the absence of any avant-garde style, any technique that could mark it historically. However, as a mutation within a certain logic of history, this process of de-realization serves also to problematize the narratives of temporal causality around which our notions of the historical present cohere.

In other words, the liquidation of the concrete present within the simultaneity of a transcendental presence serves to actualize ideology, serves, one might say, to "stand Marx on his head." While it is important to keep some distance from this conception of history, it is also important to take seriously the crucial importance both fascism and the avant-garde would acquire within such a logic. Indeed, it is not altogether necessary to place oneself within this logic in order to observe in Fascist Modernism a historical redefinition of the relationship of base and superstructure—a redefinition not merely internal to that discourse, but which in fact makes that discourse possible. It is possible, that is, to analyze in socioeconomic terms the historical displacement of economic determinism's categories.

I would illustrate this historically determined and determining movement away from established narratives of historical causality by referring to Wilhelm Reich—one of the earliest analysts to take fascism seriously as a mass phenomenon.[6] Tracing the origins of fascism back to the lower middle class and the proletarianized petty bourgeoisie, Reich argues that "owing to its character structure, the middle class has a social power far in excess of its economic importance" (Reich, *Mass Psychology*, p. 44). The political emergence of the petty bourgeoisie, in other words, runs counter to its economic impoverishment and consists less in an arrogation of socioeconomic power than in an assertion of a specific "character structure." In other words, traditional models of hegemony are questioned by the recognition that political self-expression and ideological domination are not, in the case of fascism, the prerogative of an economically dominant class. This splitting of the political and the economic realms in fascism is of great importance. Once the hegemonic homology of ideology and economy is problematized, the aesthetic acquires a new determinant power in the vacuum created by a self-absenting monopoly capitalism.

No longer the prize of economic power, no longer simply a tool for the entrenchment of economic interests, aesthetic ideology now functions as a relatively autonomous locus of resistance and class *ressentiment*. This anti-economistic impulse in fascism can be understood in two ways. Subjectively, of course it reflects a class *ressentiment* that results in a hollow anticapitalist rhetoric: the lower middle classes reject capitalism because capitalism seems to have rejected them. As a class economically constituted by the process of impoverishment, the petty bourgeoisie denies the reality of class, and its "false consciousness" thereby acquires an objective historical legitimacy. Objectively, the hegemonic emergence of this class despite its economic enfeeblement does indeed mark a qualitative shift in the social dynamics of capitalism. Consequently, if fascism really does break with the economic rationality allowing Marxist cultural theory to assume the hegemonic equalization of social and political power, then it also demands a new interpretive paradigm. This paradigm will be sensitive to the material and economic conditions motivating the move beyond a strict materialist analysis, but will not seek to explain away that move with reference to those determinants.

Fascist Modernism, then, does not vitiate socioeconomic analysis, but it does necessitate a rethinking of the relationship of ideology and economy. This qualitative shift, moreover, is not without consequence for the aesthetic project of the avant-garde. Stated crudely, the historical displacement of any monodirectional base-superstructure causality will be reflected aesthetically in the avant-garde's movement beyond an aesthetic of referentiality. Once socially reflective narratives and mechanisms (such as the base-superstructure model) begin to lose explicative power, both the project of reflection and the aesthetics of mimesis seem increasingly impossible and untenable. In analyzing Fascist Modernism as a political and aesthetic response to a loss of faith in narratives of social and cultural reflection, however, we must live with the temporal paradoxes of what I have just asserted. The paradox lies in asserting that the end of reflection-theory is itself reflected. In the avant-garde the movement beyond a reflective understanding of the relationship of base and superstructure is itself paradoxically reflected in the movement beyond a reflective, mimetic aesthetic. The newly anachronistic categories retain an explicative value precisely because in the synchronic logic of full unfolding it is the category of anachronism itself that is most radically anachronistic. From what historical perspective is the end of history to be proclaimed? This is a question that presses upon us in our consideration of the avant-garde no less than it did upon Marinetti in his confrontation with modernism.

In speaking of Marinetti's relation to a certain socioeconomic history, then, I am not speaking of socioeconomic determinants, but of an ideological reconstruction of the history of capital. This subjective reworking, however, must be understood as itself a historically objective mode of consciousness: an ideology made possible by a potential dissociation of economic and ideological power. Rather than taking economics as the determinant of systems of representation, the avant-garde, for the first time, is capable of reading capital *as* a system of representation. That is, the avant-garde is capable of developing a poetics that examines and reformulates the ideological contradictions necessary to the functioning of an economic and linguistic economy. Thus, when Marinetti confronts modernism in the person of Mallarmé, he engages not in a system-immanent critique across stylistic borders but rather in a critique of the representational system that renders capitalism logical, and which capitalism in turn seeks to perpetuate.

In my analysis Marinetti is neither within capitalism as it developed historically nor outside or beyond it. Instead, he champions a radicalized, less "fixated" capitalism—of the sort sketched so dizzyingly in the Communist Manifesto—in which the inherent and violent contradictions of the system of commodity fetishism are allowed to play themselves out.[7] In the chapters dealing with Marinetti's characterization of his symbolist mentors as poets who attempt to reify and arrest the logic of capital, I aim to demonstrate the political shifts made possible by the avant-garde's rupture with modernism. As exemplified by Marinetti, Fascist Modernism feeds neither from the desire to regulate and administer the philosophical aporias of capital, nor from the desire to sublate them within a logic of progress that has already been invalidated. Fascist Modernism is the paralogism of capital.

Before outlining the direction my analysis will take in the pages to follow, I feel I should flag at least those aspects of Bürger's analysis that are of fundamental importance to my work. As I have already indicated, I do not seek to manipulate the historical paradigm of full unfolding as a value-free analytical tool, but to situate it in turn within the logic of rationality and rationalization that makes both fascism and the avant-garde thinkable in the first place.

Clearly, the element of Bürger's analysis most important to any consideration of Fascist Modernism is that reconciliation of art and life which he sees as fundamental to the avant-garde project. This reconciliation, however, will be overdetermined by the discursive reconciliation of aesthetics and politics. The question that must be faced with respect to Fascist Modernism, then, is the extent to which the aestheticization of politics can (as Benjamin proposed) be countered by a politicization of the aesthetic. For once the parameters for defining autonomous discursive subsystems have been questioned by the avant-garde, to what extent will it still prove possible to discern the contours of the dominant discourse? The necessity of posing this question alone legitimates placing Fascist Modernism at the very heart—rather than at the margins—of any consideration of the avant-garde.

On the one hand, then, Bürger's analysis naturally suggests affinities with the Benjaminian analysis of the aestheticization of politics and attempts, albeit unsuccessfully, to work through the avant-garde as a means of developing a counter-discourse through the politicization of aesthetics. At the same time, however, Bürger's formulation—despite a somewhat studious avoidance of the question of Fascist Modernism—suggests further parallels with analyses of fascism. For example, his notion of an aesthetic and stylistic "simultaneity of the radically disparate" (P. Bürger, *Theory*, p. 63) resulting from the process of full unfolding is reminiscent of Bloch's analysis of fascism in terms of objective social nonsynchronicities.[8] In his study, Bloch too seeks to examine the historical present for the elements of nonsimultaneity and anachronism inherent in it. Thus, for example, he examines the role of the peasantry or of the student population as incommensurate with any political analysis that would seek to totalize or homogenize the historical present. At the same time as I examine the development of the bourgeois public sphere as a synchronic system, then, I wish consistently to recall that the collapse of historical diachrony in the realm of the avant-garde aesthetic, as outlined by Bürger, is paralleled by similar nonsynchronous developments in other areas of the social and political sphere.

To observe this similarity, however, is not to assert the identity of the phenomena or any causality operating between them, and I should perhaps take this opportunity to elucidate the value I attach to such homologies, which occur and reoccur across the discursive boundaries of aesthetics and politics. On the one hand, we are observing a development within the aesthetic sphere that is replicated elsewhere. This might seem to give the aesthetic a certain paradigmatic or even causal importance I would not intend. For, on the other hand, the observation of a similar full unfolding in areas outside the limits of the aesthetic might also be taken to suggest that the development within the aesthetic merely reflects the broader development of the public and political sphere. This latter conclusion would be equally wrong. What I wish to observe by pointing out these intradiscursive homologies is the way in which the process of discursive differentiation—whereby, for example, aesthetics and politics begin to seal themselves off from each other—partakes of a broader logic of rationalization, which will be examined in the first chapter. To this extent the avant-garde will be read symptomatically, as a response to the rationalization of the public sphere.

At the same time, however, it is precisely in the aesthetic realm that certain developments in the theorization of discursive autonomy first become apparent and first acquire normative value. Thus, when we speak of the aestheticization of politics, what we are observing is the application of an aesthetic experience of full unfolding to the analysis of history. What Bürger fears is that the historical stasis implicit in his model of truth and presence as unfolding will serve to deprive narratives of progress and liberation of potential. But Marinetti, the Fascist Modernist, is himself equally suspicious of any such metaphysic. His protofascistic impulses derive from a desire to accelerate rather than halt the march of progress. Consequently, I will argue that Fascist Modernism cannot be reduced to the ideological instantiation of that moment of presence that the progressive model of history must invoke and continually defer.[9]

It is within the same logic of full unfolding that I situate the sociological model of rationalization that underpins the discursive arrangement of the bourgeois public sphere. It is as a scandal of that model that the avant-garde serves to deconstruct the logic of plenitude upon which (according to Bürger) it is itself grounded. The primary objective of this book is to manipulate the apparent scandal of Fascist Modernism in order to move the consideration of fascism's relationship to the broader progressive project of the Enlightenment beyond the simplified parameters of the rationalism-irrationalism debate. I wish neither to stigmatize aesthetic modernism with the charge of protofascistic irrationalism, nor to dignify fascism with the name of rationality. Instead, I think it is important to frame the question of rationality within the broader terms of an analysis of rationalization. If each discursive subsystem moves inevitably toward its own autonomous self-realization—if, in other words, full unfolding is the ground as well as the telos of discursive autonomy—then it must be in a paradoxical assertion of its own irreducible autonomy that each individual discourse rejoins the broader project of rationalization. In other words, the overarching logic of rationalization, the category holding it together, is the very process of differentiation itself. The full unfolding that seems necessary to the logic of each subsystem reveals itself to be a broader systematic imperative.

It is not surprising, then, that problems of aestheticization and politicization occur at precisely the moment when the distinction between the two discourses seems to have become most apparent: in the aesthetic sphere Bürger would identify this moment with Aestheticism. Paradoxically, the structural uniformity of social rationalization only becomes apparent when the individual autonomous discourses have been differentiated to where the process of differentiation is itself revealed as a source of commonality. In the excursus that constitutes the second chapter I will deal with this seeming paradox in terms outlined by Lukács in his earliest attempts to deal with Expressionism as a potential form of Fascist Modernism. These will be terms of fragmentation and totalization—terms necessarily questioning critical common-places about the cultural context of modernity. In short, it will prove necessary to read the experience of fragmentation—so often taken as central to the modernist style—as symptomatic of a more fundamental process of the totalization of capitalism beyond the limits of individual experience.

In the first chapter I begin by working through the structural and ideological presuppositions of existing theories of the avant-garde. It seems clear that the definition of the avant-garde with which we now work is to some extent the product of a post–World War II revisionism that has tended to formalize the terms within which we judge "progressive" aesthetic endeavor.[10] Rather than re-constructing the category of the avant-garde historically, however, I use this curious critical *Nachträglichkeit* to uncover the philo-sophical presuppositions of existing theories of the avant-garde in order to isolate the valorized polarities around which debate is still organized. Thus, for example, I concentrate on notions of time and space as categories that have traditionally allowed us to think progress and reaction in aesthetic terms. Likewise, I question the mobilization, in critiques of cultural modernity, of categories of reality and representation—categories to which the dubious and reified distinction of art and life can ultimately be traced. It is in problematizing the relationship of reality and representation that the avant-garde breaks with modernism. If (and I insist upon the doubt implicit in that "if") modernism risks reducing reality to text, ignoring the referent and celebrating the play of signification, then the avant-garde will insist upon the reality of the text, rather than upon the textuality of the real. Examining the possibilities of a mediating term—production—in rethinking the relationship of reality to representation, I seek to prepare the ground for the later examination of Marinetti's immanentist poetics of the manifesto.

The excursus on the autonomy of literature that follows this introductory chapter marks an attempt to work both with and against hypostatized entities such as "art" and "life" in the theorization of the avant-garde. While the categories may indeed be reified, they have their own history in the emergence of cultural modernism and their own ideological objectivity in the shaping of the avant-garde. In this chapter I also attempt to mark a shift in the legitimation strategy of aesthetic autonomy. Consequently, the main objective of this second chapter is to reformulate the question of rationalism and irrationalism within the parameters of a consideration of rationalization itself as a historical and social phenomenon. The legitimation crisis I identify will necessarily alter the way in which we think of fascism as aestheticization, since it results in a shift away from an aesthetics of compensation and false reconciliation. At the same time, however, there is in the logic of legitimation a renewed emphasis on models of representation and adequation, which were rapidly becoming anachronistic as aesthetic practice. Despite Bürger's assertion that we must "understand the history of art in bourgeois society as a history in whose course the divergence between institution and content is eliminated" (P. Bürger, *Theory*, p. 24), in Fascist Modernism institutional theory and discursive practice are at odds.

The third chapter, dealing primarily with questions of decadence, is a direct application of the hypotheses ventured thus far. If, as I have claimed, the avant-garde obliges us to rethink the utilization of time and space in the construction of historical narratives, how does it think the historical and geopolitical realities of its own era? What, for example, would be the terms in which it would confront questions of decadence in the concrete political context? Since, as Bürger has claimed, the avant-garde impulse emerges from the absolutism of aesthetic autonomy in aestheticism, how can the avant-garde position itself vis-à-vis the logic of temporal decline? What would a "postdecadent" aesthetic look like? And politically, in the period of imperialist expansion—much delayed in the Italian context—how does the avant-garde think its relation to the project of imperialism? It is in this chapter that I most consistently confront the implications of a historical full unfolding— a history, that is, in which such a stage is thinkable.

In the chapter on the politics of the manifest, I seek to undertake both a substantive examination of Marinetti's rejection of Mallarmé and his own symbolist past, and a structural analysis of the newfound importance of the manifesto form. Essentially, I will argue that Marinetti sees in Mallarmé the last vestiges both of a mimetic aesthetic and of a bastardized, self-stabilizing capitalism. What Marinetti offers, perhaps for the first time, is the crucial recognition that aesthetic theory must desist from its dualized opposition of the real and its representation, in order to recognize the reality of the text. It is one thing to recognize the semiotic structure of an economic system and quite another to analyze the economy of a semiotic. I seek to demonstrate Marinetti's divergence from Mallarmé primarily at the level of a poetics and a syntax, but by the end of the chapter I hope also to have outlined what looks like a new political configuration: a politics of the manifest, in which the play of signifiers has been displaced by the immanence of the referent in the movement toward a poetics of performance. But how radical (and such will be the question framing the final chapter) is this break with mimesis? To what extent does Marinetti reinscribe, in radical form, the metaphysics of presence he scoffs at in the impossible aspirations of modernism?

Of course, these are questions that must be framed by a consideration of the broader context of modernity, and in the fifth chapter, on the machine, I undertake such a consideration. At this point, after the consideration in the previous chapter of Marinetti's relation to capitalism, I work through modernization as a process of rationalization and technologization in which the key issue is the relationship of Man and Nature. Once again, I am examining the possibilities and limits of a hypostatized set of conceptual oppositions, and once again I am reading the avant-garde as an attempt to move beyond this dualism. In particular, I examine the sense in which, within Futurism, the body represents the locus of confrontation between nature and machine, and the ultimate harnessing of these two potentialities to capitalism's libidinal project of self-destruction. It is in this chapter that I will crystallize what I take to be the logic of aestheticization, the technology of its functioning, and the nature of the discursive ruptures it inaugurates. This is a rupture with—and a rupture within—the self-understanding and self-representation of capitalism.

If I begin with a consideration of theories of the avant-garde, to some extent I move in a full circle by finally confronting theories of postmodernity. It is perhaps no coincidence that theories of the avant-garde begin to be elaborated at precisely the moment when the first whisperings of postmodernism begin to make themselves heard. If anything, a reassessment of the cultural productions of the avant-garde serves to temper our attempts to ground the notion of postmodernity aesthetically. It is not my objective to condemn postmodernism on aesthetic grounds from the perspective of a critique of anachronism. Ironically, such charges would themselves be anachronistic in their fetishization of a progressive logic of temporality. Nor, indeed, is it a question of entering into the polemical framework of postmodernism itself. Instead, what I seek is to illustrate the way in which the avant-garde's insistence upon the theatricality of politics is reassessed and revised in thinkers such as Lyotard and Lacoue-Labarthe. More fundamentally, however, I seek to demonstrate the ways in which the theatricality of power, so often identified with the aestheticization of politics, is inscribed from the very outset in the bourgeois construction of the public sphere. Presenting itself as the essence of the political, fascism emerges—in fact—as its virtual form.

If such are my conclusions, and such the trajectory of my analysis, I feel compelled to close this introduction with an explanation of my starting point: Marinetti and the Italian Futurists.[11] In disavowing for my analysis any totalizing claims about the fascism inherent in modernism or the modernism inherent in fascism, I nevertheless claim a central paradigmatic value for Marinetti, a figure too consistently omitted from analyses of the avant-garde for that omission to be mere coincidence. Focusing upon Marinetti in the analysis of the avant-garde would be legitimate from a purely literary-historical perspective, so fundamental was he to the emergence of an avant-garde aesthetic that privileges performance over the finished art-object. Through his travels and endless proselytizing, the second-rate symbolist, surrounded by a coterie of largely derivative artists, nevertheless managed to maneuver Futurism to the center of the European cultural stage for several crucially important years. If only for the vehemence with which former admirers subsequently disavowed him, Marinetti must be seen as a seminal figure.

And if (as Poggioli insists in his *Theory of the Avant-Garde*) Marinetti's work was lacking in innovation, this "lack" surely marks precisely that paradigmatic shift that Bürger speaks of—the shift, that is, away from a historically legitimated aesthetic of innovation toward that avant-garde "simultaneity of the radically disparate." Marinetti effects a rupture—the avant-garde's break with modernism—that cannot be reinscribed within a modernist temporality of progress. In fact, his career might be said to telescope the historical deformations upon which Bürger grounds his theory of the avant-garde. Bürger, for the first time in the theorizing of the avant-garde, foregrounds Aestheticism as the movement out of and against which the avant-garde's desire to reconcile art and life develops. Marinetti is one of the few figures in whom this development can be traced biographically. He starts his career as a symbolist, moves into the futurist period, and delineates his aesthetic project in a direct attack on his former masters, the Symbolists, and through an analysis of Mallarmé's poetics.[12] By focusing upon Marinetti's confrontation with his own symbolist past, I seek to make clear the political considerations arising from the avant-garde's development out of the full unfolding of aesthetic autonomy in Aestheticism.

But I envisage more than a simple reconstruction of literary-historical precedents or a genealogy of the avant-garde. Why should Marinetti merit only one mention in Bürger's theory? Why should Poggioli persistently denigrate his work as "vulgar experimentalism, formless and imitative" (Poggioli, p. 137)? What model of modernity condemns Marinetti's "external and vulgar modernity, more of matter than of spirit, a modernism considered only as a snobbist variant of romantic 'local color' " (p. 220)? What is the connection between the apparently contradictory charges of vulgarity and snobbism? What is literary theory holding at bay when it rejects "the dross of that cheapened modernism which afflicted Western culture just before and after the First World War" (p. 220)? What is the force behind this rejection of "dross," of "the cheap"? What is the relationship of theories of the avant-garde to the consumer capitalism that historically marks both Marinetti and ourselves? These are the concerns motivating my own interest in the relationship of the avant-garde to the phenomenon of aestheticization, both in theory and in its historical practice.

CHAPTER I

Avant-Garde and Modernism:
A Theoretical Introduction

．

W hen, in 1962, Renato Poggioli embarked upon one
of the earliest attempts at a systematic theory of
the avant-garde, it had long been assumed that the artists of the
so-called avant-garde had been by and large politically inclined to
the left. By the 1960's, however, this assumption could no longer
be made so readily. The art of the historical avant-garde had long
since been commodified on the art markets where it commanded
huge prices, and the new generation of (neo-)avant-garde artists
were taking an enthusiastic and ambiguous interest in the mass-
production techniques of capitalism. Talk of the "crisis," or even of
the "death," of the avant-garde was in the air and Poggioli's work
was intended, to a certain degree, as a refutation of those fears.[1]
Indeed, crisis seems to determine the very existence of theories of
the avant-garde, right up to the most recent—and most convincing—*Theory of the Avant-Garde* of Peter Bürger, which likewise
positions itself as a response to the historical disappointment of
the postwar avant-garde.

　　The focus in the current work upon what has come to be called
the "historical" avant-garde should be understood as the reflection
of an interest in the historical legitimation strategies of modernity.

Insofar as the primary textual references will be to Marinetti as a paradigmatic and influential avant-garde figure, it is intended that the cultural and aesthetic analysis will be more readily generalizable across the field of Western modernism than will the more tentative political conclusions. In returning to this period, however, I wish to reevaluate the sense of crisis motivating theories of the avant-garde, and to understand that crisis not as a postwar historical contingency but as a categorical ambiguity of the avant-garde itself. I do not wish simply to refute the common alignment of aesthetic and political revolution, and I wish even less to defend it. Instead, I intend to take the avant-garde as a paradigmatic moment in the temporal self-understanding of western culture.

In the most basic terms, the avant-garde marked a shift not simply in our understanding of art or culture but in the broader episteme that alone makes categories such as "art" and "culture" thinkable. Thus, for example, while Bürger is doubtless correct in observing the desire of the avant-garde to reconcile art and life, the epistemic thrust of the avant-garde was such that neither art nor life can be thought in quite the same way as they might have been before that attempted reconciliation. The utopian projects of the avant-garde were oriented toward a re-invigoration of stale academic aesthetics, but also toward the aestheticization of life itself. And it is here that the question of fascism in its relationship to the avant-garde necessarily poses itself with the force of a categorical self-questioning rather than as a simple historical accident. If the period from 1910 to 1939 can be characterized as the period of the historical avant-garde, it must also be characterized as the period in which fascism emerged in its most fully developed forms.

Why? This, in a sense, is the question that frames the current study, that will lead to a consideration of both the political appeal of the avant-garde and the aesthetic appeal of fascism. The avant-garde was not simply political by analogy—"revolutionary" in the most banal sense of the word. Nor can the aesthetic appeal of fascism be explained away by means of analogy—by reference to its reliance upon falsely harmonious aesthetic models, refashioned from the ideological stock of the nineteenth-century bourgeoisie and offered as a political placebo or false reconciliation. What is the political experience of the avant-garde, and what the aesthetic experience of fascism? Better still: Can these experiences be differentiated in a period characterized by the attempt to reconcile art and life? Certainly, the ambiguities of such a reconciliation seem to have led at least one theorist—Bürger—toward a strategic and provisional rejection of the avant-garde project.[2]

At the level of artistic praxis, the crisis of the avant-garde resulted from the sheer exhaustion of formal innovation and the restitution of what Bürger refers to as the "work-character" of the avant-garde manifestation (P. Bürger, *Theory*, pp. 55–59). The self-surpassing of modernity became apparent in the almost paradoxical surpassing of "surpassing" and innovation themselves as aesthetic imperatives. At the level of both theory and discursive organization the crisis of the avant-garde takes the form of a dismay at the renewed dissociation of an autonomous and studiedly formal discourse of art from any recognizably political content. (And this despite the artists' rediscovery in the 1960's of the "everyday.") In both instances, however, the crisis seemed to revolve around the phenomenon of formalization, understood either as an examination of the real creative limitations of aesthetic material or as the sociological isolation of the aesthetic from social praxis. It is this notion of formalization that will prove central to my own analysis of the *historical* avant-garde (not just the postwar, or neo-avant-garde).

However, it involves a certain paradox to bewail the formalist isolation of art from life, given that formal specialization is itself the precondition of any autonomous discourse. Art would quite simply not be art if it were life—at least not in the sense that we understand art. Moreover, I do not wish to engage in fruitless and simplistic debates about the relative merits of form and content in art. This is not the essence of formalization either. Instead, I understand formalization as precisely that epistemic and sociological articulation that constitutes the bourgeois public sphere as a structure of relative discursive autonomies. When I speak of formalization in the context of the avant-garde, I speak of neither formal innovation or stagnation (which would re-inscribe the avant-garde within the parameters of a modernism to which the category of "the new" was still pertinent) [3] nor of art for art's sake (which is, nevertheless, most important for any understanding of the avant-garde).

Instead, it is a question of examining a broader ideological structure in which art—by defining itself autonomously—rejoins life in and of itself, insofar as life is thought in philosophical terms as the historical coming to consciousness of the parts through the totality. This model of historical consciousness, or full unfolding, is not offered arbitrarily as an interpretive paradigm, but rather as a reflection of a specific ideology, the ideology that subtends the bourgeois public sphere and makes comprehensible the twin phenomena of fascism and the avant-garde. In brief, the entirety of this study—beginning with the lengthy excursus making up the next chapter—offers an examination of the terms of a certain paradox: it is an attempt to understand how, the more art becomes art, the more it can seem to conjoin with life; and how both fascism and the avant-garde are alternative manifestations of that paradoxical conjunction.

The sense of crisis informing the theories of the avant-garde (a crisis all the more present for being in certain cases denied) is, of course, nothing new. It is indeed the historical *sine qua non* of the avant-garde itself; but the crisis is not simply an intra-aesthetic affair—not simply an exhaustion of aesthetic innovation. It finds its clearest expression in Benjamin's famous essay "The Work of Art in the Age of Mechanical Reproduction"—with specific reference not to the avant-garde, but to the rise of fascism. The question of the sublation of art and life is posed there quite clearly as a choice between the aestheticization of politics and the politicization of aesthetics. Since Benjamin's analysis of fascism as the aestheticization of political life will serve to structure the analysis of the current study, it is important to underline the strict parameters within which he offers the analysis, but which I, in turn, do not take as binding upon my own reworking of the problem.

If Benjamin implicitly articulates a crisis, he does so only to offer a solution: the rhetorical opposition of aestheticization of politics and politicization of aesthetics settles the question for him.[4] For my part, not only do I find it hard to keep to this opposition, but I also have grave doubts about the liberating value of the mass reproduction and de-auraticization of art celebrated in this essay. Benjamin's analysis is too constricting in two regards; first, while it sets out to portray the individual work of art's loss of aura, it does not seriously question the existence of a discourse called "art."[5] Indeed, the iconoclastic power of the gesture of de-auraticization itself requires some continued awareness of the discourse. By limiting his analysis (at this point) to the work and its production, he fails to articulate the fundamental, structural reorganization of discursive realms envisaged by the avant-garde and effected by fascism. Second, the model of aestheticization rests upon a stigmatization of fascism as (aesthetic) anachronism, as a false restoration of art's aura. As the analyses of fascism offered elsewhere by Benjamin tend to confirm, and as I shall examine in chapter 3, the aesthetic in the name of which politics is aestheticized is assumed to be decadent and reactionary. By "aestheticization" Benjamin means false reconciliation, the aesthetics of *schöner Schein* and illusion, the soporific aesthetic exemplified by Hitler's own tastes and the paraphernalia of Nazi kitsch.

There is, of course, ample historical legitimation for Benjamin's assessment—but the empirical evidence of the policy of fascist regimes toward culture and the arts should not lead us to accept this assessment as it stands. Is fascism reactionary because it aestheticizes politics, or because its own aesthetic sensibilities happen to be "reactionary"? To accept Benjamin's model of political aestheticization as an orientation toward aesthetic anachronism—and then to bolster this with a (selective) observation of subsequent empirical evidence—is surely to trivialize the more fundamental power of the argument. More than this, to posit political reaction on the basis of aesthetic reaction is, in fact, to fall prey to aestheticization oneself: to confuse, in turn, the political with the aesthetic. Perhaps it was Benjamin's own engagement with the avant-garde of his time that prevented him from examining more closely its implication in the process of aestheticization. But whatever Benjamin's reasons, it is nevertheless just as important to read fascism through the avant-garde as it is to investigate the avant-garde for vestiges of fascism. This is where theories of the avant-garde have consistently proved inadequate.

If one had to isolate one major weakness in the (Anglo-American) tradition of the critical treatment of modernism, it would be the acceptance of the synonymity of political and aesthetic progress. The crisis that motivated renewed interest in a theory of the avant-garde at precisely that historical juncture where an avant-garde praxis seems increasingly impossible is nothing less than the recognition of the nonalignment of political and aesthetic "progress." Poggioli's study was timely, then, in its claim that "the hypothesis (really only an analogy or symbol) that aesthetic radicalism and social radicalism, revolutionaries in art and revolutionaries in politics, are allied, which empirically seems valid, is theoretically and historically erroneous" (Poggioli, p. 95).

"Empirically," Poggioli concedes, the equation of aesthetic and political progress "seems valid"; but when he places the empirical in opposition not only to theory but to history itself, the meaning of his assertion becomes unclear. On the one hand, it would seem, the "empirical" evidence (i.e., the equivalence of political and aesthetic radicalism) cannot be understood historically; nor, on the other hand, is history itself to be understood strictly empirically. Even when, as here, it seeks to re-instate linear, progressive models of history, the theory of the avant-garde seems to necessitate a move beyond a simply empirical understanding of history. The avant-garde itself is more than a simple empirical historical event. It is as if history—in the avant-garde, and in its theorization— were being cleansed of its empirical nature, as if it were becoming, in some sense, purely historical.

By unwittingly uncoupling history from the empirical, Poggioli tacitly relies upon a discursive opposition of aesthetics and politics. For to characterize an action as "empirically" but not "historically" revolutionary is to posit a realm of the empirical existing outside history. This realm (such is the implication of Poggioli's analysis) would be the aesthetic; and thus Poggioli's unstated insistence upon an empirical yet ahistorically self-legitimating discourse serves to implicate him in the ideological tradition of aesthetic autonomy. Revolution in art is to the discourse of the aesthetic as revolution in politics is to the realm of the political. By rejecting the identity of the acts, by seeming to dismiss the coincidence of political and aesthetic as "only an analogy or symbol" Poggioli achieves two things. On the one hand, he inaugurates a new critical perspective on modernism in which the adjective "revolutionary" must be used more cautiously, but on the other he lends great weight to the system of analogy itself. It is the illusion of the analogy that guarantees the reality of discursive autonomy. A division of art and life must be assumed if their realignment by means of "analogy" is to be taken as the principle of the avant-garde.

The tradition in literary and cultural criticism that implicitly aligns categories of political and formal progressiveness culminates in the point where the political tendency of a given text can be measured in terms of its formal innovation. This critical assumption not only betrays a naïve faith in the monolinear and synchronized nature of historical progress across various social discourses, but also serves to depoliticize theories of modernism. Once political judgments can be displaced onto formal considerations—once a text can be called "progressive" by virtue of its formal qualities, and that judgment extended to its political aspects—the political itself becomes superfluous as a critical tool. The division of historical and formal readings of "modernism," "high modernism," or the "avant-garde" has tended not simply to depoliticize the object of study (the works themselves) but also to disguise the political implications of critical reading.

At the same time, however, we must beware of hurrying Poggioli toward a more radical formalism than he would wish to espouse. For we are still some way here from the assertion that formal structures might be politically coded *in and of themselves*. Even the reading of form as ideology—ushered in by readers substantially more critical of modernism, as we shall see—is itself ambiguous. If the "analogy" of political and aesthetic revolution tacitly assumes the autonomy of the aesthetic discourse, it nevertheless draws back from a reading of the specific text as a self-sustaining political economy. A more radical critique of form as ideology, however, must follow one of two routes: either it asserts just such an internal ideological economy of form, and thus positions itself as the apotheosis of formalism, as form's self-sublation into content; or it returns to the analysis of analogy. Such, at least, would seem to be the dilemma of a postformalist reading of modernism—a dilemma the avant-garde of Marinetti helps us resolve (or evade) by effecting a shift in reading paradigms.

To remain with Poggioli for the moment, it seems to me that his theory involves certain extremely important consequences. First, there is the implicit need to distinguish between the historical and the empirical. This recognition involves both a rereading of the modernist canon and a rethinking of the very temporality of modernity itself. The downside of the dissociation of the historical from the empirical is a somewhat willful historical revisionism on Poggioli's part; a revisionism in which Futurism, for example— the cornerstone of the current study and the most obvious threat to the political intentions of the theory of the avant-garde as practiced from Poggioli through Bürger—is consistently marginalized and denigrated. More fundamental to the current study, however, is the implicit recognition in Poggioli that with the avant-garde history ceases to function merely as a chronology, as an amalgam of empirical facts, and must be understood "theoretically." This is not, I will argue, simply a question of offering an *alternative* view of history, but rather the recognition of a paradigm shift that is itself historical. The avant-garde will come to stand for the empirical de-empiricizing of history, for the empirical "becoming-theory" of history.

But how, first of all, are we to understand the privileged insight that Poggioli's theory affords into the political machinations of canon formation? What political agenda, in other words, shapes our current understanding and definition of modernism? We must begin with the division—by means of that "analogy" which both conjoins and separates—of aesthetics and politics. Analogy is at once separation and conjunction of the political and the aesthetic, for it does not simply separate two purely distinct and autonomous discourses, but conjoins two entities that are always already marked by the separation, by analogy. Rather than the separation of aesthetics and politics, what this analogy produces is a politics of separation and an aesthetics of separation: two discourses marked by an originary rupture. The ground of the analogy linking the terms is, in fact, the symmetry of the separation: what the discourses have in common within the critical discourse is the mark of their separation from each other. Aesthetics and politics are *constituted*, rather than simply differentiated, by the act of separation.

This can be examined more concretely. On the one hand, Poggioli characterizes the avant-garde aesthetic as tendentially apolitical, but this apoliticism itself takes a political form. "The only omnipresent or recurring political ideology within the avant-garde," argues Poggioli, "is the least political or the most antipolitical of all: libertarianism and anarchism" (Poggioli, p. 97). Antipolitical positions—fundamental to the autonomy of the aesthetic—articulate themselves in a specific politics: the politics of "libertarianism and anarchism." Likewise, the political sphere within which such a culture can develop is characterized as a sphere predisposed toward the establishing of discursive autonomy. The antipolitical politics of the avant-garde are matched by a quite specific political and social formation. "Such considerations," observes Poggioli of his own work, "lead to the reaffirmation that avant-garde art can exist only in the type of society that is liberal-democratic from the political point of view, bourgeois-capitalistic from the socio-economic point of view" (Poggioli, p. 106). As a structure, "bourgeois capitalist liberal democracy" seems to maximize the proliferation of autonomous discourses under a principle of nondetermination. Ideologically, it seems (at least to Poggioli) to isolate no dominant principle of control.

The relationship of nondetermination that Poggioli seems to have in mind describes very well the analogous relation between aesthetics and politics, which has traditionally justified the assumption that political and aesthetic progress go hand in hand without either term impinging upon the other. More concretely, Poggioli's analysis of "the rapport between avant-gardism and the capitalist bourgeoisie" (Poggioli, p. 94) culminates in this critique of totalitarianism: "The avant-garde, like any culture, can only flower in a climate where political liberty triumphs, even if it often assumes a hostile pose toward democratic and liberal society. Avant-garde art is by nature incapable of surviving not only the persecution, but even the protection or the official patronage of a totalitarian state and a collective society, whereas the hostility of public opinion can be useful to it" (Poggioli, p. 95). The avant-garde emerges as the product of a kind of free-market aesthetics. It is important to locate the antitotalitarianism of Poggioli's aesthetic historically, for it is symptomatic of the political environment in which our own notions of aesthetic modernity have been formed. The formalization of the avant-garde—and the canonization of figures such as Joyce, Proust, Mondrian, Dali, Klee, and Schönberg—is a relatively recent phenomenon, which owes more to the cultural politics of the Cold War than it does to the history of modernism in the first third of this century.[6] It is in this tradition that Poggioli's analysis should be read. A modernism that takes as its point of reference the movement toward abstraction in the visual arts and toward linguistic experiment in literature is a modernism defined in formal terms, which can be developed only within a specific autonomous discursive configuration—the bourgeois public sphere. Antitotalitarian models such as Poggioli's serve equally effectively as a critique of "reactionary" socialist realism as they do as a critique of fascist neoclassicism. "Progressive" form and the tendency to abstraction as the primary criteria for the establishing of a modernist canon serve a specific and historically located political function. It is not only a question of the political environment favoring an avant-garde aesthetic but also of the critical reaffirmation of that environment through the construction of formalist aesthetic criteria.

If it is possible to read theories of the avant-garde within such a political framework, however, it is also possible to isolate in them a moment of crisis in the ideological self-understanding of liberalism. Poggioli's antitotalitarian aesthetic has some disturbing features—disturbing, that is, for the very liberalism from which they seem to emerge. For in the avant-garde we have on the one hand an apoliticism bodied forth as "libertarianism and anarchism" and on the other hand this aesthetic is framed at the level of social structures by the politics of "bourgeois-capitalist liberal democracy." What we seem to be left with is an uneasy alliance of anarchism and bourgeois capitalism facilitated by an ambiguous affinity between the "liberal" and the "libertarian." Throughout this work I will build upon this apparent theoretical anomaly in order to argue that the avant-garde is constituted as a historical moment in which capitalism confronts its own anarchic impulses. The theorization of the avant-garde attests to a similar self-recognition.

While Poggioli's *Theory of the Avant-Garde* broke with criticism's previously unquestioning alignment of political and formal progressiveness, then, what it affirms is the happy coexistence of the avant-garde and capitalism. In recent years, theoretically informed criticism of modernism has built upon this important assertion from a critical perspective in order to develop an attack on cultural modernism. It is from this more recent tradition that a new ideological topos has emerged that inverts pre-Poggioli models of modernity; the study of what Jameson has called "the Modernist as Fascist."[7] It can certainly be argued with some force that the canon of Anglo-American modernism admits of little affiliation with a left-wing political project. From the fascism of Pound to the conservatism of Eliot, from Yeats's involvement in the nascent protofascist organizations in Ireland to Lewis's early enthusiasm for Hitler—the depoliticizing formalization of modernism within the English canon has certainly served to gloss over a rather consistent picture of political reaction.[8] The focus on Futurism in the current study is intended to problematize Jameson's observation that "the familiar split between avant-garde art and left-wing politics was not a universal, but merely a local, anglo-American phenomenon."[9] For while the continent did, indeed, produce a greater number of committed avant-garde artists of the left, it also produced its fair share of Fascist Modernists. If, then, the dissociation of the left from the avant-garde was "merely a local, anglo-American phenomenon," the same cannot be said of the more troubling collaboration of the avant-garde and the right. The move in critical writings away from the equation of aesthetic and political progressiveness toward a recognition of the more complex mediations governing the relationship of form and ideology has nevertheless failed to problematize sufficiently the very category of form itself. Jameson has gone further than most in the assertion that "the perfected poetic apparatus of high modernism represses History just as successfully as the perfected narrative apparatus of high realism did the random heterogeneity of the as yet uncentered subject." [10] His argument concludes that after a moment of "peculiar heterogeneity" in the work of Conrad, a movement toward the totalizing forms of high modernism results in an effacing of political referentiality. [11] It is this notion of "the repression of History" that has since become the battle-cry for a reexamination of the political affiliations of modernism. Based on the assumption that modernism's most salient formal feature is the privileging of space over time, more recent criticism has attempted, as Jameson does above, to see in that privileging a formal occultation of History. [12] Nevertheless, this particular attempt to reverse the assumptions of previous critical elisions of political into formal progressiveness itself takes root within formal categories that resemble the grounding terms of the liberal, formalist tradition. [13] Again, the assumption is that form and ideology necessarily coincide: the privileging of linear or metonymic structuring principles is equated with an introduction of the category of history into the work. Whereas the all-important analogy was between the valency of the aesthetic as *act* and the political ramifications of that act, now the analogy is internalized within the form of the work itself. The study of form as ideology is both the end and the absolute of formal criticism.

But what sort of theory, then—what sort of reading—can be sufficiently sensitive to the phenomenon of Fascist Modernism?

This theory cannot simply consist of a formal text-immanent criticism, for the formalization of the avant-garde, as I have argued above, is itself a historically specific phenomenon. At the level of theory, it is necessary that the very possibility of formal analysis be placed in a historical context.[14] The cognition of formal structures *as* formal structures already implies a process of distantiation from the ideological content of literature, a distantiation possible only within a specific historical context—for example, when formal elements are revealed as manipulative structural principles and lose their semblance of naturalness. Form, like ideology, is recognizable only as anachronism; thus formal readings necessarily articulate a historical relation to their object, even if that relationship is merely one of supersession.

There is, however, one obvious way to develop Jameson's critique without hypostatizing form as an ideologically generative category. The analysis of "the repression of History" is based upon the assumption that a progressive politics is possible only on the back of a linear or progressive view of social evolution. The non-spatial, or temporal, text articulates just such a notion, it is argued. By insisting upon the opening up of the closed formal economy to the heterogeneity of history, we have indeed moved beyond the simple elision of aesthetic into political revolution, but we have not fully escaped the realm of analogy. It seems that the temporality of the linear text must be understood as historical time by means of analogy, within a logic of the micro- and macrocosm. Or must it? Is there not, perhaps, a second way to build upon Jameson's analysis, a reading that would take account of the materiality—the reality—of aesthetic time? In such a reading, the temporal/spatial opposition would center around the question of the text's production of its own consumption in time. Literature would no longer exist within a temporality alien to history, but would itself be a specific experience and articulation of historical time. It would no longer be a question of high modernism *excluding* something ("repression"—to insist upon Jameson's term—is anything but exclusive). It would, rather, be a question of high modernism *using* time—the actual time of aesthetic consumption—as a constructive element in its own production.

This change in understanding makes room for a reading strategy that responds to the textual practice of the avant-garde itself. It involves a move beyond the traditional mimetic paradigm. More concisely, the question would no longer be: How does the micro-time of the aesthetic *represent* the macro-time of history? Instead, one would ask: What *happens* to time in the high modernist text, to that time which cannot be divided into the micro- and macro-, to the only time there is, to the time which is the time both of production and of consumption—in other words, to history? The type of reading that such a position encourages would be a "productive" reading—or alternatively, a reading *of* production. It would read the text as a process of production existing within reality, rather than as a signifying system situated outside reality by virtue of the very distantiation inherent in representation. This shift in reading paradigms is not simply a methodological modification, for it is around precisely this question of representation and production that the avant-garde defines itself in opposition to modernism. A thematization of these two types of textuality— text as production and text as representation—is, for example, at the very heart of Marinetti's project: in his work the machine is not simply topos but modality. Marinetti's texts are not just about machines, they *are* machines.

Reorienting the reading of avant-garde texts around the paradigm of production addresses several problems inherent in those readings in which politics and history figure as analogy. First, and most obviously, there is a problem in creating the temporal-spatial dichotomy in the first place. The opposition can be offered only somewhat schematically. However, if (as I have suggested) one takes time literally in one's understanding of form (rather than as a metaphor for a certain effect of the text) one need not be too embarrassed by the term "temporal form." Form, in this sense, would need to be understood dynamically. Second and more problematic is the political thrust of the prevailing opposition, namely the assumption that "progress"—itself an ambiguously spatio-temporal concept, like the *avant*-garde itself, which refuses to locate itself in the either/or of space and time—is possible only on the basis of a specifically temporal and linear understanding of history. Of course, the notion of linearity is itself borrowed from a spatial geometry, and the equation of temporal linearity with political progress has been questioned by critics who see in the privileging of the spatial a possibility for the emergence of new areas of political struggle in the redefinition of public and private. This possibility is marked institutionally by the expansion of a politicized discourse of culture into areas such as feminism, lesbian and gay studies, and African-American studies.[15] (Certain French feminists, for example, have been particularly concerned with developing what Luce Irigaray has referred to as an "architechtonics" that "confounds the linearity of an outline, the teleology of discourse, within which there is no possible place for the 'feminine,' except the traditional place of the repressed, the censured." Her argument that "we need to proceed in such a way that linear reading is no longer possible" offers but one example of the way in which the opposition of a "progressive" and a "repressive" discursive structure must be organized around coordinates other than the spatio-temporal.)[16]

The debate concerning the value of the terms "spatial" and "temporal" in a reading of literary texts—and the doubts as to whether the terms can ever be more than tropes—would be dreary indeed, were it not for the specific historical context in which the avant-garde emerges and reworks the opposed terms. Particularly with reference to the phenomenon of modernism—to the aesthetics of relativity, so to speak, to the art of a post-Newtonian era—the division of time and space in this fashion must surely be problematic. If anything, the texts Jameson deals with should be understood as confronting the scientific (and historically localizable) elision of time and space and the collapse of an ideological structure oriented around the opposition of these terms. Moreover, the valorization of the categories itself presents problems: Is time necessarily more progressive than space? Might there not be ways in which the paradigm of space—public space—could be reconfigured, could change its functions in a libertarian way?

In *The Emergence of Social Space*, for example, Kristin Ross has examined the emergence of a synthetic discourse of "spatial history" at precisely the moment when the avant-garde begins to collaborate in the political sphere. She comments here upon Brecht's reading of Rimbaud's "Bateau ivre" as a politicized narrative.

> At the same time that Brecht affirms the narrative, diachronic power of Rimbaud's verse, he is concerned with portraying historical development in terms of a massive, synchronic expansion or spatial movement: the late nineteenth-century European construction of Space *as* colonial space. In Brecht's statement Time and Space are not where they should be: history has gone spatial, and the lyric—that unique, evanescent, exceptional moment—tells a story. (Ross, pp. 75–76)

In other words, precisely in the case of the avant-garde it is important to orient criticism not in terms of the opposition of time and space, but rather around the problematization of those categories. There are also political reasons for reevaluating the category of space as something other than just a congealing of the temporal flow. The politicization of space within the discourse of colonialism and imperialism (examined in the third chapter with reference to Marinetti) would be just one of those reasons.

In fact, Ross herself works with an opposition of Mallarmé and Rimbaud in order to highlight the political implications of the concept of modernism in which our own critical, structural language is mired. Taking the Mallarméan text as emblematic of the modernist tradition, she argues that "instead of the Mallarméan problematic of signifier and signified—consider, for example, such spatial experiments as Mallarmé's typographical arrangements of words on a page in 'Un coup de dés'—Rimbaud's concern is with the referent" (Ross, p. 89). The Jamesonian "repression of History" now resurfaces as the occultation of the referent within the signifying process. It is argued that the synchronicity of the structuralist paradigm, like the spatiality of the high modernist text, lends itself to repression.

Ross's observations are well-taken, and the implications she draws for contemporary theory and its privileging of signification as the primary cognitive category are extremely important. By radicalizing Jameson's position into an epistemological critique of a certain structural form of reading, she tends to undermine the grounds on which a formal critique of a spatializing ideology would be possible. At the same time, however, the implicit valorization of time at the expense of space is retained: Rimbaud is praised for his historicization of space, while Mallarmé is criticized for spatializing the historical temporality of the referent. Though it is important to stress the way in which—particularly at this time—the category of space is imbued with the sense of history-in-the-making, the recognition of this fact cannot be confined to the literary tradition of Rimbaud and to the political tradition of the Commune. Marinetti also, as an avant-gardiste of the right—as a Fascist Modernist—is well aware of the fact. Even in this more nuanced form, the opposition of time and space will not afford a political taxonomy.

It is primarily in opposition to Mallarmé that Marinetti, the former Symbolist, sets himself up as an artist of the avant-garde. And yet, in spite of that opposition, Marinetti engages in precisely those typographical experiments that Ross takes to embody the dehistoricizing tendencies of literary and critical modernism. It is the attempt to reconcile this seeming paradox that leads me to question Ross's overcoding of politics and representation. For the mimetic project of Marinetti's work should not be restricted to the model of signification and representation. It insists, instead, upon a model of production, of reference: of reality and its generation. Rather than accepting that all reality is text and bemoaning the loss of the referent, Marinetti's writing demands that we stress the reality of all texts and the irrepressibility of the concrete text itself as referent. The shift from the reified dyadic sterility of signifier and signified leads, in the case of Marinetti, to a poetics of the performative, or indeed to performance itself. The futurist "text" *is* the performance. Such, it seems to me, is the key to a delineation of Futurism as avant-garde: rather than the modernist obsession with text, one finds instead the avant-garde's obsession with the real.

The inextricability of time and space in Marinetti's texts operates beyond the level of textual representation and enters (as in Rimbaud) the immediately political sphere. Whereas the opposition of time and space tends to characterize space as stasis, the apparently spatial typography of Marinetti is nevertheless process-oriented and productive—just as, indeed, the synchronicity of the Saussurean paradigm itself serves not to fix but to deny the stasis of all positive terms. More important, the implicit equation of space with inertia and time with action has very real political implications. Ross is quite right to observe that "the privileged and exclusive status of space as a natural referent corresponds to the needs of Western colonialism" (Ross, p. 87), for what is at stake in the historical moment of the avant-garde's emergence from modernism is the question of imperialism, of capitalism and its historical progress into the domain of the spatial.

The opposition of time and space forecloses at the level of theory the historical (temporal) becoming-space of history in the age of imperialism. This does not mean that historical progression has simply stagnated in the broad spatiality of empire, but rather that space itself has become dynamically, historically significant and can no longer be understood as self-contained and inert. It is this confusion and reevaluation of time and space in the avant-garde and in the politics of imperialism that will ground my consideration of the colonial impulse in Marinetti. "Time and Space," declaims Marinetti, as if foreseeing the terminological difficulties of the subsequent critical debate, "died yesterday" (Marinetti, *SW*, p. 41). For the Fascist Modernist space is effraction, production, and transgression.

In proposing an alternative model for reading the avant-garde text—a model of production suggested by the texts themselves—it is important also to differentiate the avant-garde from modernism. By concentrating in this work upon a literary tradition alien to the Anglo-American canon I wish also to overcome a terminological embarrassment to which the passages quoted from Jameson attest; namely the assumed interchangeability, within the critical community, of terms such as "modernism" or "high modernism" with the term "avant-garde." In English studies the differentiation of modernism from a specific avant-garde has not fully established itself.[17] Given the formal criteria generally taken as constitutive of modernism in the English context, the difficulty of sustaining such a division is not surprising. Once modernism is defined in terms of a tradition of innovation the specificity of the innovation itself becomes irrelevant within the broader tradition of infraction. As a continuous series of breaks, modernism as a critical category does not allow of any radical break *with* modernism which would not always already exemplify the very movement *of* modernity itself. Modernism becomes an all-enveloping category precisely insofar as it embraces everything which is not itself; that is, by virtue of its definition as a movement of self-negation or self-transcendence. The formalized definition of modernism enshrined in the Anglo-American canon leaves no place for the avant-garde.

In questioning the conflation of modernism and the avant-garde, I oppose also that strain of theory exemplified by Calinescu, which sees in the avant-garde a phenomenon differentiated from modernism only by virtue of its radicality. Calinescu's position is that "there is probably no single trait of the avant-garde in any of its historical metamorphoses that is not implied or even prefigured in the broader scope of modernity. There are, however, significant differences between the two movements. The avant-garde is in every respect more radical than modernity."[18] This necessarily subordinates the avant-garde to the trajectory of modernism. More radical than modernism, it is the modernism of modernism, so to speak, rather than a historically motivated break *with* modernism. The chapters to follow will insist upon the historical specificity of a cultural avant-garde that can be distinguished from a broader project of modernism. Moreover, the fact that the emergence of the avant-garde as the dominant group within the cultural sphere broadly coincides with the emergence of fascism as a political movement, and that the waning of the avant-garde is marked by the emergence of National Socialism as a world political force, is also taken as being of central importance. In positing modernity as the overarching problematic in terms of which both fascism and the avant-garde must be examined as responses within specific discursive fields, this book attempts to trace the common sources from which both phenomena draw, and the resolutions each offers to the inherent contradictions of modernity. In posing this issue, however, my analysis moves some way from the strict aesthetic division of modernism and avant-garde insisted upon by Bürger and questions the continuing critical validity of the categories he uses to assert that distinction.

I have already indicated what I take to be a central ideological division between modernism and the avant-garde in the cultural sphere—namely, the insistence in the former upon the textuality of the real, and in the latter upon the reality of the text. Retaining the critique of signification outlined by Ross, this shift might also be characterized as a move into a poetics of utterance and performance and away from a semiotic. The differentiation between modernism and avant-garde must itself be placed within the broader context of the cultural discourse in its relation to the social totality, however. This much, at least, must be retained from the theory of the avant-garde exemplified by both Poggioli and Calinescu. Calinescu's observation that "at some point during the first half of the nineteenth century an irreversible split occurred between modernity as a stage in the history of western civilization—a product of scientific and technological progress, of the industrial revolution, of the sweeping economic and social changes brought about by capitalism—and modernity as an aesthetic concept" (Calinescu, p. 41) has been reworked to both liberal and conservative ends. For Calinescu, the break within modernity as a unified sociocultural concept serves to place the artist necessarily on the side of resistance and opposition to capitalism. In Daniel Bell's analysis *The Cultural Contradictions of Capitalism*, meanwhile, the same break serves to isolate the cultural sphere as a contradictory and subversive moment operative within capitalism itself—as the sphere in which enjoyment and consumption are encouraged as necessary to the cycle of production, but also as the moment at which the very ethic of productivity itself is questioned.

Holding back, for the moment, from the futile impulse to take sides—"for" capital, "against" culture, or vice versa—I would simply like to note the way in which the constitutive nature of this break is underplayed in each of the theorists. This rupture within modernity does not mark a point at which "culture" breaks with "politics," a moment in which something which already exists re-defines its relation to something else which also already exists. It is, instead, the moment at which aesthetics and politics themselves become thinkable as autonomous discourses. Moreover, this dif-ferentiation and distancing between the political and the cultural spheres should not be thought of in terms of a rupture threat-ening the coherence of a more broadly defined modernity, but rather as an epiphenomenon of an essentially dis-ruptive moder-nity. Modernity *is* rupture; is the subject, rather than the object, of disruption. This rupture should be understood not as the collapse of a discursive structure, but as its precondition, as the precondi-tion of the relative autonomy of the bourgeois public sphere.

The semblance of rupture must be understood within a more complex process of totalization. At the level of the social, one might wish to invoke Max Weber's notion of rationalization as a process in which the processes of fragmentation and articulation of the totality are coextensive. In my work here, however, I wish to stress instead the philosophical implications of this interplay of fragmentation and totalization within the modernist discourse of rupture. In sketching out the emergence of the avant-garde within the realm of cultural discourse, I wish to invoke the category of formalization *not* as an unfortunate characteristic of a (decadent? depoliticized?) aesthetic, but as the principle of modernization itself, as the principle that ultimately reunites those differentiated spheres established by the internalized operation of formalization itself. As a way of rethinking totality, the category of formaliza-tion creates a new context for conceptualizing the relationship of aesthetics and politics. In a nutshell, the problem of theories of the avant-garde has been, all along, a problem of political para-digms. Modernity—at its virtual point, the point of its impossible completion—has always been thought in terms of totality and fragment, or (to use Poggioli's terms) as the struggle between totalitarianism and anarchy. Consequently, as a weapon against the forces of totalitarianism, fragmentation can be valorized in bourgeois theories of the avant-garde: liberalism finds an ally in anarchy.

From another perspective, analyses of "the repression of History" stigmatize the attempt to replace the totality of the historical process with the illusionary totality of the perfectly spatial work of art. Anarchy and totalitarianism, fragmentation and alienation should not, however, be thought as alternatives. This, if anything, seems to be the message of Fascist Modernism: totalization is necessarily a coexistence of totality and fragment; it is a totalized process of fragmentation and of the articulation of those fragments within an organized whole. Totalitarian bureaucracy, not a repressive authoritarianism, should be the model: totality as an organization, not as the simple self-identity of power.

The interplay of totalization and fragmentation within the logic of rationalization is fundamental to the historical self-understanding of modernity. Reinhart Koselleck, in an examination of the emergence of a discourse of modernity, has observed the ways in which the category of history itself serves to reunite fragment and whole by temporalizing and deferring the notion of totality. "Since the second half of the eighteenth century," he observes, "there have been a growing number of indications of a concept of a new age [*neue Zeit*] in the emphatic sense. Time is no longer simply the form in which all history plays itself out; it acquires a historical quality of its own. History no longer takes place in time, but by means of time. Time becomes dynamic, itself a force of history." [19] What he is describing is precisely that process of formalization and self-reflection, operative at the level of history, which takes place within the aesthetic discourse. In other words, the process of self-reflection and formalization that supposedly distances or alienates the modernist aesthetic discourse from the broader project of modernity is itself typical of that rationalizing modernity. Formalization as self-reflection and autonomy is, then, a unifying principle within modernity, rather than the source of fragmentation. By differentiating itself, the aesthetic discourse reenters a totality that is itself predicated upon the principle of differentiation. Discourse does not become modern or antimodern within the neutral parameters of its own autonomy; only in becoming autonomous does it become modern. The development of a notion of history that realizes itself *through* time, rather than just *in* time—in which the medium or form is transfigured into quality and concept—is mirrored in the self-reflexivity of the aesthetic subdiscourse upon its own formal medium. Thus the apparent isolation of art from life actually manifests a more general and paradigmatic historical reexamination of the principles of discursive legitimation and historical progress. Art reflects upon art as history reflects upon history.

As I have indicated, a sociological model for the understanding of this philosophical position might be sketched out around the Weberian notion of rationalization. All I wish to note here, however, is the way in which autonomy does not foreclose the possibility of social totality. As Koselleck implies, at a certain historical juncture—coextensive with the emergence of modernism in art and culminating, I would argue, in the avant-garde—history begins to reflect upon itself, to constitute itself as discourse. Consequently, the historical sublation of autonomous discursive fragments into a notion of history as totality—that is, the process of totalization—should not be thought as a movement out of discourse into the tyrannical self-identity of philosophized history, but rather as a passage *into* discourse, into the discursive praxis of history. Just as political options cannot be rigorously organized around the dichotomy of space and time, so it is necessary to locate political action beyond the partisanship of fragment and whole. A politics or theory of centralized action cannot foreclose the process of fragmentation, but neither can the championing of the fragment—be it the individual as fragment, the amorphous desire, or the unchained signifier—deny its own compatibility with totalitarian structures.

By placing the emergence of the avant-garde in the context of that more general process of historical self-reflexivity, it is to some extent possible to overcome the apparent dichotomy between those who see the avant-garde as an assertion of political and cultural solidarity and those who see it as a result of a radical dissociation of art and politics. The act of dissociation must be seen not only in terms of the specific social environment from which the avant-garde sought to dissociate itself (namely, the apparent entrenchment of bourgeois power in the latter part of the nineteenth century) but also in terms of that paradigm shift (outlined by Koselleck) whereby history becomes the material, rather than just the medium, of social progress. This shift allows us to view the process of rationalization and specialization not simply in terms of an ideological Taylorism, a division of ideological labor, but rather as an insistence upon the full articulation of discursive subsystems and their respective mediations as the prerequisite for any historical progress or for any progress *into* history. The discursive organization of modernity (as Poggioli observes approvingly) encourages a maximum of apparent discursive autonomy. What this means, in effect, is that the realization of modernity is at one with its liquidation, its totalization at one with its fragmentation. Modernity is entrenched as a central organizing principle only when it has apparently decentered any such central principle and disseminated power to the various autonomous discourses.

What does this mean for the traditional cultural model that takes modernity to consist in a tradition of innovation? The tradition of innovation entails a process of self-affirmation through self-negation. Progress is seen as the negation of what has gone before, and yet the repetition of the gesture of negation displays the complicity of the new with what has gone before. Within a modernity structured as the interplay of (discursive) fragment and (social) totality, however, the principle of negation as a temporal and progressive impetus has been spatialized and rendered structural. No longer must negation follow in historical sequence: negation is itself a structural principle, the modality of the relationship of discursive parts to each other and to the whole. Negation is a structural possibility—indeed, the structural precondition—of a modernity based on discursive autonomy, as well as being a historical eventuality. Consequently, progress and reaction cannot be thought simply as movements away from or closer to the self-fulfillment of modernity, but as contemporaneous but non-synchronous impulses within modernity itself.[20]

The problem, then, is this: How to think modernity, or modernization as a process, without thinking it purely in terms of time? One response might be to drop the terminology of modernity altogether, and indeed, the study of Fascist Modernism has led one critic to argue that "there is no such thing as modernity in general. There are only national societies, each of which becomes modern in its own fashion."[21] What can this mean? Jeffrey Herf (from whom this statement is taken) clearly wishes to move beyond Eurocentric or teleological models of modernization, but the statement involves a certain paradoxicality. If "modernity in general" is to be stripped of any meaning, then how is the adjective "modern" to retain the meaning necessary for the assertion that a society "becomes modern in its own fashion"? Modernity as something general is being explicitly rejected and yet implicitly retained. Rather than refuting Herf's position on the basis of this paradox, however, I take it to be indicative of the very process of modernization itself; of modernization, that is, as "formalization." Rather than seeing modernity as the development of a system "in its own fashion," one can make sense of this assertion only if one accepts that becoming modern and the discovery of one's "own fashion" are one and the same process. Such a formulation would provide a basis for the examination of Fascist Modernism by indicating a form of discursive eugenics in which both the political and the aesthetic discovery of "one's own fashion"—both nation and culture—are thought as coextensive.

In other words, there is no identity of the national society that is fulfilled in the process of modernization. Rather, it is a question of identity being constructed in the process of modernization as something originary. This I take to be another example of the process of formalization, whereby discursive subsystems, and even national societies, assert their autonomy only through a process of self-reflection. Moreover, Herf's model, reworked as a model of precisely that general modernity he wishes to refute, makes it easier to understand how and why the phenomena of fascism and National Socialism—the insistence upon a German *Sonderweg*, for example—are not altogether incompatible with the process of modernization and cannot simply be rejected as reactionary in terms of a teleological model of modernity.

The ramifications of the formalization model of modernization are great, and my ambitions for this introduction of the topic are somewhat more modest. So where does all of this leave us vis-à-vis the avant-garde? First, it seems that what is required is a model of institutional and discursive modernization, a model that accounts for historical progression in terms of its impact on the structure of the bourgeois public sphere and the relations existing between specific discourses within it: a model of dynamic synchronicity. This model should also take account of a division of the avant-garde and modernism, for even if the former is taken to be the completion or radicalization of the latter it is a completion as something entirely other than that which it completes. The essence of modernity as we have traditionally thought it is its incompletion, the impossibility of ruling out yet more radical negation, yet more startling innovation. A modernism that is somehow "completed" will be decidedly anti- or postmodern; it will be an avant-garde.

To end this introduction, however, I would like to point toward the ends and the end of this book, to the concerns underlying it, which resurface in the final chapter. The political implications of the transmutation of history in the era of the avant-garde must also impact upon my own theory. The attempt to address this problematic informs the final chapter of this study, in which I begin to deal with fascism, the avant-garde, and the postmodern. If it is no longer possible simply to rally forces around the banner of temporality, what theoretical and practical options are left? Certainly it is not enough to stigmatize spatialization as a willful antihistoricism on the part of aesthetes and theorists. At a certain historical point—that of the avant-garde—time seems to "go spatial." What we must attempt is not to reverse this process but to understand it, and to locate it historically (to use a spatial metaphor that may not be a metaphor). To what extent is it possible, then, to argue, along with Kristin Ross, that contemporary theory is caught in the same antihistorical, antireferential movement that characterizes the Anglo-American modernist canon? To argue that "Contemporary theory's canonization of Mallarmé and Saussure at the expense of Rimbaud goes hand in hand with the priority given epistemology and aesthetics over social thought and the celebration of a romantic 'politics' of textuality, that ludic counterlogic of semantic instability that characterizes much of French theory, and especially French theory readily imported in America, today" (Ross, p. 89). In the final chapter I take this observation seriously by examining the status of "postmodern" theory as a response not only to the aesthetic project of the avant-garde but to the political phenomenon of fascism.

That a confrontation with the avant-garde as well as with fascism should raise questions as to the legitimation of theory is, perhaps, apposite. For the avant-garde itself must be understood as part of a broader legitimation crisis. Throughout this chapter I have attempted to demonstrate the ways in which the avant-garde is not simply a historical event, but history *as* event, or an event that happens *to* history as well as *in* it. According to Bürger, the avant-garde liquidates the notion of historical style: "Through the avant-garde movements, the historical succession of techniques and styles has been transformed into a simultaneity of the radically disparate. The consequence is that no movement in the arts today can legitimately claim to be more historically advanced, as art, than any other" (Bürger, *Theory*, p. 63). All the formal possibilities of art hitherto thought of as historically contingent (and which had, in turn, been deployed sequentially in order to create an effect of history *within* the aesthetic realm itself) reveal themselves synchronically, as structural possibilities of the present. Style is dissociated from its historical specificity—but this dissociation itself is historically specific. With the avant-garde, western culture creates something it can no longer legitimate in its own terms. The intrinsic unity of production and legitimation within bourgeois capitalist ideology has been broken.

If there is to be one recurring theme throughout this study, it will be this notion of the "simultaneity of the radically disparate." For as a characterization of the avant-garde it also provides an important way of thinking political anachronism and the coexistence of progressive and reactionary social impulses in and around both fascism and the avant-garde. History has ceased, with the avant-garde, to function as a legitimating instance. One cannot simply return to a premodern linearity, either in theory or in aesthetic practice. The so-called repression of History has proven itself to be the last historically legitimated act, the last adequate response to a modernity in which art and politics become dissociated as cosequential narratives. Both politically and aesthetically, "progress" and "reaction" can no longer be fully disengaged as historical concepts. The stage is set for Fascist Modernism.

CHAPTER 2

Excursus on the Dialectic
of Autonomy and Rationalization:
History and Theory

I have attempted, in the previous chapter, to give some sense of the theoretical issues surrounding contemporary theories of the avant-garde. In the light of Poggioli's reconfiguration of history, theory, and the empirical, however, I have consciously avoided any attempt to reconstruct the avant-garde as a historical reality with antecedents and heirs. In returning, now, to some such contextualization of the avant-garde, my objective is to examine not the "historical" reality of the "empirical" avant-garde, but rather to trace the philosophical metadiscourse within which the historical and the empirical were thought in the nineteenth century from the perspective of an emerging avant-garde. Of course, to offer any such overview is necessarily to condense and schematize a heterogeneous and disparate body of thought.[1] But once again, my objective is less to do justice to the historical reality of a certain mass of thought than it is to enter into the discourse of aesthetic autonomy itself. For this reason, the current chapter will begin with a brief overview of trends that presaged the emergence of the avant-garde only to move onto a philosophical recontextualization of those developments in the latter part of the chapter.

While the avant-garde that we have come to identify with movements such as Futurism, Dada, Surrealism and Constructivism emerged from or fed upon the political and ideological tensions which sparked off World War I, it is obviously possible to trace its origins back to the nineteenth century and to a critical rupture in the relationship of the artist to society. In the previous chapter, I used the term "formalization" to characterize both a specific historical ideology—according to which discursive subsystems both attain autonomy and reintegrate themselves into the totality of the paradigm of self-reflection—and a certain revisionist postwar art criticism that has shaped our own view of modernism and of the avant-garde. Despite the suspicion that the formalization of the avant-garde was largely a product of postwar criticism, an examination of its origins in the nineteenth century shows that the critical division of formal and political aspects of the avant-garde has not been solely the product of revisionist literary histories. As an emergent phenomenon, the avant-garde itself also tended to such divisions. The coincidence of a movement toward a realization of full discursive autonomy (as a momentous cognitive rupture from the slow process of formal evolution) with a desire to extend this principle of self-reflection to the broader social realm is a constitutive element of the emergence of the avant-garde from a modernism that saw itself more in terms of evolution than revolution.

Although the use of the adjective "avant-garde" to describe purely formal characteristics of a work seems to point to a process of art becoming distinct from life, this movement toward a self-immanent autonomy in fact reflects that broader historical movement outlined in the previous chapter: a movement toward a qualitative rather than merely quantitative notion of historical time.[2] It is in terms of this drama of association and dissociation, acted out around the question of just *when* the political and the aesthetic avant-garde became uncoupled, that theories of the avant-garde are staged.

On the one hand, there is what might be called the "Lukácsian" interpretation of literary history;[3] namely, the assumption that up until the revolutionary year of 1848 literary producers were necessarily at the forefront of bourgeois historical progress and that subsequent to this their insistence upon merely formal innovation reflected a loss of faith in the historical mission of their class and an attempt to paper over the loss of impetus with an aesthetic of affirmative innovation. Others, such as Mario De Micheli, insist upon the vital links that existed between political and cultural avant-gardes even after the emergence of *l'art pour l'art* as a cultural force.[4] Thus, while De Micheli's parameters for periodization are in many senses "Lukácsian," he differs from Lukács in taking not the revolutions of 1848 but the abortive Paris Commune of 1871 as the final rupture of political and aesthetic modernism. In this he is in broad agreement with the analysis of Matei Calinescu, who situates the rupture in the decade of 1870–80. Poggioli, meanwhile, in his *Theory of the Avant-Garde*, cites *La Revue Indépendante* of 1880 as the final collaboration of political and aesthetic progressives in the nineteenth century (Poggioli, p. 11). The vital difference between such analyses and a standard Lukácsian analysis, then, is that while Lukács would place the bourgeois artist in a purely affirmative position after 1848, the assertion of a continued collaboration of cultural and political "progressives" after 1848 situates the artist (after the failure of a workers' uprising in 1871) in a position of opposition not to society in general, but rather to entrenched bourgeois values that had proved their resilience in the face of revolution. Thus De Micheli's analysis allows a much more positive evaluation of the isolationism of the proto-avant-garde of the late nineteenth century.

Consistent with De Micheli's analysis, the notion of the avant-garde as a cultural phenomenon capable of defining itself in immanent, formal terms does, in fact, first become common around 1870 in France.[5] That the use of the term in this sense coincides with the political upheavals of the Paris Commune is significant; the use of the term is surely ambiguous. On the one hand, the borrowing of the term indicates a collaboration of the political and the aesthetic, and yet this borrowing might on the other hand be read as a displacement. The term can be used with an aesthetic meaning precisely because the political usage of it begins to lose force. In other words, the emergence of the cultural avant-garde as a terminological commonplace results not simply from a political collaboration but, one might suspect, from the fundamental political *failure* necessitating that collaboration.

Just as our own revisionist literary histories tend to overlook the emergence of *Neue Sachlichkeit* and other directly political cultural movements that arose during the decline of the historical avant-garde, so histories of the nineteenth century (and theories of the avant-garde such as Bürger's) are all too ready to trace a continuum from the aestheticism of *l'art pour l'art* to the aestheticism of the decadents and *Jugendstil*, overlooking the collaboration of artists and revolutionaries in the midpart of the century. It is important to resist such a historical elision, and to insist upon the vitality of a politicized cultural sphere of a "middle period" in the nineteenth century, made up of movements caught between these two aestheticisms.[6] What is also important to note is that already in the early part of the nineteenth century the notion of a cultural avant-garde had begun to gain currency. In the writings of Saint-Simon and his followers, the metaphor of a cultural avant-garde had already been used in speaking of artists—albeit in a somewhat more functional and instrumentalized sense than we might accept today.[7] However, whether one wishes to stress the emergence of the term "avant-garde" in the early part of the century or its popularization toward the end of the century, it seems that one confronts the same phenomenon in both cases. For in both cases, the term seems to emerge outside the normal parameters of class analysis. In the first (Saint-Simonian) scenario, the term would reflect the emergence of a new leading "class" (or nonclass) of technocrats; in the second, it would result from the social alienation of cultural producers and the establishment of a form of *Lumpenproletariat* consisting of *déclassés* intellectuals.

I would argue, however, that it is not a question of the avant-garde defying traditional class analysis, but rather of its emergence from within that same sociological nexus in which class itself becomes scrambled in the period of high capitalism.

With the acceleration of social mobility enabled by the bourgeois revolutionization of the conditions of production, the possibility of orienting political affiliations around the poles of left and right is also problematized. Whereas Saint-Simon's notion of the cultural avant-garde privileged artists, the entrenchment of the avant-garde at the end of the century seems to result from the opposite phenomenon: from their social underemployment. It begins to look as though the nineteenth century either lionizes or marginalizes artists and the aesthetic sphere as a countervalue to the prevalent discourse of class. Saint-Simonian technocracy and the intellectual *Lumpenproletariat* seem equally fertile ground for the avant-garde. From an examination of this common pedigree, the question necessarily poses itself: Might not fascism, as a form of technocratic organization of the *Lumpenproletariat*, feed from ideological sources similar to those of the avant-garde?

Avant-garde: left or right? The historical provenance of the term itself from within the Saint-Simonian camp perhaps serves as an indication of its historical and political ambiguity in a way not entirely irrelevant to the phenomenon of Fascist Modernism. Is it possible that the historical origins of the avant-garde might provide a framework within which the subsequent collaboration of avant-garde artists with fascistic political movements would be more understandable? In the essay in which the term "avant-garde" (or "vanguard") is first used, for example—"The Artist, the Scientist, and the Industrial" of 1825—it is characterized thus:

> We—the artists—will be your vanguard. The power of the arts is in effect the most immediate and most rapid of all powers. We have all kinds of weapons. When we wish to spread new ideas among men, we inscribe them on marble or canvas; we popularise them in poetry and song; we use, in turn, the lyre or the tabor, the ode or the ballad, the story or the novel; the drama is open to us and through it, above all, we are able to exercise an electric and victorious influence. We address ourselves to man's imagination and sentiments; consequently, we are always bound to have the sharpest and most decisive effect. (Saint-Simon, p. 281)

It is important to bear in mind the particular configuration of forces in which the notion of a cultural avant-garde first emerges.

Though emanating from an early form of socialism, the artistic avant-garde also enters into a pact with the powers of science and industry. Far from advocating the primacy of the aesthetic as an autonomous realm of ideological production, moreover, Saint-Simon's use of the term "avant-garde" is essentially functional, and refers less to the social or ethical content of art than to its value as a means of popularizing ideas developed in the scientific or industrial spheres.

In this essay, the collaboration of art, science and industry is valorized: "Unity, the virtue and protector of the weak, is also one of the requirements of strength. . . . Let us combine our forces and mediocrity, which triumphs from our disunion, will be ashamed of its own feebleness, and will take its place beneath us, overshadowed by our peaceful power and our triple crown" (Saint-Simon, p. 281). The "triple crown" of the arts, science, and industry functions as something considerably more important than a mere metaphor in Saint-Simon's political thought. In fact, the alliance of these three forces characterizes the role that Saint-Simon sees them playing within his model of a redefined monarchy: "Our attachment to monarchy is sincere, and our system is entirely favourable to monarchy, since it would immediately place the throne on firm foundations and give it more complete stability than the armed forces of Europe could provide" (Saint-Simon, p. 285). The political credentials of the avant-garde, then, prove to be somewhat ambiguous when traced back to the nineteenth century. The antibourgeois thrust of the artist's rhetoric in this dialogue is tied to a notion of absolute centralized power embodied in the sovereign—a combination not entirely alien to twentieth-century fascist rhetoric.

In his essay "The Idea of Avant-Garde in Art and Politics," Donald D. Egbert concentrates upon the ambiguities of Saint-Simonism to account for the gradual splitting of the cultural avant-garde into two camps. On the one hand, there are those who—in the Saint-Simonian tradition—continue to view the role of the artist in the cause of social progress in purely functional terms. This, claims Egbert, would account for those politicized movements that formalistic histories of the avant-garde tend to overlook, as well as for a tradition of Marxist orthodoxy within certain strains of the avant-garde. On the other hand, there is an avant-garde tradition—a tradition that has since come to monopolize our understanding of the historical avant-garde—which, disenchanted with the reactionary social organization and centralization of the Saint-Simonian monarchy, gravitates toward a form of early anarchic socialism, epitomized by Fourier.

Egbert's analysis is valuable not only for its reconciliation of some of the conflicting models of the avant-garde, but also for the way in which it opens the door to an examination of the interaction between fascism and the avant-garde in the twentieth century. The isolation of an anarchic form of socialism (Egbert's Fourierist strand), from which will emerge both the avant-garde and fascism in the early part of this century, is a crucial commonplace in studies of Fascist Modernism, most notably in analyses of the collaboration of Mussolini and Marinetti in Italy in the years preceding the fascist regime.[8] The characterization of the avant-garde as a culture of the *"déclassés"* obviously suggests parallels with the emergence of fascism as a political expression of those same *déclassés*, otherwise disenfranchised in the division of power between industrialists and workers. Thus, one analyst of National Socialism has even gone so far as to see fascism and the creation of an antibourgeois ("avant-garde") subculture as parallel strategies of the lower middle class in the face of its social and political marginalization, arguing that

> the hypothesis seems to arise that the division between the educated and the uneducated may have developed in the nineteenth century into the true dividing line between the ruling oligarchy and its subjects. If this is true, subjects seeking emancipation had two ways to respond: either forming a subculture or resorting to barbarism. The first was the solution of the socialist labor movement; the second was the way of the Nazis, and it was the true revolutionary way.[9]

The problematic comparison being made here between National Socialism and the socialist labor movement might, with a minimum of modification, be extended to fascism and the subculture of the avant-garde. In this case, the relationship between the two phenomena would be one of alternativity: they would constitute two possible responses to one and the same sociopolitical problem: that of cultural literacy and political oligarchy.[10] However, the excessive claims made in the preceding passage as to the "revolutionary" nature of National Socialism (I would not refute its revolutionary nature, but I would not wish to measure it within the same parameters as the revolutionary praxis of the avant-garde) might serve as an indication of the need for some mediating category that would disrupt the simple transference of ideological material from one discursive realm to another. From Saint-Simon through to the historical avant-garde, what is at stake is not the political and ideological content of the discourse of art, but the political and ideological constitution of the discourse itself. What is at stake, in other words, is the "institution" of art.

As Bürger argues in *Theory of the Avant-Garde*, "works of art are not received as single entities, but within institutional frameworks and conditions that largely determine the function of the work" (P. Bürger, *Theory*, p. 12). This notion of the institution should be understood both materially and ideologically as referring to the "productive and distributive apparatus and also to the ideas about art that prevail at a given time and that determine the reception of works" (P. Bürger, *Theory*, p. 22). It is necessary for an understanding of the institution to study not only the relationship of art to life, of aesthetic to social praxis, but also the relationship of the discourse of the aesthetic to other discourses and, further still, to the legitimating metadiscourse framing it.[11] History becomes a problem of theory rather than of the empirical: a problem of the theory of the empirical, of the possibility of thinking specific phenomena in the generic sequentiality of history.

I do not wish to enter into the terminology of autonomy outlined in Bürger's theory, but for the purposes of this study, it will be necessary to reformulate a popularized understanding of the autonomous work of art.[12] In common usage, the term is often taken to denote a work of art free from the constraints of the marketplace: that is, "noncommercial" or even "high" art. In its most extreme forms, this concept of autonomy culminates in an aestheticist position of art for art's sake, or in an art which in some way thematizes its own opposition to the process of cultural commodification. This formulation of the concept of the autonomous work is the result of a process of vulgarization occurring throughout the nineteenth century, which is linked to a specific strategy for the legitimation of the notion of aesthetic autonomy.[13] I shall refer to this legitimation strategy as the "structural legitimation theory" because of the way in which it characterizes art in terms of its compensatory structural relationship to other social spheres. Its claim is that art either represents reality as it "should" be, or that it is in the realm of the aesthetic that certain human potentialities unacknowledged and suppressed in everyday life continue to have free play. Within such an understanding art first truly becomes "affirmative" (in Marcuse's sense)[14] by internalizing as a structuring ideological principle the claim to autonomy. Rather than using the status of autonomy as the basis for a critique at the level of content or form, such works would serve merely to celebrate the (false) autonomy of art as a social fact and thereby reconcile themselves with a reality in which the principle of autonomy is suppressed.

In modifying the popularized conception of the autonomy of the *work* in favor of a study of the autonomy of the *institution*—a modification that will in turn involve a revision of the legitimation strategy outlined above—it is nevertheless necessary to see the process of vulgarization as something more than a simple betrayal or obfuscation of the realities of aesthetic autonomy as it evolved from the period of the Enlightenment. The popularized or vulgarized form of autonomy represents the historical playing out of certain dialectical tensions within the original notion of autonomy itself. In its original form, the notion of the autonomy of art (as opposed to later ideologies of the autonomous *work* of art) offers a double dialectic. First, autonomy must be understood dialectically in terms of the definition it provides of the relationship of the cultural producer to the relations of production and exchange prevailing in bourgeois society; autonomy is the guarantee of art's exclusion from these relations and its critical attitude toward them. Second, autonomy entails a dialectic in the legitimation it offers for art as a discursive field among (or even above) others.

The popular notion of autonomous art as an art standing in opposition to the money-motive is, in fact, diametrically opposed to the historical conditions that rendered that ideology possible. The precondition for a form of art free from direct ideological control is a mechanism for the mediation of that control. In bourgeois society this mediation of power takes the form of the marketplace. Commercialization is the guarantor, rather than the opponent, of autonomous art. It is only from the eighteenth century on that literature as we would now understand it can be said to exist, for it is only at this point that the production of literary texts ceases to serve a purely representative function under the patronage of the court or the church and begins to offer an ostensibly depoliticized forum for a politically underrepresented bourgeoisie.[15] The dilemma of the eighteenth-century bourgeoisie, whose economic power was accompanied by political disenfranchisement, clearly favors the emergence of a politicized aesthetic discourse, for the power to buy guarantees the power to speak—through art. Autonomous art must be examined, then, as a function of commodification; and its autonomy must also be thought in *relation* to, not in *opposition* to the political. The popular notion of an ideologically unencumbered art is itself radically political; and where such a strategy might appear today to be a way of masking ideological concerns, in the context of eighteenth-century authoritarianism, the establishing of such a "neutral" discursive field was tendentially subversive.

The break with the dependence on a system of cultural patronage is possible only upon the assurance of alternative economic support to the new species of literary producer—and this assurance is found in the literary marketplace. It is important, however, in characterizing this shift in the economic basis of cultural production, to recognize that it is not simply a question of a new financial resource becoming available for the continuation of an existing mode of literary production. The change in economic structure both determines (by means of the economic control exercised through the marketplace) and reflects (in the sense that literature now stands in a new set of social relations) a new function for literary production. Just as one cannot speak of preautonomous art as an art "controlled" by the court or the specific system of patronage (since the representative and propagandistic needs of the feudal system generated for "literary" production a specific function from within its own machine of power), so it is important to realize that it is only when a change in the conceptualization and exercise of power allows for the mediation of social control through the marketplace that the instance of control itself as something extrinsic to the artistic process becomes thinkable. In externalizing from itself the moment of control and mediation (that is, in developing the vulgar notion of autonomy) bourgeois culture actually defines and specifies the very idea of control.

The autonomous work of art as it evolves in the bourgeois era necessarily defines itself in terms of a lack, or in terms of the relativity of its own autonomy. Only by consistently evoking and opposing the instance of control (in this case, money as the mediation of that control) can the autonomous discourse isolate and in some way externalize the idea of control from the terms of its own discourse. In order to circumscribe an "inside," a discursive field, it was necessary for early autonomous art to conceptualize an "outside," figured as money or the market. Consequently, the seeds of the subsequent vulgar notion of autonomy as freedom from financial control are sown in the real conditions determining autonomy. Thus the relationship of "actual" to "vulgar" aesthetic autonomy cannot be thought as a falling away from philosophical truth into political ideology.

The phenomenon of autonomous art is not, however, exhausted by reference simply to the material conditions of its possibility. It is necessary also to understand the ways in which art establishes itself as an autonomous, organized discourse within the discursive hierarchy of the bourgeois public sphere, which it helps to create. In this broader sense, autonomy must be understood as the demarcation and isolation of a set of practices as a coherent and recognizable ideological sphere, not only free from control by economically mediated social power but also independent of any other, overarching discourse. If the first dialectical moment of the autonomy aesthetic consists in the problematic nature of the relationship of the discourse to a social praxis defined by relationships of commodification and exchange, the second consists in the relationship of the aesthetic sphere to other discourses that also claim to exist outside those relationships.

One might refer to this problem as the relationship of autonomy to autonymy. Is a discourse that does not name itself as discourse truly autonomous? But then, if a discourse does bear within itself the principle of its own autonomy, can that autonomy be grounded, since it is legitimate only in terms of the discourse it attempts to establish? In one sense, a fully autonomous discourse can only be a discourse in which the claim to autonomy is in some way immanent, legitimated in terms of that discourse itself rather than by reference to an external legitimating principle to which, through the relationship of definition, it would necessarily be subjugated. It is just such a model of immanent autonomy that the nineteenth century begins to develop in that division of art and life emphasized by Bürger. In respect of its relationship to philosophy, however, the autonomy aesthetic developed at the end of the eighteenth century is clearly problematic. If capitalism provides the material preconditions for autonomous art, then it is the philosophical tradition of German Idealism that provides its ideological legitimation.[16] At the end of the eighteenth century the emerging literature is assigned a place within a discursive hierarchy regulated by the philosophy of Idealism. Thus, while art might be said to resist at the level of content capitalism's tendency toward economic rationalization, it can do so only within a prerationalized set of philosophical relationships. Contrary to its ideological status in the nineteenth century as an escape from ubiquitous social forces of rationalization, autonomous art is also a product of those forces.

Clearly, the legitimation of the autonomy of art in terms of a philosophical metadiscourse is at the root of the structural legitimation theory. It is the philosophical discourse that fixes, controls, and itself discourses upon the series of relationships that define art in terms of its opposition to the everyday. Thus, as discourse, art can be said to be external to the discursive practices structuring social existence only because, as object of the metadiscourse of philosophy, it can be described *in relation to* those other discourses. This difference, later ontologized in the practice of *l'art pour l'art*, is still defined in terms of a relativity within the philosophical meta-discourse. It is important, therefore, to hold onto the fundamental difference between the theory of discursive autonomy developed by Idealism (a theory that in its very metadiscursive legitimation of that autonomy entails a dialectical moment of self-negation) and the practice of aesthetic autonomy exemplified in *l'art pour l'art*. In the move from theory to practice, from discourse to work, from metadiscursive to immanent legitimation, there occurs a loss of the self-critical moment of the autonomy principle, and the pos-sibility of ideological manipulation presents itself. In describing the crisis of, or attack upon, autonomous art that manifests itself in the historical phenomenon of the avant-garde, it is important not to simplify the dialectic of autonomy as merely a question of the institutional relationship of art to life. The dialectic must also be viewed in the light of the prolonged struggle between the discourses of art and philosophy that occurred in the nineteenth century.

Indeed, the very opposition of the terms "art" and "life" is itself symptomatic of the historically specific set of discursive rela-tions established within a philosophy of consciousness. Within this model, the full articulation of artistic autonomy necessarily entails a self-sublation; for art, once it attains a state of self-consciousness, ascends to the status of philosophical truth. Built into this model of aesthetic autonomy, then, is a moment of self-negation that en-sures the primacy of the philosophical metadiscourse. The truth value of art—at least at this stage—is not a value intrinsic to the discourse *as* art, but rather a measure of art's potential for attain-ing a philosophical status as truth.[17] Within the epistemology of a philosophy of consciousness, the attaining of consciousness (in this case, through a full articulation of the structural possibilities of a discursive subsystem) is itself a historical moment; and since an art, which is in the vulgarized sense autonomous, supposedly stands outside the categories of history, the full articulation of the discursive autonomy of art necessarily goes beyond the realm of the aesthetic by reintegrating art and life as history. Thus the Idealist tradition allows both for the vulgarized absolutism of the autonomy aesthetic and for the ultimate subjugation of the aesthetic to philosophical categories.

It is tempting to oppose an original dialectical notion of autonomy and its subsequent nondialectical vulgarization in terms of a "true" and a "false" autonomy, but such an opposition serves only to ignore the inherent structural paradoxes of the dialectic, which renders possible as one of its consequences the undialectical autonomy principle.[18] Moreover, it was the so-called false autonomy developed in the course of the nineteenth century (but only really canonized at the end of that century) that served as the ideological background for literary producers in the early part of this century. Both the notion of a crisis of art and the attempt, in the form of the avant-garde, to go beyond the ideology of autonomy become explicable only when the historical restructuring of autonomy is made explicit. In fact, the early twentieth century marks not a "moving beyond" autonomy, but a reengagement in some of the paradoxes of the concept, which had been gradually ironed out in the preceding century.

The entrenchment of the autonomy aesthetic is, then, co-extensive with its vulgarization. What was once the precondition for the literary *institution*—an autonomy defined in relational terms and framed by a philosophical metadiscourse—becomes, in the course of the nineteenth century, an aesthetic imperative at the level of the work itself. "The division of art and life, which figures in Schiller as the definition of the status of art," argues Christa Bürger, "is interpreted in later vulgarized aesthetics as a direction for aesthetic production. The idealization of reality is demanded" (C. Bürger, p. 108). This model of autonomy already implies a shift from the level of discourse to the level of work, and in this privileging of the work itself marks the first step in a gradual distantiation of the autonomy principle from the philosophical metadiscourse. The vulgarization of the autonomy aesthetic therefore takes place at the cost of philosophy as a framing discourse. It is at the moment when autonomy no longer functions as the form of enunciation of a discourse, but rather as the object or content of that discourse (as exemplified in the development of the vulgarized autonomy aesthetic toward a self-referential *l'art pour l'art*) that art becomes affirmative. Or rather, art that was already affirmative in its structural function—as controlled medium of expression for residual needs—becomes thematically affirmative once it self-consciously rejects social norms. Autonomy, once "a critique and expression of alienation" (C. Bürger, p. 109), now becomes mere ideology.

The problem of affirmative art brings us to the question of legitimation. Recent critical attention paid to what I have termed the "structural legitimation strategy" (exemplified in the Frankfurt School critique of affirmative art) has tended to obscure a crucial paradigm shift occurring in twentieth-century theoretical legitimations of an autonomous literary discourse. If, in the era of the avant-garde, there is a legitimational crisis of sorts, it is not the structural legitimation theory but a second model that has failed. Let me outline briefly the two models I propose. On the one hand—in the structural legitimation model—art offers a refuge from an increasingly reified social sphere and encourages the development of faculties left untapped by a rationalized Lifeworld. In this form (as critiqued by Marcuse) cultural production becomes merely affirmational, despite its utopian value, insofar as it functionalizes art as a channelled expression for the repressed. This affirmational tendency is complete at the moment when art begins to thematize its opposition to a reified Lifeworld merely as a means of perpetuating its own existence. Art becomes affirmational only by taking real discontents and offering ideological gratification, thereby serving a real social function. The energies tapped by art are real life-energies, while the expression these energies find remains ideological, not because of the nature of the aesthetic per se, but because of the position given it by the philosophical metadiscourse. The notion of affirmative culture lays bare the way in which the structural legitimation model actually fuses notions of autonomy and integration.

There is, however, a second model upon which the autonomy of art will come to be grounded: a model stressing the mimetic and interpretive value of the aesthetic discourse. So long as it can claim to reflect a social totality—and even the act of affirmation, as an act of judgment, is a form of reflection—art can lay claim to a form of autonomy predicated upon its externality from the totality it reflects. While this model also necessitates a theoretical division of art and life, its understanding of the function of art is radically different. No longer is art a process of beautification, but an interpretive, representational, or even cognitive code. I shall refer to this model as the "representational legitimation strategy." This model tends to displace the metadiscursive structures of philosophy in favor of a framing discourse modeled upon the aesthetic itself; more specifically, upon the notion of mimesis or representation. The externality of the aesthetic is not fixed within the terminology of a framing discourse (philosophy) that acts as theoretical mediation between art and life; rather, it is fixed by the distantiation implicit in the very act of representation and reflection. The autonomy of the aesthetic is explained in terms of its own mimetic modality. The discourse of aesthetic representation presupposes its own externality from that which it represents. Autonomy is legitimated immanently, as mimesis.

In what follows, I wish to suggest that the so-called crisis of representation that has been taken to be a central impulse in modernism in fact reflects not a move beyond the notion of autonomous art, but an attempt to legitimate autonomy in this second way. In short, I wish to suggest that both the aestheticization of politics and the attempt, in the avant-garde, to offer a new and critical perspective on social praxis stem from an attempt to refashion problematic notions of discursive autonomy in the light of a new aesthetic metadiscourse, which by virtue of its functioning as metadiscourse rejects the Enlightenment philosophical paradigm, but which in its aestheticized structural principles owes much to the vulgarized nineteenth-century aesthetic of idealized realism.

Having demonstrated how the dialectical tensions that give birth to the avant-garde in the first half of this century derive not only from the problematic nature of the relationship of art to life but also from the relationship of art to the discourses of philosophy and, increasingly, politics, it remains to examine the reconfiguration of these discourses and their mediated relationship to a specific historical reality. Perhaps the most sophisticated analysis of a specific literary phenomenon in its relationship to the socioeconomic conditions of this period can be found in Georg Lukács's analysis of Expressionism.[19] Taking Lukács as a starting point, I wish now to sketch in the theories of a discursive collapse that seem to underlie models of both fascism and the avant-garde, and to work toward a methodology for the reading of texts that transgress established discursive barriers.[20]

Lukács argues that the imperialist stage of capitalism does not mark a structural change in the organization of bourgeois society, but that it simply extends the organization of that society to an extent no longer accessible to individual understanding, or to the interpretive powers of any existing discourse. Rather than accept the fragmentation of experience and the disempowering of traditional ideological forms, however, the bourgeoisie responds by ontologizing the experience of fragmentation itself (which is, in fact, merely an experience of incomprehension in the face of a process of totalization, which is quite the opposite of fragmentation).[21] It is not reality that is fragmentary, but experience itself. Thus— and this would seem to be the major contribution of Lukács's theory—the experience of fragmentation poses problems of representation rather than effecting an objective interruption of the process of totalization. With the collapse of traditional interpretive paradigms in the face of an ever-expanding capitalism, the bourgeoisie responds by placing its faith in reified notions of art. The autonomy of art is breached by an ideology that, in its attempt to mask and depoliticize the totalization of capitalism, necessarily introduces a negative form of politics into art. Discursive collapse and discursive totalization are one and the same thing: a totalitarian discourse is always implicitly a discourse of fragmentation, and vice versa.

What Lukács allows us to posit (contrary to the critique leveled at him by Bloch)[22] is a noncontemporaneity of ideology and discourse, whereby a discourse prolongs its own existence by cannibalizing and thematizing its own demise, thereby entering the realm of mere ideology. No longer valid as a philosophy of relations, as a philosophy that itself discourses upon the mediations of the individual's integration into the totality, traditional philosophical systems collapse, seeming instead to offer a structural *analogy* to the experience of fragmentation. Art assumes the mantle of philosophical reconciliation. The double fragmentation—the "false" (in Lukács's terms) fragmentation of experience and the actual fragmentation of rationalized discourse—is recast as a mimetic relationship whereby one fragmentation is taken as representative of the other. The collapse of the mimetic possibilities of theory is itself mimetically represented. Thus the possibility of the representation of a totality—lost in the original experience of fragmentation itself—is recovered by means of an essentially aesthetic redefinition of the relationship of philosophy to life. The persistence of an aestheticized philosophy (*Lebensphilosophie*) in the early part of the century is possible only within the terms of a new aesthetic paradigm: "representational" rather than "structural" legitimation. In the light of this crisis of rationalization, whereby the subdivision of discourses reaches the point where no one discourse is capable of conceptualizing the relationship existing *between* those discourses, the entire rationalism / irrationalism debate must be reexamined.[23] Clearly, this paradigm shift from the structural to the representational has implications that go far beyond the realms of the aesthetic or the philosophical, and must impact upon our reading of political discourse in this period. The rise of "the aesthetic," and the possibility of a movement of aestheticism, is due to its ability to articulate a mimetic relationship in which the experience of fragmentation is overcome: the ability to *represent* fragmentation reasserts a representational totality in which the problem of fragmentation is itself implicitly negated.

To summarize the value of the preceding analysis to the following examination of Fascist Modernism, we should emphasize the way in which it allows for a broadening of the notion of the aestheticization of political life. Aestheticization now offers a description of fascism that foregrounds the way in which both the avant-garde and fascism are symptoms of a shift of legitimation strategies, which also led to the privileging of an essentially traditional aesthetic principle (mimesis) at a time when that principle was itself becoming increasingly unworkable from an aesthetic standpoint.[24] It is within this broader framework—art as a legitimation strategy for philosophy—that Bürger's model of the fusion of art and life in the avant-garde must be reexamined. Moreover, it is in the context of this rethinking of social rationalization that the question of rationality and irrationality must be confronted with respect to fascism. What Lukács's study does allow us to retain from Bürger's analysis is the move beyond the essentially compensatory or affirmative analysis of the relationship of art to life, since the development of a representational model marks a shift from this structural legitimation strategy. Clearly, the new centrality of the aesthetic involves a rejection of the marginal function of residual gratification accorded to art in the earlier model. Furthermore, it now becomes possible to envisage a fusion of the utopian and the totalitarian, which would be sensitive to the way in which the experience of fragmentation demands a discursive reconstruction—a totalization—of "fragmented" life as a utopian moment. This reconstruction is actually no more than an accommodation of the interpretive system to the apparent fragmentation of everyday existence, since discursive fragmentation, by means of its analogous relationship to "fragmented" reality, can, within the representational model, now appear to be an adequate (i.e., integrative and totalizing) interpretive system.

If (and it is a large "if"), as Lukács claims, the seeds of fascism are already sown in the aesthetic of Expressionism—and indeed, in modernism in general—then it is not the collapse of the mimetic tradition that is responsible for this implication of aesthetic modernity in political reaction. The problem, instead, lies in the ideological retention of the mimetic tradition, or rather, in the ontologization of its collapse as itself the mimetic representation of a more general ethical and ideological collapse. If the avant-garde as an aesthetic responds to the failure of representational strategies, it is fascist aestheticization in the political realm that paradoxically represents and obviates that failure.

CHAPTER 3

Decadence and Nationalism

Fascism eludes classification. It disorients political analysis in the confusion of left and right, refuses to point the way forward by conflating progress and reaction. Fascism was and is a scandal, both historically and theoretically. No wonder, then, that political theory must reach beyond itself to characterize the phenomenon. Radically heterogeneous indeed, fascism introduces the forces of heterogeneity into the political not only at the level of history but also at the level of its analysis. Formulated as the aestheticization of political life, not only does fascism introduce the mechanisms of aesthetic control historically into the public and political realm, but it likewise obliges political analysis to borrow its terminology from aesthetics. Thus analysis is compromised by fascism, its object: for is there not, perhaps, something inadequate, something, ultimately, aestheticizing in the portrayal of fascism as aestheticization?

In this chapter, I wish to examine the way in which the superimposition of an aesthetic taxonomics upon the analysis of the political phenomenon of fascism has both disarmed and empowered analysis. Building upon the implications of Bürger's model of full unfolding, and the paradigmatic place accorded Aestheticism within this model, I wish to orient this chapter to the category of decadence. The intention is to examine the ways in which the notion of decadence might straddle the political and aesthetic discourses, and to assess the importance of the category in establishing our contemporary critical position vis-à-vis the avant-garde. Within the context of an aestheticization of political life, what might decadence be, what might it enact? Is the aesthetic the end point of decadence, that to which the political is reduced once it has, from within its own dynamic, become decadent? Or is aesthetic decadence merely an external precondition for aestheticization, the *model* for political decay? And if this were so, would it not be necessary, all the same, to propose some model of decadence from within the political itself to explain its subsequent acceptance of an external, aesthetic model?

The answer lies between these possibilities. The political and the aesthetic, in the heyday of their autonomy—that is, broadly speaking, in Enlightenment theory—have traditionally been defined in terms of a mutual exclusion, and each necessarily bears within itself, therefore, the trace of that which has been excluded. One might, then, think fascism in terms of the sublation of the externalized aesthetic discourse within the autonomous discourse of politics as a historical return of the repressed, as the articulation of that "internal external" at which politics sets its limit. Thus Bürger, in his insistence upon the role of Aestheticism in the development of the avant-garde, argues that "the self-criticism of the social subsystem that is art can become possible only when the contents also lose their political character and art wants to be nothing other than art. This stage is reached at the end of the nineteenth century, in Aestheticism" (P. Bürger, *Theory*, pp. 26–27). In other words, the process whereby both the fascist aestheticization of politics and the avant-garde reconciliation of art and life become thinkable demands a prior stage of radical discursive distinction or full unfolding.

I shall concentrate here on those cultural analyses that treat of the fin de siècle ideology from which both aesthetic and political decadence might be said to emerge. Politically, the interpretive possibilities can be polarized around the figures of Georg Lukács and Walter Benjamin. On the one hand, there would be a model of decadence holding that historical periods follow on in a cycle of decay or—stated more positively, following Lukács—that prior to the emergence of the proletariat as the objective subject of history, decadence and progress are indivisible. The decadent self-liquidation of the bourgeoisie is progressive, active, destructive—but ultimately constructive in its unleashing of concrete historical forces. But there is another analysis of decadence, rooted in the writings of Benjamin: in "The Work of Art in the Age of Mechanical Reproduction," in "Theories of German Fascism" and, perhaps most tellingly, in the first "Pariser Brief."[1] Here, decadence is displaced: no longer simply the inevitable and autonomous development of a political cycle, the ideological expression of a class in a state of decay, fascism seems to root itself in an extrinsic *aesthetic* form of decadence. In other words, fascism is not for him, as it is for Lukács, the product of a purely political and economic decay, but rather a hybrid, the superimposition of a specifically decadent aesthetic on the political realm. When Benjamin talks of the aestheticization of political life, it is specifically a decadent aesthetic that he has in mind.

And perhaps inevitably so. For the transference of aesthetic qualities into the political realm necessarily presupposes a decadence or decay of sorts; namely, the decay of the categories of the political and the aesthetic themselves as autonomous entities. But there is a potential paradox here. For traditionally, decadence as an aesthetic phenomenon is identified with Aestheticism, that is, with those movements which most stridently asserted the irreducibility of the aesthetic to any other discourse, and which sought to isolate the aesthetic experience from all praxis. To insert a decadent aesthetic into the political realm—to realize it—is, then, to destroy it. If fascism does indeed mark the aestheticization of political life—and an aestheticization effected in the name of a specifically decadent aesthetic—then it simultaneously brings about the end of a decadence defined in purely aesthetic terms. Fascism would necessarily be a decadent decadence: the decay of decadence in its aesthetic form.

This is a paradox (paradoxically, a paradox of tautology), which I will attempt to explore here. In plain terms: if Lukács's socio-economic analysis disgorges, not surprisingly, into an assertion of the inseparability of fascism and high capitalism as mere stages in the same bourgeois dynamic, can a similar assertion be made at the ideological level? Do fascism and the avant-garde, in other words, share a common ideological root in the decadent movements of the fin de siècle, and if not, what differentiates them either from aesthetic and ideological decadence, or from each other? More fundamentally, is decadence the adequate ideological expression of the bourgeoisie in the stage of high capitalism?

I have already hinted at the ways in which fascism unseats cultural critics and seeks to implicate them in the very process from which they seek to distantiate themselves, drawing them into this ineluctable escalation of the aesthetic which fascism may or may not be. I will therefore try to avoid the terminology of "progress" and "reaction," not in order to keep an open mind but in recognition of the inevitable relativity of the terms and of their disempowerment by fascism. This is not to say that fascism cannot ultimately be judged as a reactionary or a progressive political phenomenon, but rather that it necessitates a form of doubling of these terms. Thus fascism, for example, might be reactionary not in and of itself, but by virtue of the discourse it inaugurates on the relationship of progress to decadence. By the same token, if a liberal critique seeks to legitimate itself as progressive, then its own articulation of the terminologies of progress and reaction must likewise be examined. What I wish to address here, then, is the way in which a literary and cultural criticism, still implicated in a certain bourgeois discourse of progress (from which I, in turn, do not claim to distantiate myself), instrumentalizes fascism as a means of a reexamining its own terms and values. What I propose is to allow barbarism and civilization to discourse upon one another, to try to understand what it is about the "civilized" ideology that the critic claims to share with the avant-garde which might differentiate it from fascist "barbarism." To reexamine the categories of barbarism and civilization, then, to take them more seriously than they are, perhaps, taken by those who use them. To characterize an ideological opposition of fascism and democracy: this is the task.

In attempting to reconstruct a workable model of decadence, one is struck by the obsessiveness with which this category of historical decay, this moment of historical unfolding and emptying out, attempts to write itself a history. It is to some of these histories I would like first to return. The problem with the aestheticism debate as it has figured in the analysis of modernism is precisely its polemical propensity to create false dualisms. Reaction and progress would be one such duality; rationalism and irrationalism would be another. In this regard, Lukács might be said to be the philosopher-historian par excellence of decadence. The philosophical concerns culminating in his *Destruction of Reason* already inform the prewar writings such as the first critiques of German Expressionism, and find a programmatic aesthetic expression in the 1938 essay "Marx and the Problem of Ideological Decay." However, a closer examination of essays such as the latter reveals Lukács's thought to be much more mediated by aesthetic categories than his better known, more dogmatic and polemical analyses of fascism might lead one to believe.

Lukács isolates two major components operative within decadence: namely, absence of mediation, and scholasticism. In the face of capitalism's movement toward greater and greater expansion in the period of imperialism, artists lose the ability to grasp the totality of the relations structuring social life. One can respond either by mistaking the partiality and fragmentation of one's own experience for an experience of the totality, or plod away positivistically gathering details whose connections one cannot fathom, but which one hopes might someday lead to a picture of the totality. In the first case, the enthusiastic and unmediated Expressionist or neo-Romantic is likely to ontologize fragmented experience in the claim that the world itself is somehow fragmented when, in fact, it is moving toward ever more dizzying degrees of economic centralization and political totalization. Alternatively, those ecstatic moments of intuitive insight might be reworked into a utopian vision of "Man" as an ahistorical figure ultimately immune to the historical contingencies of experience. In this latter case, art's ability to articulate the limits of cognition would be taken as a sublime negation of those limits. In the second scenario, meanwhile, the pedantic Naturalist would work in the absence of any social vision and clutter the surface of his text with accidental detail, ignoring the causal relations subtending that surface.

Both politically and aesthetically, then, Lukács's position is marked by its insistence upon the totality of the forces and relations of production. In the programmatic literary essays a claim is made for the reestablishment of a literature of the totality, a literature that, mediated through class consciousness, would allow the individual some form of overview. When he is not being prescriptive, however, Lukács seems more aware of the need to thematize the disjunction of (fragmented) experience and the totality of social relations. In the essay on ideological decadence, for example, he traces not only aesthetic but also political decadence back to specifically literary roots: "If the mendacious and demagogic slogans of fascism about 'blood and soil' were able to find so rapid a reception and seduce such large sections of the petty bourgeoisie, then the philosophy and literature of the decadent period, which awakened these instincts in its readers—very often, of course, without even an inkling of how they might be used, often indeed vigorously rejecting such consequences—is in large measure responsible, for it helped in fact to cultivate those feelings" ("Marx," p. 131). Though very different, lack of mediation and descriptive positivism share a common philosophical root in a specific form of modernism that Lukács traces back to the Romantics. It is with the Romantics that decadence begins: "The first artistic theory of the era of decay was the German romantics' concept of 'irony,' in which this creative subjectivity was already absolutized, with the subjectivity of the work of art already degenerated into an arbitrary play with the self-created characters" ("Marx," p. 146).

For Lukács, the key to Romanticism's implication in the development of a specifically fascistic *politics* lies in its recasting of the category of subjectivity. Subjectivity is rendered absolute, but at the same time that absolute is gambled upon an imaginary play, upon the author's interaction with his own imaginary projections. Romantic irony—an aesthetic of incompletion—locates the subject simultaneously both within and beyond the epistemological horizon of the narrative itself. Or rather, the romantic narrative acknowledges the existence of something beyond itself in its deployment of irony. This "beyond" might subsequently be interpreted as the locus of a putative subject, but as such, this subject would function as no more than the horizon of the totality of the work. Consequently, the Romantic subject is capable of experiencing himself only insofar as he is excluded, alienated, ironic.

The subject is not a positive concept, but rather the ideological recontainment of that which cannot be contained in the text itself. The subject is, or is marked by, a textual lacuna, an absence not of subjectivity but of any possibility of objective perspective. In other words, the subject is defined precisely by the failure to grasp the objective totality and functions, at the same time, as just one element of that totality which the work itself cannot grasp. Insofar as it is aware of its own self-externalization (an externality which, of course, it seeks to express *within* the text) the Romantic aesthetic retains, in however compromised a form, some degree of ideological self-awareness. Lukács's fundamental assertion is that in the course of history this ironic subject nevertheless seeks to positivize itself, to experience itself as plenitude rather than as lack. Thus, in Symbolism (and here we arrive at full-fledged decadence) the experience of fragmentation spills over into an epiphanic, but nevertheless ideological, assertion of the unity of the subject. The symbol, as "the artistic means for reconciling at least in appearance what is in actual fact irreconcilable" ("Marx," p. 162), grounds this aesthetic of self-deception: "For Symbolism in no way offers any solution for the contradictions of this realism, but means on the contrary the perpetuation of these contradictions at an artistically lower level that is still further from grasping reality" ("Marx,"

p. 162). As the bearer of such a reunification in consciousness, the category of the subject itself becomes fundamentally "symbolic" and ideological.

Lukács does not limit his critique to the aesthetic realm, however; he asserts that this paradoxically included / excluded, self-aggrandizing / empty subject provides the social and psychological subject of fascism, realizing in the political sphere the decadent aesthetic tradition originated by the Romantics. "The social connection between the over-refinement of vacuous individuality and this unleashed bestiality might strike many readers as paradoxical, caught as they are in the prejudices of our time. But they can readily be shown in the whole intellectual and literary production of the decadent period" ("Marx," p. 131). For Lukács, then, the key to understanding the way in which aesthetic decadence finds its way into and shapes fascism as a political form of decadence lies in the historical constitution of bourgeois subjectivity through the medium of literature. Decadence, in Lukács's more fully developed formulations, is not simply a question of a decadent society producing a decadent literature. The real decadence of literature lies precisely in its attempt to reconstruct notions of subjectivity rendered problematic in the social and political realm. And fascism, it seems, results from the application of a specific form of aesthetic, ironic subjectivity to the political realm. Implicitly invoking a decadent transgression of discursive subsystems, here Lukács is reminiscent of Benjamin—but the trajectory of his analysis (based, as it is, upon the idea of a political reworking of an impoverished and ideological model of subjectivity drawn from the aesthetic realm) would seem to direct itself more toward an analysis of the prior politicization of the aesthetic than toward a straightforward aestheticization of politics.

This is perhaps the key problem. If one wishes to see in aestheticized politics an intermingling of otherwise mutually exclusive and even contradictory discursive systems, how does one decide which shapes which? Thus when Lukács refers to "the crudeness and animal bestiality that marks the portrayal of emotional life in the bourgeois literature of the period of decay" ("Marx," p. 143) does literature feature as just one modality of a broader concept of decadence (in this case the decay of a specific class) or is it the privileged term? In response to this dilemma, Benjamin's proposals—specifically, his work on Brecht[2]—seem clear enough. However, his analysis necessitates a simultaneous separation and integration of the aesthetic and the political in a way that makes it difficult to formulate the problem in the oppositional terms he outlines. Although his characterization of decadence is fairly traditional in the figures it cites, and agrees, by and large, with those figures named by Bürger,[3] Benjamin is more keenly aware than either Bürger or Lukács of the paradoxes inherent in translating aesthetic constructions of subjectivity into the political realm. He characterizes the mutation of the necessary mediation between the aesthetic and the political realm which takes place in fascism as an "*inherently contradictory juncture.*" What is important for Benjamin is that the passage from the aesthetic to the political, from Aestheticism to fascism—or (stated in the extreme terms that demonstrate the problems with the very idea) from Symbolism to National Socialism—occurs at precisely that moment when the aesthetic most decisively severs its links with any other discourse.[4]

To talk of fascism as Aestheticism "in practice," however, is to ignore the fact that Aestheticism defines itself precisely by means of its distantiation from practice. For Benjamin, then, fascism would be the conclusion Aestheticism defers: "Decadence never turned its interest toward monumental art. It remained for Fascism to unite decadent theory with its monumental praxis. There is nothing more instructive than this inherently contradictory juncture."[5] The "inherently contradictory juncture" of which Benjamin writes entails the encounter of a certain decadent theory with its own "monumental praxis." There is, in fascism's enactment of a decadent aesthetic, a simultaneous assertion and negation of decadence. Decadence, whose very principle is its divorce from all praxis, unfolds and negates itself in praxis. Benjamin's description of this praxis as "monumental" questions, I think, the possibility of conceiving of a specifically decadent history, of history as an adequate modality for the working through of decadence. For the static quality of decadent praxis, its monumental presence, seems at once to place in question a whole thematics of history and to indicate the aesthetic as the discourse into which history will eventually be displaced.

Attempts to read the avant-garde historically—that is, not simply as a historical periodization but as a historical "modality," as a qualitative form of history rather than as a phenomenon merely located within it—run into that same paradox, that same dialectic of self-realization and self-negation, which we have just observed in the case of the decadent aesthetic. It is only a decadent decadence that could possibly realize itself in practice—and yet, as a decadence within the very category of the decadent itself, such a decadent decadence might indeed be the purest form of decadence. In the same way, the avant-garde marks a point at which aesthetic autonomy both realizes and liquidates itself, and, more important, a point at which history is realized and terminated as a meaningful term of ideological legitimation. Such, at least, is the implication of Bürger's analysis.

If Benjamin and Lukács mark out the political terrain, it is Bürger who, for the first time, most fully demonstrates the centrality of what have traditionally been labeled decadent movements to the constitution of the avant-garde.[6] Arguably the most frustrating aspect of Bürger's analysis, however, is the ambiguity and generality of the term he uses to develop his argument: "Aestheticism." For methodological reasons it seems that Aestheticism cannot simply be reduced to a specific historical instance, although its instantiations within literary history are, in the narrative Bürger provides, clear enough. To locate Aestheticism *within* history would be paradoxical precisely because Aestheticism represents an *end* of history—or at least the point at which literary history liquidates itself in History (that is, in a self-conscious realization for which Bürger uses the term "full unfolding"). In what follows I will use the word "history" (with a small "h") to differentiate the historical process, which grounds the possibility of sequential or developmental narratives, from "History" (with a capital "H") which shall stand for both the "full unfolding" of the former "history" but also the liquidation of its self-narrating, sequential process.

In the context of the full unfolding of History in the extra-aesthetic sense, argues Bürger, specific discursive subsystems are nevertheless capable of unfolding themselves in advance of the broader social conditions that frame them. Thus, at the end of the nineteenth century, art reaches a stage of full unfolding in advance of society as a whole. This privileging of the subsystem of art as a forerunner of the historical phenomenon of full unfolding renders absolute the notion of the avant-garde.[7] In a sense, it is no longer the avant-garde within art which is at issue, but art per se as the avant-garde of social and historical self-realization. In a sense, then, as a paradigmatic moment of full unfolding, Aestheticism is already an avant-garde of sorts. The historical avant-garde would thus be the application to the broader social and historical realm of an aesthetic consciousness gained in Aestheticism. Could it be, then, that the avant-garde, and not fascism, stands in a relation to Aestheticism as its "monumental praxis"?

Once we take seriously the coincidence of progress and decadence in the guise of Aestheticism, the avant-garde, normally examined only in terms of its progressive formal innovation, must be reexamined in terms of its relation to decadence. Such an avant-garde is not to be thought in terms of an aesthetic modernity, for it can no longer be the formal innovation of the avant-garde that is progressive. The liquidation of aesthetic autonomy has already deprived the subsystem of any telos in respect of which progress might be measured. In aesthetic terms, the avant-garde seems to be progressive precisely by dint of its movement beyond—or outside of—any autonomous discourse of aesthetic temporality within which the notion of progress would make sense. As Bürger points out, it is through the avant-garde movements that art disgorges into that "simultaneity of the radically disparate" which undermines the legitimational value of history in the aesthetic field. What might previously have been accounted for chronologically as a developmental and historical mastering of technique is now displaced into the presence of historical consciousness itself.

What matters now is not the seriality of techniques, the sequence of the history, but the synchronic consciousness *of* that history. The sequentiality of the historical narrative is subordinated, in aestheticist eclecticism, to the moment of the narration itself as a moment of self-conscious plenitude.

Clearly, there is something disturbing about the way in which history cancels itself in order to unfold itself in History. The historical present empties itself into a spatially figured, cognitive presence. The primary difficulty presented by this emptying out of historical narrative—the negative face, perhaps, of full unfolding—is its tendential delegitimation of traditional modernist aesthetic value judgments. If an age defines itself in terms of a passage beyond style as a historically determined concept, then one can no longer criticize specific techniques in terms of their untimeliness or historical anachronism.[8] The "simultaneity of the radically disparate" makes a nonsense of the value judgments linked to such epithets as "progressive" and "reactionary" in respect to art. It becomes more and more difficult to differentiate between a legitimate passage beyond historical style and cynical pastiche or even plagiarism. What had seemed merely to be the liquidation of aesthetic autonomy has proven, in the avant-garde, to be a liquidation of history itself as a legitimating instance.

This crisis marks a turning point in the history of modernity, for (as Habermas has argued in his essay "Modernity—An Incomplete Project") the specificity of modernism has always lain in the way in which it thinks of its own relationship to tradition. Habermas argues that with the emergence of a modernity in the Enlightenment sense, the new is no longer evaluated in terms of the "classic," but rather a "classic" is instead defined as something that has once been authentically modern. If such is the case, then we must conclude that the avant-garde has left any such modernity far behind, for there is no longer any historical narrative within which the epithet "authentic" could be applied to the modern. In the avant-garde, the modern denies modernity, so to speak, in favor of that "simultaneity of the radically disparate" in which the historical provenance of the disparate is effaced.

The recognition of this antimodernism, which would dispute the presentation of the avant-garde as merely an exaggerated, purified, or merely quantitively differentiated form of modernism, might give rise to philosophical speculation on the problem of periodization. For example, is the historical avant-garde already in the realm of the postmodern? I defer any consideration of such questions until the final chapter, but we should from the very outset be wary of any apocalyptic assertions of a postmodern end of history. Perversely, in the avant-garde, history is neither dead nor at an end, it is simply "out of date"—historically speaking. "Time and Space died yesterday," declares Marinetti; and this paradox obliges us to speak of death—that is, of the end of history—only in strictly historical terms. History pursued to its own death is history in its most radical form, history in the infinitely extensive modality of its own finitude. History as full unfolding, as something qualitatively different, necessarily bears the scars of a historical discourse of temporality that has become anachronistic, but within which the category of anachronism is itself the most fundamental of anachronisms. History as narrative—history with a small "h"—was itself the last barrier to its own full unfolding in History. In much the same manner that art, as an autonomous sphere, must negate itself in order to realize itself, so, it would seem, must history. The end of history is—the end of history.

The point of this disquisition upon the historicity or ahistoricity of the avant-garde is to raise the possibility of a discussion of decadence that moves beyond the polemical terminology of progress and decline; or, to state more clearly the political implications of such a possibility, beyond the terminology of progress and reaction. It is such a discussion, I believe, that both the avant-garde and fascism (in its more apocalyptic moments) seek to inaugurate. It is not a question of simply rethinking decadence as a modality of progress (in the Lukácsian mode), but of rethinking progress itself in terms of decadence, of thinking self-liquidation as the aim of History, as history's end. Nor is it simply a question of revalorizing decadence (the more ancient discourse, we are told)[9] as a metatheory of History, as History's history, but rather of thinking of historical full unfolding as a self-negation of history in a moment of historical self-consciousness. The decisive importance of Aestheticism for the avant-garde should not be thought causally but imperatively: Aestheticism is the consciousness and conscience of the avant-garde. These, then, are the terms in which I would like to reopen the question of decadence.

The parallels between the paradoxical and simultaneous self-realization and self-negation of aesthetics and history, and of decadence as a historical aesthetic, are not entirely fortuitous. As the historical moments at which these paradoxes become clear, both fascism and the avant-garde could be above all else the last inheritors of a metaphysical tradition in which it is possible to think of history as a process of full unfolding. And yet, in the light of Bürger's analysis of the avant-garde as an attempt to liquidate the division of art and life—an attempt that resulted in the liquidation of the legitimating value of history itself—I think it is important to expand our analysis of the failure of the avant-garde beyond the aesthetic consequences detailed by Bürger.[10] We should take seriously the possibility that fascism, like the avant-garde, represents an attempt to reconcile a certain aesthetic (decadence) with the praxis it both entails and resists, and that *both* fascism *and* the avant-garde result in a certain "false sublation" of art and life. Taking seriously this parallel, one faces the question as to whether the real failure of the avant-garde is reflected not in the pseudo-avant-garde of the postwar period (which prompted the writing of theories of the avant-garde) but in fascism, which both shares and treacherously realizes the avant-gardiste historical perspective.

Before leaving the question of periodization, however, I think it is important to problematize and flesh out Bürger's notion of Aestheticism. Within the critical vocabulary, of course, Aestheticism stands as a cipher, as a politically loaded term. Eschewing the directly political concerns of Marxism, the nineteenth-century aesthete would, presumably, introduce into the aesthetic realm the anarchic tradition of Fourier.[11] As the political ideology best suited to the assertion of aesthetic autonomy—or, in so banalized a critical form, to the assertion of autonomy of any kind—

aestheticized anarchism is rooted in an individualism that resists political closure. In its confrontation with the potential commonality of fascism and the avant-garde, subsequent criticism gratefully returns to this old saw of nineteenth-century anarchic and aesthetic individuality. For the liberal, the avant-garde thus inherits the mantle of a solid bourgeois individualism that could have no truck with a fascist politics of the masses, while for the left any possible links between progressive aesthetics and reactionary politics are consigned to the netherworld of the incorrigibly bourgeois, schismatic overvaluation of the superstructure.[12]

By virtue of what mediations, though, is it possible to think of the avant-garde as emerging from Aestheticism? That is to say, in what way might the avant-garde be both a product and a rejection of Aestheticism, its realization and its negation? Answering these questions leads us into a better understanding of the way in which Aestheticism was, in fact, uniquely suited to bridge the gap between aesthetics and politics, despite its insistence upon discursive differentiation. In a study of the phenomenon of the dandy, Giovanna Franci has attempted to differentiate divergent ideological strands from within the complex of Aestheticism itself. Taking the dandy as an explosion of the hermetic aesthetic realm of Symbolism into the everyday, she argues that the simplifying term "Aestheticism" must ultimately be discarded.[13] According to Franci, three developments are possible from within Symbolism. First, "*estetismo*," characterized by the dandy, who represents the attempt to render life aesthetic: this would mean the victory of the aesthetic. A similar unification of art and life is attempted by "*Liberty*," (or Art Nouveau) but this time in the name of a commercialized aesthetic, in the name of the commodity. Finally, the avant-garde itself represents the end of the aesthetic, its death. Whereas *estetismo* represents a movement away from the Symbolist duality of art and life that attempts to recast life itself in terms of art and to establish a *vita estetica*, Art Nouveau positions itself as a form of ornamentation of the everyday, a rendering palatable of the increasingly alienated and alienating objects of industrial society: "*it is the beauty of the new, technical beauty, industrial art*" (Franci, p. 221; emphasis mine).

While this model modifies and differentiates Bürger's chronology of the avant-garde in certain important ways—most specifically, by characterizing the avant-garde as a reaction not against aestheticism *tout court*, but against the particular form of reified aestheticism of Art Nouveau—it nevertheless retains the privileged position of the avant-garde itself as an ultimate negation of the very problematic, as the liquidation of art. For reasons we have already indicated, this is unsatisfactory. Death serves a specific purpose in the self-perpetuation of bourgeois history, and is no less at work in the supposed "death of art" exemplified by Marinetti's assertion that "Time and Space died yesterday."

But, to stick with Marinetti for a moment, even Franci's opposition of Art Nouveau's "beauty of the new" and "industrial art" to both the figure of the dandy and the negation of art by the avant-garde collapses when confronted by that avant-garde dandy Marinetti, the aesthete of the machine. Tendentially, Franci's tripartite model simply serves to legitimate a binary opposition of the dandy / avant-garde to the inauthentic and affirmative aesthetic of Art Nouveau. In a sense, then, the Benjaminian distinction between the aestheticization of politics (fascism) and the politicization of aesthetics (communism) has already been prefigured— *within* the confines of what we have hitherto simply termed Aestheticism—in the opposition between *estetismo* and Art Nouveau. What this differentiation within the realm of Aestheticism would suggest is that the link of fascism to decadence might best be traced through Art Nouveau (or, as Sontag suggests, through its successor, Art Deco).[14] A certain history of the aesthetic (or is it an aestheticized history?) begins to outline itself.

The implicit dualism, which entails an aesthetic and political stigmatizing of Art Nouveau, is of interest precisely because it collapses in the face of Futurism. Franci's characterization of Art Nouveau is so clearly reminiscent of Marinetti, and Marinetti in turn is so clearly a twentieth-century avant-garde dandy, that the terms of the analysis must be revised. The celebration of technical beauty, which Franci places squarely in the camp of Art Nouveau and against which the avant-garde supposedly reacts, in fact enters into the avant-garde through the figure of Marinetti. Moreover,

the opposition to industrialized representation is further problematized by Benjamin's model of aestheticization, which (at least
on the surface) is sympathetic to the forces of technology that for
Franci serve merely to legitimate Art Nouveau. Short of excluding Marinetti from the pantheon of the avant-garde—and such
an exclusion would be willful, given the indubitable influence of
his methods of provocation and self-promotion on other avant-
garde movements—one would have to reject the simple opposition Art Nouveau–avant-garde (in Bürger's terms, Aestheticism–
avant-garde) and, potentially, that broader distinction between
aestheticized politics and politicized aesthetics.

Let us recapitulate the terms framing the political problem of
avant-garde and decadence. On the one hand, there is the dandy,
the outsider, the individual; on the other, Art Nouveau, an aesthetic indicative of capitalism in its imperialistic phase, which reduces beauty to a mass-produced norm. In Franci's analysis it is
mass production that carries forth the decadent tradition into the
twentieth century—a conclusion that clearly poses problems to
a Benjaminian analysis of fascism developed in the name of the
liberational possibilities of the work of art in the age of its technical reproducibility. At the same time, the dandy also serves to
problematize some of the historical categories used by Bürger in
his characterization of Aestheticism. If, as we are told by Franci,
Art Nouveau is "more homogeneous with the imperialistic phase
of Capital" (Franci, p. 220) in that it limits the aesthetic to the em-
bellishment of the commodity, to the enhancement of its price, or
simply produces the aesthetic as an object of mass consumption,
then what would be the implications of linking both this tendency
and the dandy tradition to the avant-garde through the figure of
Marinetti?

Franci will begin to address the problem by characterizing the
opposition of the dandy to the marketplace in the following terms:

> The opposition of the dandy is *substitution* or *inversion*. In general-
> ized exchange, in which art and the commodity are equivalent terms,
> there is no antithesis, only permutations [*permutabilità*]. This is why
> the dandy-aesthete substitutes and inverts, because the conditions of

inversion are the rejection of reality and life in favor of dandyism, aestheticism [*estetismo*] as real life. But it is not enough simply to reject: inversion also means substitution. It is necessary to assert that the true reality is the reality of the dandy; "L'idéalisme, c'est vrai." The third moment is therefore one of inversion as *regression*, not in a historical or historicist sense, for the dandy's process of inversion is antihistorical and antitemporal. (p. 34)

Her attempt to valorize the dandy's aesthetic of substitution is immediately problematized within its own oppositional dyad. As a critique of capitalist systems of exchange, the aesthetic of substitution reveals its affinity with that permutability of the marketplace which it supposedly rejects. The dandy's attempt at an aesthetic substitution and the marketplace's set of profit-oriented permutations function as modalities of each other within a broader economy of exchange.

More interesting, however, is the isolation of this permutability as an aesthetic rooted in a specific stage of capitalism. The notion of permutability, with which Franci characterizes that commodification of all difference that the avant-garde opposes, in fact describes the formal and structural makeup of the avant-garde itself in its rejection of a given historical style. By expanding the paradigm of permutation, by indicating its grounding of a progressive aesthetic of substitution, one is obliged to reevaluate the avant-garde's "simultaneity of the radically disparate." One arrives at a preliminary conclusion that the posthistorical formal permutations of the avant-garde and the permutations of the commodity are intrinsically linked. History, to the artists of the avant-garde, is available as commodity; and the commodity, in turn, is intrinsically "historical," second-hand. Perhaps, after all, the avant-garde *does* develop a style, one of *bricolage*, in which the commodification of history and the historicization of the commodity (that is, aestheticization and politicization respectively) converge.

But what of the persona of the dandy itself as work of art, as the precursor of the avant-garde's reintegration of art and life? Within the mythology of decadence the dandy's function is to reassert a form of individualism which serves either to redeem or to condemn a specific political position. It is Calinescu who most clearly foregrounds this issue of individualism, which also subtends Lukács's analysis. He asserts, quite simply, "A style of decadence is simply a style favorable to the unrestricted manifestation of aesthetic individualism, a style that has done away with traditional authoritarian requirements such as unity, hierarchy, objectivity, etc." (Calinescu, *Faces*, p. 171). The key to the ambiguity of this assertion lies, I think, in the term "aesthetic individualism." Calinescu seems to imply by it the entry of the irreducible individual into the realm of the aesthetic and the subsequent collapse of hierarchies implicit in the autonomous discourse of the aesthetic itself. Insofar as one might wish to map this position along the Benjaminian continuum of aestheticization and politicization, then, the disruption of the aesthetic by something extrinsic and dysfunctional to it would seem inimical to any project of aestheticization. And yet Calinescu's position involves us in a paradox: it is only possible to position him on the "good," "antiaestheticizing" side of things by invoking the individual as something extrinsic to the discourse in which this individual is subsequently lodged. What this means, however, is that this individual is something displaced—displaced, that is, from the political in the broadest sense of the word, from the day-to-day functioning of his or her society. In other words, it is no longer a question of decadence subverting the aesthetic with something intrinsically political, but rather of the becoming-political of the individual through a transgressive passage into the aesthetic.

Aestheticization and politicization become synonymous, or at the very least, co-originary. Politicization is the entry of the individual excluded from politics into the realm of the aesthetic. The aesthetic, in turn, is the realm in which the political becomes actionable for the subject. Is this "aesthetic individualism" anything different from the "vacuous individuality" that Lukács traces back to Romanticism, and which he sees asserting itself in fascism? Is it, in other words, not the entry of the individual into the aesthetic, but rather the *construction* of individuality itself as a specifically aesthetic category; as (to insist upon Calinescu's own formulation) "*aesthetic* individualism"? The aesthetic begins to function not only as the refuge of the political, but also as the birthplace of a surrogate individuality. As a figure whose very person prefigures that form of reconciliation of art and life attempted by the avant-garde, the dandy has implications for political as well as aesthetic analysis. I would like to suggest that the dandy represents a rethinking of the possibility of revolutionary action in the age of high capitalism. In the crudest of terms, one might even speak of a disappropriation of revolution, its separation from the proletarian subject-object of history. The failure of the proletariat to materialize as a historical subject will have been rectified by the reworking of bourgeois subjectivity in the figure of the dandy. As both creative subject and created object of the aesthetic—as subject and object in one—the figure of the dandy points the way toward an avant-garde aesthetic project on the one hand, and marks the displacement and replication of the political dynamic of the historical dialectic into the realm of the aesthetic on the other. If, as our reading of Bürger's analysis indicated, the avant-garde operates within a certain historical modality that at least gives the effect of an end of history, this is because the displacement of the historical dialectic of subject and object from the level of the collective to the level of the individual (the dandy), and subsequently into the aesthetic of the avant-garde (which goes even further by negating the distinction between individual and collective at the level of production), curtails certain historical and political possibilities.

In brief, the aesthetic project of the reunification of art and life appropriates and aestheticizes the political dynamic of history's subjective and objective realization in and through the proletariat. It is certainly within a class dynamic that Baudelaire sees the dandy emerge. He argues:

> Dandyism appears above all in periods of transition when democracy is not yet all-powerful, and aristocracy is only beginning to totter and fall. In the disorder of these times, certain men who are socially, politically and financially ill at ease [*déclassés, dégoûtés, désoeuvrés*], but are all rich in native energy, may conceive the idea of establishing a new kind of aristocracy, all the more difficult to shatter as it will be

based on the most precious, the most enduring faculties, and on the divine gifts which work and money are unable to bestow. Dandyism is the last spark of heroism amid decadence.[15]

The class analysis is somewhat confusing here. The argument is that the dandies form a class of *déclassés* in opposition to the emergence of the commercial bourgeoisie in the period of the decline of the aristocracy. It is not, however, the dandy who figures as a standard-bearer of historical decadence: it is the bourgeoisie that is decadent.

Progress, in this Baudelairean formulation, is conflated with decadence. History is a history of decadence, and as a class outside that historical continuum of class struggle, the dandies escape decadence. But the situation is more complex. The dandies escape precisely by virtue of their "decadent" refusal of historical progress as the inevitable succession of classes. The experience of the *déclassé* offers a suspension of history as a teleological principle, in much the same way as the avant-garde offers a "simultaneity of the radically disparate" and problematizes historical teleology as a legitimating category. It seems to me that this analysis of the dandy—as one who, through decadence, opposes the decadence of history—dislodges a more conventional analysis of the dandy in terms of the modernist impulse to "*épater le bourgeois.*" For in this latter model, the dandy would exist merely as a *determinate* negation of the bourgeoisie. Moreover, the ideological hegemony of the bourgeoisie is established precisely by virtue of such a negation of the notion of class hegemony: in humanism. When the modernist dandy, as opposed to the avant-garde dandy analyzed by Baudelaire, opposes the bourgeoisie, he or she actually does no more than the bourgeoisie itself, which is perpetually concerned with denying and concealing its own class character.

It is to this latter model of the dandy, this essentially bourgeois, modernist dandy, that Calinescu appeals in his celebration of aesthetic individualism. By moving beyond the parameters of class, however, the dandy of the avant-garde has the potential for disrupting the teleology of a modernist politics. Unwittingly, perhaps, this dandy opens up—among other things—the space of fascism. According to Calinescu, the political valency of the dandy must be measured within the historical context of his emergence. As a historical phenomenon dandyism is intrinsically inimical to the pressures of nationalism and imperialism, rooted as it is in a form of stubborn individualism. "If we admit that the concept of individualism is central to any definition of decadence," Calinescu posits, then "it is clear that, besides having their disadvantages from the point of view of nationalism and sheer military might, decadent periods should be favorable to the development of the arts and, more generally, should eventually bring about an aesthetic understanding of life itself. To prefer decadence to its radical opposite (that is, barbarism) appears, at least culturally, a legitimate choice" (Calinescu, *Faces*, p. 171). Decadent individualism is invoked in opposition to both nationalism and militarism, as it constitutes civilization's last bulwark against what Calinescu calls "barbarism." Since the dandy is identified with the spirit of (bourgeois / antibourgeois) insubordination, we are asked to believe that decadence only poses problems to a specifically nationalistic and militaristic politics of "nationalism and sheer military might." Whereas Lukács refers to "unfettered bestiality" as the modality of decadent subjectivity, Calinescu is proposing a specifically aestheticist counterdiscourse to fascism (whose barbarism would seem to lie in the effacement of bourgeois subjectivity). Of course, Calinescu's analysis fails to question the ideological status of the individual itself in the light of the coincidence of overrefinement and barbarism to which Lukács refers. Decadence is not simply a narrative of the bourgeois subject's self-assertion, but rather the modality of its very constitution: the modern (fascisticized) individual is the product of decadence rather than the reverse.

As a social and political agent, Calinescu's civilized subject is already the product of a process of aestheticization, a subject constituted in the aesthetic sphere and accustomed to experiencing him- or herself only within the aesthetic realm, as *schöner Schein*. Whether or not one accepts the Lukácsian critique in its undercutting of Calinescu's position, there is nevertheless something profoundly paradoxical in Calinescu's deployment of the individual as the basis of a counterideological ideology. For, as Paolo Valesio has pointed out, "individual-ism" is by definition a charismatic construct indicative of a potentially fascisticized mass ideology.[16] Valesio points out that individualism is a "collective ideology of the unique," made possible as an "-ism" by precisely that dynamic of charismatic authority, that interplay of collectivity and uniqueness, within which fascism is generated.

Ironically, it is the demons of liberalism unleashed by Calinescu's analysis that point toward this conclusion. For we should not forget that there is something anarchic in Calinescu's rediscovery of the bourgeois subject as filtered through the lens of Aestheticism, something that threatens the very liberal order it seeks to affirm. Could it be that through a political reassessment of the avant-garde our society discovers its affinities with anarchism as one virtual polarity in the opposition of individual and collective? Thus, rather than seeking the sociological continuum of high capitalism and fascism in the realm of the economic, should we begin to see fascism as an ideological response (entailing economic compromise) to the aporias of bourgeois individualism? The charismatic fusion of individual and collective effected by fascism, far from being anathema to capitalism, might actually be its accentuated grimace.

Indeed, one of the paradoxes of capitalism is the inherence within it of a dialectic of negation and affirmation. Since it establishes and renews itself through a relentless revolutionizing of the means of production, while at the same time presenting itself as the sole guarantor of social order, capitalism is embroiled in a consistent and systematic underestimation of its own destructive powers.[17] This I take to be the condition of modernity in the very broadest of senses—a condition in which revolutionization and conservatism necessarily coincide, in which the hegemonic economic and ideological powers assert themselves by their very ability to change. In terms of this broad definition of modernity, it is not necessary to effect a division of economic and cultural modernity (as does Daniel Bell in *The Cultural Contradictions of*

Capitalism) in order to explain the antagonism between artist and society. Presenting itself as the representative of order, the bourgeoisie in fact thrives on disorder: one need only look at the tensions in Marx's writing to appreciate the way in which he "unveils the modern bourgeois as consummate nihilists on a far vaster scale than modern intellectuals can conceive" (M. Berman, p. 100).

As an escalation and manipulation of a form of individualism, then, fascism draws its ideological force quite precisely from a reconciliation of those "alternatives" of civilized decadence and barbaric militarism with which contemporary, liberal champions of decadence such as Calinescu would confront us. There is no necessary opposition between the barbaric hordes Calinescu seeks to hold at bay with decadence and the aestheticized individual. The individual, the nation, rationalization, aestheticization—these, then, are the questions raised by the very category of decadence. The charismatic idiom of individualism articulates the barbaric language of the objectified masses. Nevertheless, the inescapable terms of opposition left us by the preceding analysis remain: individualism and / or barbarism.

In a sense, then (indeed, in a sense that Lukács himself did not fully recognize and would have forcefully resisted) the more dogmatic assertions of Lukács (his association of aestheticism with decadence, and ultimately with the barbarism of fascism) ring truer than the liberal analysis of Calinescu. For is there not something too conciliatory about a decadence whose most potent expression consists of nothing more than a form of "aesthetic individualism"? Characterized thus, decadence as an attack on bourgeois social structures would leave intact the most fundamental philosophical underpinning of those structures: the subject itself. But what is at stake here? Barbarism serves as more (or less) than a name for the empirical phenomenon of fascism; it responds at the level of theory to the loss of an objective historical subject. Having construed aestheticization as intrinsic to the very constitution of the bourgeois subject, would it be going too far to trace it to the very root of barbarism also? Would it, in fact, be too barbaric (in the face of fascism) to construe barbarism as an essentially aesthetic notion, as a field of representation? And if one were to offer such a construction, would it be possible to think barbarism as in some way constitutive of the historical mission of the bourgeoisie? Barbarism, in this sense, would figure not simply as social injustice or even cruelty, but as a system of representation, as a framework within which justice, civilization—even the subject—become thinkable.

Although characterizing barbarism as a system of representation seems to contribute to that escalation of the aesthetic to which fascism constantly invites us, there is in fact a tradition of such categorization within Western thought as it tries to think its own relation to representation. I would like to conclude this chapter by addressing this issue of barbarism as a representational as well as a political idiom. Grounded in an Enlightenment tradition of ethnology, the periodization of history by means of its relation to language and representation had long been forgotten by academic disciplines marked by a nineteenth-century positivism. Only with the work of thinkers such as Michel Foucault, Jacques Derrida, Gilles Deleuze and Félix Guattari does this tradition re-emerge (albeit in very differing terms and, in the case of Derrida, in deconstructed form).[18] Rather than reading *for* barbarism as a thematic situated beneath the surface of modernist texts (and one need not read very far beneath the surface in the case of writers such as Marinetti) it is a question of reading barbarism as the condition of possibility of these texts. Barbarism needs to be read not as a given object scrambled in the code of Aestheticism, not as the ugly reality aestheticized in the symbolic representations of decadence, but rather as itself the system of representation informing the decadent aesthetic, effecting, in turn, an overcoding of its latent social codes.

Barbarism as I would wish to use it here is more (or perhaps less) than a pejorative term based on a notion of human rights; it describes a specific social and symbolic order that makes possible the coexistence of modernity, in a certain form, and fascism. In utilizing the work of Deleuze and Guattari in what follows, my aim is not to suggest a model of historical regression, wherein literary decadence would be regressive or reactionary because it harks back to anachronistic, barbaric systems of representation, but rather to examine the barbarous representational possibilities of that "simultaneity of the radically disparate" alluded to by Bürger. At a certain point—and that point, for Bürger, would be the avant-garde—such harking back is actually most timely. Or, to slip into the terminology of Deleuze and Guattari, at a certain point, the prevalent representational practice consists, in fact, of a system of historical "de-coding."

For Deleuze and Guattari, barbarism functions as the name of one of three social "machines": the savage, the barbarian (or despotic), and the civilized, each of which generates its own system of representation:

> We have distinguished among three social machines corresponding to the savage, the barbarian, and the civilized societies. The first is the underlying territorial machine, which consists in coding the flows on the full body of the earth. The second is the transcendent imperial machine, which consists in overcoding the flows on the full body of the despot or his apparatus, the Urstaat: it effects the first great movement of deterritorialization, but does so by adding its eminent unity to the territorial communes that it conserves by bringing them together, overcoding them and appropriating their surplus labor. The third is the modern immanent machine, which consists in decoding the flow on the full body of capital-money. It has realized the immanence, it has rendered concrete the abstract as such and has naturalized the artificial, replacing the territorial codes and the despotic overcoding with an axiomatic of decoded flows, and a regulation of these flows; it effects the second great movement of deterritorialization, but this time because it doesn't allow any part of the codes and overcodes to subsist.[19]

The terms of the analysis clearly lend themselves to a critical rhetoric, though they are bafflingly hermetic in so schematic a presentation, and it is in the light of such a scheme that I hope to undertake a reading of Marinetti in the following chapters. For now, however, I wish to concentrate on the passage from the barbarian to the civilized—a crucial rallying point in the ideological reconstruction of the avant-garde through figures such as Calinescu—which is marked by the movement away from the vertical, hierarchical, or directly oppressive organization of significant material to the less structured, "de-coded" axiomatic of signification characteristic of modernity.

It is crucial to remember that the civilized "machine" shares with the barbarian the characteristic of deterritorialization, that is, the dissemination of signifying practices and their dissociation from any necessary material instantiation. Clearly, the project of civilization sketched here is extremely precarious. It consists of a system of representation becoming ever more totalized and schematic, and ever less dependent upon any moment of fixation. The "de-coding" constituent of the civilized social machine promises two possibilities of escape from signification: the escape into the real—out of code and into what it represents—and at the same time (and diametrically opposed) an escape *from* the real, from the necessary tying of code to something preceding it, to the thing that is the code itself. Modernity, then, would be at once translation and destruction—the destruction of that which is translated.[20] It risks destroying and translating any code within which it can itself be understood, for among the codes to which it assigns archaic function is the virtual code of its own potential meaning. Modernity, then, courts a collapse into meaninglessness, a collapse that would be a fall into reality—or into pure ideology. It is by its very nature always already anachronism. Is there then a point (and would barbarism be the name of that point?) where modernity recoils from itself? Recoils, that is, not only historically, as in the avant-garde's "simultaneity of the radically disparate," but also from its own potentially anarchic project of de-coding? Or does the process of de-coding, and the process of totalization in which capitalism is engaged, find its own historical equilibrium—politically in the project of imperialism, and culturally in the avant-garde?

That the leap from Deleuze and Guattari to the concrete or political level should be so vertiginous serves as warning, perhaps, that their categories should not be read in any conventionally historical sense. And yet it is, I think, possible to locate the ideological nexus of fascism and the avant-garde within that scheme.

By way of a beginning, I would like to recall Franci's insistence upon the homogeneity of Art Nouveau and imperialism. At the time, we noted the difficulties inherent in isolating the tradition of the dandy—and with it, the tradition of the avant-garde—from Art Nouveau, but refrained from commenting upon the value of her invocation of imperialism. In the passage noted earlier, Franci already seemed to sense the convergence of those traditions of imperialism and avant-garde which she sought to isolate when she argued that in imperialism "art can only die as art." At the same time, she characterized the avant-garde as "the death of art in the bourgeois sense of the word." This idea of the death of art—a death necessitated both by imperialism and by the avant-garde—seems to point toward that ideological nexus in which a repressive politics and a progressive aesthetics potentially meet. As a working hypothesis, one might read Franci's analysis against the grain to suggest that a certain form of decadence—more specifically, the form that infiltrates the avant-garde—is consonant with the project of imperialism and cannot simply be limited to the categories of traditional bourgeois aesthetics.

I would like to suggest that imperialism is, in fact, the "becoming-barbarian" of civilization, but not in the limited sense that imperialism, to our sensibilities, is somehow barbaric, distasteful, an outrage or a crime. The assertion is made, rather, in the conviction that it is in imperialism that capitalism finds an outlet for the imperative of de-coding, but an outlet that functions as a natural limit, that saves capitalism not only from its own economic aporias but also from the impossibility of self-representation, from the inevitable collapse into historical autism. The self-limitation of capitalist de-coding is effected by a superimposition of what can only provisionally be termed the "literal" and the "figurative" senses of "territorialization." For in linking imperialism and barbarism we place ourselves in the awkward position of linking imperialism and "deterritorialization"—linking, that is, a political phenomenon based on territorial conquest to the category of deterritorialization. But perhaps this is the point: for it is in the project of imperialism that civilization once again encounters ter-

ritory. In imperialism, it is in the act of de-coding and deterritorialization that territory once again asserts itself with the force of
the literal. The project of deterritorialization is played out across
the global territory, and the territorial ambitions of imperialism
realize the imperative of de-coding by fracturing the integrity of
the encrypted possibilities of the nation-state.

How, then, to situate the avant-garde, fascism, and imperialism
in relation to one another? How, in other words, does decadence
play upon the relationship of civilization to barbarism? In a sense,
the confusion of territoriality and deterritorialization we find in
imperialism—the breaking of the national code and the establishing of a code based upon the notion of transgression (of borders),
a code always already "broken"—is indicative of the impossibility
of locating precisely the function of any one of these moments
within the ideological confines of capitalism. We can, however, put
forward some provisional hypotheses concerning the ideological
relation of fascism and the avant-garde to the age of imperialism.

The starting point would be the move beyond the codifying
possibilities of the nation-state. The problem of nationalism and
imperialism and its centrality to a consideration of Fascist Modernism has already been noted by Fredric Jameson in his study
of Wyndham Lewis, *Fables of Aggression*. In the chapter entitled
"From National Allegory to Libidinal Apparatus" (pp. 87–104)
Jameson asserts that prior to World War I it was still possible,
thanks to "the objective existence of a system of nation-states, the
international diplomatic machinery of pre-World-War-I Europe
which, originating in the 16th century, was dislocated in significant ways by the War and the Soviet Revolution" (p. 94), to
construct a novelistic narrative within "an essentially allegorical
mode of representation, in which the individual characters figure
those more abstract national characteristics which are read as their
inner essence" (p. 90). The national stereotype resulted from a
system of coding and over-coding which Jameson identifies with
diplomacy.

Thus far, Jameson's analysis of Fascist Modernism is most suggestive, indicating as it does a way of understanding the interaction

of "objective" historical data and the possibility of narrative organization—and, indeed, of an alignment of signifier and signified.

He goes on to argue that "national allegory should be understood as a formal attempt to bridge the increasing gap between the existential data of everyday life within a given nation-state and the structural tendency of monopoly capital to develop on a worldwide, essentially transnational scale" (p. 94). The position Jameson is attempting to reserve for Lewis's brand of modernism is that representational space opened up by the collapse of the allegorical narrative possibilities inherent in the system of nation-states. In this he is quite right, and while his argument would clearly exclude the *völkisch* extremes of National Socialist ideology, this position likewise characterizes a continental tradition of Fascist Modernism typified by Marinetti. However, the problem with his analysis arises when he offers a tentative characterization of what lies *beyond* this late form of national allegory, when he suggests that "the empty matrix of national allegory is then immediately seized on by hitherto unformulable impulses which invest its structural positions and, transforming the whole narrative system into a virtual allegory of the fragmented psyche itself, now reach back to overdetermine the resonance of this now increasingly layered text" (p. 96). The straining of impulses is clear in such passages. On the one hand, there is the desire to break out of national allegory into the realm of "libidinal economy," and on the other a recognition of the structural limitations of any economy of desire.

I would like to suggest that imperialism offers a paradigm that at once expands upon and negates these "allegorical" possibilities of nationhood. What lies beyond national allegory is not the libidinal economy of language itself, but the de-coded libido of the deterritorialized, territorial body politic. As a source of inspiration for the avant-garde aesthetic, the project of imperialism—understood as a form of adventure, a transgression and flirtation with death, rather than as a simple expansion of capital—holds a particular fascination for the Fascist Modernists. However, it is useful in the examination of the role of the avant-garde aesthetic in the development of imperialism to insist upon the distinction between nationalism and imperialism, a distinction that can be observed most markedly in the case of Marinetti.

Applied to Marinetti, the imprecise taxonomy of "nationalism" confuses two divergent ideological strains. Originating in the irredentism of pre-war Italy, Marinetti's "nationalism" was already marked by a call for national expansion. Whereas irredentism drew its ideological legitimation from a notion of plenitude and the reconstitution of lost unity, Marinetti's imperialism celebrates transgression and the tendential negation of any such plenitude. Such is the paradox of imperialism: for expansion negates the unity not only of the invaded country but also of the aggressor nation, which thereby bursts through the boundaries of its own territory. The forms of legitimation in (irredentist) nationalism and imperialism are, aesthetically speaking, quite diverse. On the one hand, irredentist nationalism musters an aesthetic of unity and completion, an essentially classicizing aesthetic, while imperialism on the other hand implies an aesthetic of transgression and incompletion, an aesthetic of the avant-garde. It is not simply a case, then, of the avant-garde emerging (in Marinetti's case) from the collapse of a system of nation-states, but rather of its emergence within the same dynamic that marks the movement of those states beyond nationhood to imperial power.

Thus, in seeking the origins of Marinetti's aesthetic of destruction, for example, it is not necessary to resort to an anarchic Symbolist youth, but rather to situate him within the destructive and transgressive dynamic of capitalism itself in its imperialist phase. The ambiguities of Marinetti's nationalism account for the possibility of his collaboration with anarchists, as well as for his political affiliations with fascism. At the same time, his deconstruction of the category "nation" also offers the clearest evidence why imperialism was a constant point of political rupture for the avant-gardiste Marinetti in his relations with the anarchists, as well as with the fascist regime.

It was over the issue of imperialism that Marinetti first broke with the anarchists in 1911 and over the same issue that he was to have his major ideological doubts concerning fascism. From the very outset, the bellicose nature of Marinetti's political ideology had been apparent: already in the political manifesto of 1909 he had opposed the occupation of Italian territories by the Austrians and called for national expansion.[21] That Marinetti's irredentism should already be expressed at this point in terms of a call for expansion is key to the understanding of his "nationalism." The incommensurability of the nationalist discourse of plenitude and the imperialist discourse of transgression is first documented in the "Manifesto a Tripoli italiana" of 1911, with its three axiomatic principles:

1. All freedoms must be granted the individual and the people except for the freedom to be a coward.
2. Let it be proclaimed that the word ITALY must dominate the word FREEDOM.
3. Let us cancel out our fastidious memory of the grandeur of Rome with an Italian grandeur one hundred times greater.[22]

As the basis for an aesthetic project, Marinetti's nationalism has to be differentiated into two contradictory moments: an aesthetic of unity and completion and an aesthetic of transgression and incompletion. Consequently, the early collaboration with the anarchists, in which a shared irredentism was not deemed inimical to the anarchist project, feeds into a more traditional aesthetic configuration, whereas the later imperialism enacts on the national scale the demand of the technical manifesto, "Destroy the 'I' in Literature."[23] In seeking the origins of Marinetti's transgressive and modernist aesthetic within a political ideology, then, it is necessary to rethink his nationalism in terms of the potentialization of the transgressive and self-destructive elements inherent in the expansion of capital in its imperialist phase. Quite contrary to the bourgeois individualist structure imposed upon decadence by Calinescu, here, in the decadent and expansionist phase of capital, the impulse seems to be toward the *destruction* both of the state and of the individual.

It is in terms of the question of imperialism that we can also begin to focus upon the concrete historical situation of Futurism with regard to fascism. Curiously, it will be Marinetti's bellicose imperialism which shall also serve to distance him from Mussolini's brand of fascism. In the manifesto of 1911, Marinetti rejects "the grandeur of Rome" as a legitimation of the project of imperialism, reveling, instead, in the illegitimacy of the transgression. Mussolini consistently resorts to the myth of a new Rome; that is, of a historical rather than territorial reconstitution of a lost unity. This difference was to remain a constant stumbling block in Marinetti's attempts at a rapprochement with fascism after the rupture of 1920. Even in the conciliatory *Futurismo e Fascismo* Marinetti insists: "Yes! Yes! we must march on and not degenerate in our sacred ambitions. Let us urge on Italian youth (already prepared and eager muscularly and spiritually) to the conquest of an Italian Empire! It shall and must be Italian, for a Roman Empire would be a restoration or a plagiarism" (p. 243). The modernist insistence upon novelty, upon aesthetic innovation, is invoked to rethink history in specifically *textual* terms: as plagiarism.

In terms of the paradigm of imperialism, then, Marinetti stands as an indication of the fact that an avant-garde aesthetic does not necessarily oppose, and may be consonant with, the political project of imperialism. Strangely enough, however, it is those last vestiges of modernism—the distaste for historical plagiarism and the insistence upon a historical aesthetic of innovation—that serve to articulate Marinetti's estrangement from fascism. It is, paradoxically, the rhetoric of modernity that constitutes the Futurist avant-garde in its most clearly delineated form.

In this exchange, Marinetti at once walks the thin line separating the avant-garde from fascism and the equally thin line differentiating it from modernism. Marinetti's belligerent imperialism most fully represents that aspect of the avant-garde originally sympathetic to the project of fascism. However, he also marks most clearly the point where the collaboration must cease. In the light of Mussolini's attempt to legitimate the Italian Fascist empire in terms of its Roman antecedent, Marinetti is finally obliged to move away from fascism. He urges us onwards "to the conquest of the Italian Empire" in the name of a modernist abhorrence of plagiarism.

Although the "simultaneity of the radically disparate" made

possible by the avant-garde—the political principle of nonsynchronicity—lends itself to invocations of a Roman past, it negates the possibility of reconstructing the past as plenitude. History as plagiarism—such is the nightmare of Marinetti's Futurism, caught between a rejection of progressivist notions of modernity and the need to articulate that rejection within the spatio-temporality of the modern. It is not the project of imperialism itself but its legitimation in terms of historical precedent that necessitates the rupture of a barbaric politics with the avant-garde aesthetic. Both spatially (in terms of the nation-state) and temporally (in terms of historical precedent) all plagiaristic metadiscursive legitimations based on plenitude are anathema to the avant-garde. Time and Space died Yesterday.

CHAPTER 4

The Politics of
the Manifest

If it is necessary to understand the avant-garde as a process of *Selbstkritik*, as Bürger insists, as an institutional
rupture with the discourse of art rather than a system-immanent
quarrel with any specific literary or artistic precedent, the preceding framing of Futurism within an analysis of the changing
legitimational strategy of the autonomy aesthetic will have proved
useful. At the same time, the consideration in the previous chapter
of the historical modality of decadence will, I hope, have served
to illustrate the way in which the radical rupture with history is
itself determined by the cultural specificity of a prevailing historical paradigm. In Marinetti's case, the ostensibly system-immanent
critique of Symbolism and the institutional critique of art as such
are inextricably linked. Culturally and politically, Marinetti's response to literary and political precedents must be related both to
Italy's belated imperialism and to its dependence upon the cultural
traditions of other countries.

Thus, while Jameson is right to point out the importance to
modernists such as Lewis of the collapse of the nation-state as a
viable allegorical vehicle, it has proved possible to go further in the
case of Marinetti, and to assert a certain historical and aesthetic af-

finity with the project of imperialism. It was particularly important to evaluate Marinetti's relation to literary precedents—specifically to Aestheticism, and more specifically still, to Mallarmé—because of the political over-coding of the aestheticist position within the body of critical theory. In this chapter, I wish to explore in more detail the terms of Marinetti's system-immanent critique of Mallarmé in order to understand the ways in which Marinetti, by way of a confrontation with his own Symbolist past, develops a political ideology which is at the same time a poetics. If nothing else, Marinetti, whose career presents itself as a telescopic model of the historical trajectory mapped out in Bürger's *Theory of the Avant-Garde*, offers a touchstone for the assessment of the current state of theory. Developing out of and against a decadent aestheticism, he stands at the very threshold of the avant-garde project of the early part of the twentieth century. It is therefore all the more surprising that he should be so consistently written out of theories of the avant-garde.

Before confronting Marinetti's critique in its specificity, let us contextualize his contribution within the political framework of the previous chapters. In his essay on the origins of the avant-garde, Egbert observes a bifurcation of artistic engagements in politics in the nineteenth century. On the one hand there was a tradition derived from Saint-Simon, which was committed to direct social intervention and which subsequently proved amenable to directly politicized aesthetics and ultimately to a form of Marxism; on the other hand there were those who wished to restrain the aesthetic realm from any direct intervention in the political. Egbert characterizes this latter strain:

> The latter in turn, if they had any social interest at all, were likely to be sympathetic to the social utopianism of Saint-Simon's chief socialist rival, Charles Fourier, who in contrast to Saint-Simon stood not for a social movement highly centralized about a controlling élite group, but for decentralizing society and government into small, closely knit, federated communities, or "phalanxes," as more conducive to the personal development of their individual members. Thus, where Saint-Simon was to be in many respects an ancestor of the Marxian varieties of communism, Fourier was to be an ancestor of modern communist

anarchism, a variety of socialism to which leaders of art for art's sake understandably became more sympathetic.[1]

Egbert does not develop his argument in strictly literary-historical terms, but the implications are clear, as is the problematic nature of those implications for any analysis of the avant-garde. If the avant-garde does indeed represent a dialectical moment within the fully articulated literary and aesthetic subsystem first made explicit in Aestheticism, then the political model it inherits is oriented not toward direct social action, but toward a form of anarchism whose very raison d'être consists in the desire to maintain autonomous discursive subsystems. This is a restatement of the paradox encountered in our consideration of decadence as an impossible attempt to realize that which opposes its own realization in praxis.

The history of the term "avant-garde," then, gives the lie to the theory of the avant-garde. The term itself derives from a Saint-Simonian tradition of instrumentalization, whereas—if Bürger is to be believed, and I think he is—the avant-garde of the twentieth century is made possible only by an Aestheticism owing much to an opposing tradition identified with Fourier. There is a fundamental tension within the avant-garde, it would seem; a tension exemplified by this ambiguity of origin. Critically, Aestheticist anarchism is identified with decentralization, with the sort of individualism championed by Calinescu. In turn, decentralization favors the establishment of autonomous discursive practices, such as the aesthetic mode, no longer subordinated to any central political or philosophical program. How, then, do we disentangle these conflicting impulses operative within the genealogy of the avant-garde?

It is tempting in the light of the attempt to understand the avant-garde project as the reintegration of art and life to stigmatize Aestheticism as a sort of historical nadir, which by its very extremity made it possible for the avant-garde to articulate a counter-position. Such a stigmatization oversimplifies, for Aestheticism's attempt to extricate art from life necessarily bears within itself a critical moment. First, in the face of an ever more totalizing Life-world, the assertion of the possibility of autonomous discourse—

an "outside"—is in itself subversive. Second, the recognition that certain affects, certain practices, certain ideas must be ideologically and discursively sequestered, by virtue of being incommensurable with the broader realm of social practice, necessarily condemns that society which excludes them. Aestheticism, then, is not simply affirmative in Marcuse's sense. When Mallarmé argues that "language, in the hands of the mob, leads to the same facility and directness as does money," he confronts head-on those realities that merely affirmative art must exclude.[2] Whereas affirmation establishes autonomy by fiat, so to speak, in Aestheticism autonomy is established as a counterdiscourse.

There is, however, a further difficulty in theorizing the relationship of the avant-garde to its aestheticist predecessors—namely, Bürger's categorial definition of the avant-garde as a reaction not against any particular movement, but against the institution of art *as such*. Beginning with this definition, how is it even possible to speak of the specific relation of the avant-garde to Aestheticism as the relationship of one aesthetic movement to another? One might begin to answer this question on the general methodological level in the light of our consideration of aesthetic autonomy. Thus aestheticism might be said to operate at the level of what in chapter 2 I labeled the "vulgarized" notion of autonomy, for its autonomy consists in a rejection of the integrative and totalizing discourse of commodification. As a product it might fall prey to relations of commodification and exchange; but it nevertheless attempts to articulate within itself an opposition to those relations.

At first sight, it would seem that Marinetti's attack on the Symbolists is out of kilter with Bürger's insistence upon the institutional rather than system-immanent modality of avant-garde critique. Despite the more fundamental Futurist attacks on cultural institutions such as the museum and the academy, the literary critique in Marinetti's manifestos has a quite specific and identifiable (even nameable) object. As a category of distinction and discrimination, then, does Bürger's insistence upon institutional rather than system-immanent critique consign Futurism to the realm of mere modernity, excluding it (as it is quite pointedly excluded from his analysis) from the avant-garde? Or might the reverse be the case? Might not the system-immanent critique of Marinetti's manifestos question the terms of Bürger's analysis?

To proffer this latter suggestion is not simply to assert that the Futurists de facto constituted an avant-garde, that they engaged in system-immanent critique, and that such critique must therefore be perfectly commensurable with the avant-garde project. Rather, it is a question of reexamining the systematicity of a historically localizable critique itself as a taxonomy. For what is the object of institutional critique if not an aesthetic construct—that is, art itself? When Bürger insists upon "the full unfolding of the constituent elements of a field [as] the condition for the possibility of an adequate cognition of that field" (P. Bürger, *Theory*, p. 17) he demonstrates the incommensurability of his own model of cognition, based as it is upon a notion of plenitude or full unfolding, with the deconstructive practice of the avant-garde. Bürger's "institution," which seems to resolve itself into the paradoxically philosophical autonomy of art rather than into a material critique, this implicit "as such" of art, is itself legitimated only within the confines of a form of temporality dear to the Symbolists of Marinetti's critique—a temporality consisting not only in nostalgia but also in a belief in the "immortal" and the "imperishable."

Thus when Marinetti proclaims, "To the conception of the imperishable, the immortal, we oppose, in art, that of becoming, the perishable, the transitory, and the ephemeral,"[3] what he is articulating is not a simple regression from the conceptual possibilities of a panoramic history made possible by that simultaneity of the radically disparate achieved in Aestheticism. This is not simply a return to the mundane historicity of the internecine, or system-immanent, literary squabbles characteristic of modernism. Rather, Marinetti's position demonstrates the inextricability of modernity and the avant-garde. For the immortality of Aestheticist temporalities is itself potentially already a "going-beyond," is itself a modernist, system-immanent critique of the modernist temporality of "going-beyond." It is what lies beyond the temporal beyond of modernity—and therefore it partakes of that modernity. Consequently, Futurism, as an inheritor of the Aestheticist position, is faced with the impossibility of articulating a negation that will not enter in turn into the spiral of negation constitutive of the progressive logic of modernity. This will be a negation of history *in* history, rather than history's transcendent negation of itself *as* History.

It is indicative of the difficulties inherent in any attempt to break with the linear temporality of historical narrative that Marinetti himself should feel compelled to describe the emergence of Futurism in terms of an individualized narrative of birth and death. The birth of Futurism was announced to the world in *Le Figaro* of Paris on February 20th, 1909, in terms clearly indicating both the Symbolist influence and the persistence of a narrative of historical emergence: "We had stayed up all night, my friends and I, under hanging mosque lamps with domes of filigreed brass, domes starred like our spirits, shining like them with the prisoned radiance of electric hearts. For hours we had trampled our atavistic ennui into rich oriental rugs, arguing up to the last confines of logic and blackening many reams of paper with our frenzied scribbling" (Marinetti, *SW*, p. 39). Futurism was born of Symbolism, it would seem. Or—since the subsequent manifesto itself is engendered only through the text's careering into a "maternal ditch almost full of muddy water" (Marinetti, *SW*, p. 40)—one might say that Symbolism exerted a paternalistic influence and impact upon Futurism. The mosque lamp, redolent of a decadent orientalism underscored by the oriental rugs and the pervasive ' sense of ennui, already harbors the secret of Futurism, yet covers it, diffuses it, filters it, renders it decorative. Such is Marinetti's own symbolic representation of the ambiguous relationship that (according to Bürger) the avant-garde maintains to Aestheticism. It is not a relationship of simple negation, but rather of Futurism's exploitation and liberation of certain energies already inherent in Aestheticism.

The Founding Manifesto is quite clearly an attempt to work through and work a way out of Symbolist topoi. The former Symbolist poet Marinetti confronts his own literary past with more than a touch of irony. Elsewhere, the tone is rather less conciliatory—as in the manifesto "We Abjure Our Symbolist Masters, the Last Lovers of the Moon." Here, while recognizing the influence of Symbolist forebears, Marinetti quite explicitly dissociates Futurism from Aestheticism, and from D'Annunzio—the champion of such literary tendencies in Italy—who is here execrated with particular vehemence for the following "intellectual poisons": "(1) the sickly, nostalgic poetry of distance and memory; (2) romantic sentimentality drenched with moonshine that looks up adoringly to the ideal of Woman-Beauty; (3) obsession with lechery, with the adulterous triangle, the pepper of incest, and the spice of Christian sin; (4) the professorial passion for the past and the mania for antiquity and collecting" (Marinetti, *SW*, p. 68). These, then, are the themes that dominate the manifesto: the loathing of nostalgia, the celebration of an androcentric machine-culture over the Symbolist "soliloquizing vegetation" and "botanical sentimentality," and above all the rejection of "a passion for eternal things, a desire for immortal, imperishable masterworks" (Marinetti, *SW*, pp. 66–68). Of particular interest in the light of the erotic project to be outlined in the following chapter is the rejection of "the adulterous triangle." Marinetti's antieroticism (belied by other highly erotic celebrations of the machine—as, for example, in the Founding Manifesto) is rooted in a misogyny that quite clearly confronts that primal "adulterous triangle" of the oedipal family.

The inspiration for Marinetti's rejection of Symbolism is consistently grounded in an eroticized confrontation with the sentimentality of those "Lovers of the Moon," the Symbolists. Nevertheless, the grounds for his rejection of Symbolism are themselves elaborated from within the topoi of Symbolism itself. "Thus we will transform," he promises, "the *nevermore* of Edgar Poe into a sharp joy and will teach people to love the beauty of an emotion or a sensation *to the degree that it is unique and destined to vanish irreparably*" (Marinetti, *SW*, p. 67). The temporality of Futurism is a temporality of deferral. Far from being the simplistic "presentism" deplored by Poggioli, it celebrates the emotion not for the here and now, but for the moment of its disappearance. The temporality is modernist insofar as the present is laden with the potentiality of the future, and yet the present is itself experienced only as a form of anteriority—from the standpoint of a future of pure negation. Nothing is to be ontologized, not even the temporality which denies all ontology. This, for Marinetti, marks the difference between Aestheticism and Futurism. Whereas the former attempts to negate the temporality of modernity as the temporality of endless commodity exchange by imagining a moment of presence projected (and absented) into infinity, Futurism aims to *accelerate* the temporality of modernity to the point where no moment of presence can be posited—except in retrospect, as a despicable symptom of nostalgia. And Futurism hates nothing more than nostalgia—which is necessarily the nostalgia not simply of one temporal present for another, but rather an ontological nostalgia for the very category of presence itself.

It is in this, and not in some outdated thematic of vintage cars and biplanes, that Futurism is a celebration of futurity, of speed. In this important manifesto we are offered much more than a thematic resumé of Futurism. What we have is nothing less than a philosophy of history—or rather, a refusal to fix such a philosophy; a refusal to fix it even in the refusal itself. In tracing the transmigration of this aesthetic into the elaboration of a consistent politics, it is interesting to note that it is precisely the same critique of a specific ideology of time that informs Marinetti's political response to anarchism in the manifesto "Trieste, our beautiful powder-keg." More importantly, however, the political manifesto serves to demonstrate Marinetti's failure to develop from the aesthetic of the earlier manifesto a political counterdiscourse that could resist the moment of presence with equal consistency. Translated into the discourse of politics, Marinetti's aesthetic concretizes around a metaphysics of presence, as when he draws the following distinction between Futurism and anarchism: "Futurism quite clearly distinguishes itself from the anarchic conception. The latter, denying the infinite principle of human evolution, limits its parabolic thrust to the ideal of universal peace and a stupid paradise consisting of embraces in the open air and swaying palms. We, on the other hand, assert as the absolute principle of Futurism the continuous development of man."[4] Once again there is that same revulsion at the moment of history's arrest in universal peace. Here, this is a moment of self-reflection and self-presence in which man can take man in his arms—quite literally—just as, in the moment of discursive full unfolding, the artist could, in a moment of cognition (*Begreifen*), take hold of and transcend the institutions framing his or her critique. More problematic, and indicative of the difficulties of articulating the postmodern temporality of Futurism as a political project, is the invocation here of notions of evolution, which threaten to reintroduce a form of progressivism.

Whereas the critique in the aesthetic realm managed to weave its way around issues of temporality, refusing to inhabit any one of them, here the political rejection of anarchism (which, it will be remembered, Egbert had isolated as a forerunner of the avant-garde, and which forms the backbone of "individualist" celebrations of the avant-garde) results in a position that falls short of the complexities of the aesthetic critique. I think it is possible to see, in this falling away of critical rigor in the passage from aesthetics to politics, the reason for Futurism's necessary but necessarily ill-fated involvement in fascism. Ironically, it is not the inhumane machinic culture proposed in the anti-Aestheticist manifesto that compromises with the totalizing and totalitarian discourse of fascism, but rather the illicit humanism, which celebrates "the continuous development of man." In the passage from an aesthetic to a political critique, then, there would seem to be a loss of clarity and of radicality. But does this inability to follow through the critique of Aestheticism with an equally philosophically convincing political critique manifest itself at the level of poetic practice?

The parallel of the critique of Aestheticism and the critique of anarchism serves to obscure the context in which Marinetti will most consistently read Symbolism—the context of capital. Marinetti's critique of Symbolist passéism articulates itself as a critique of the arrest of capitalist self-destruction, or takes that arrest as the paradigmatic expression of both an aesthetic and a morality to which Futurism is opposed. Opposing the notion of aesthetic immortality, Marinetti explains, "We on the other hand think that nothing is lower or meaner than to think of immortality while creating a work of art, lower or meaner than the calculated, usurious idea of the Christian heaven, which is supposed to reward our earthly virtues at a million percent profit" (Marinetti, *SW*, p. 66). This passage marks an important turn in the Futurist critique of Aestheticism, for it problematizes the assumption that the temporality of modernity is synonymous with the evaluative potentialities of capitalist exchange. Whereas one might generally think of the disposability of the modernist aesthetic—caricatured in Marinetti's conviction that "when we are forty, other younger and stronger men will probably throw us in the wastebasket like useless manuscripts—we want it to happen!" (Marinetti, *SW*, p. 43)—as being necessarily predicated upon a system of exchange and replacement that fosters consumerism, Marinetti seems to be pointing toward the investment of that system in notions of aesthetic immortality. Immortality is invoked as an accretion of the mortal, as its usurious escalation—as the point of fulfillment and realization of value toward which the system of exchange is necessarily oriented but which it must never attain. Likening this notion of value realization to the Christian notion of heaven, Marinetti opens up the possibility of reading his system-immanent critique of Symbolism as indicative of a much broader social, political, and moral critique. In effect, by reading the Symbolist aesthetic tropologically, he questions the very possibility of any limitation of critique to the aesthetic system.

History, then, is historicized as a legitimation strategy of capitalism. "History, in our eyes, is fatally a forger, or at least a miserable collector of stamps, medals and counterfeit coins" (Marinetti, *SW*, p. 67). This critique of the counterfeit, of history as a miserable collection of the inauthentic, clearly recalls Marinetti's critique of plagiarism against Mussolini's Romanizing imperialism. History, it would seem, is necessarily plagiaristic, necessarily a counterfeiter, and yet it figures as the discourse grounding all exchange, as the temporality in which all values will eventually come into their own. It is, in fact, the principle of capital itself, the principle of amassed value, the withdrawal of exchange values from actual exchange; and therefore, the discourse in terms of which all value (as something extrinsic to the act of exchange itself) reveals itself to be counterfeit. History is at once the transcendence of historical contingency within which all events are potentially exchangeable, and at the same time the gold standard against which all such events might be exchanged and valorized. Marinetti does not seem to be suggesting a move beyond or outside the exchange relations of capitalism as an alternative to the modernist temporality, but advocates rather the refusal to re-collect those relations (and in this re-collection, history is necessarily, even when future-oriented, a passéist discourse) in the omnipresence of History. Such is the ideological framework within which the critique of Mallarmé and the Symbolists is articulated.

While in his simultaneous acceptance and rejection of Symbolism as a literary precedent he seems to confirm Bürger's analysis of the central importance of Aestheticism to the development of the avant-garde, Marinetti's pronouncements at the same time problematize some of the categories Bürger develops to characterize the avant-garde itself as a historical phenomenon. To pursue the political implications of what seems at first glance to be a specifically literary or system-immanent critique, it is necessary to delve deeper into the terms of the debate on poetry inaugurated by Marinetti in the manifestos. The "futurism" of Futurism consists in something other than the simple celebration of technology and futuristic topoi. It consists in a historical perspective that situates itself outside the ontology of History in its full unfolding without falling back into the historical self-narration typical of modernity.

There is a second crucial element to the "futurism" of the movement, however: a critique located at the level of signification and representation itself. Marinetti abhors the passéism inherent in *any* act of representation, in the primacy it affords to the "thing" represented, to the signified over the signifier. The dual terms of signification stand, for Marinetti, as markers of a temporal ideology, an ideology that privileges the passive past of the signi*fied* over the active present of the signi*fier*. The yoking of the signifier to the signified, which supposedly preexists it, is for Marinetti the most fundamental expression of our culture's indebtedness to a past identified with the self-sufficiency of the prelinguistic signified. Marinetti's attack on the signified is implicitly an attack on the conceptual framework of rationality. A consideration of the temporality of signification mediates the philosophical position outlined in Marinetti's model of history and vice versa; to understand how this is so it will be necessary to think in terms of the relation of the temporal present to the philosophical presence of cognition.

What remains to be elucidated, then, is the relationship of Marinetti's valorization of the evanescent *present* to his rejection of the cognitive *presence* implicit in the aestheticized notion of historical full unfolding. This question is particularly difficult to answer precisely because what is at issue is not simply an insistence upon the uniqueness and irreplaceability of the temporal (of the present) as opposed to an ontology of presence, but rather a valorization of an "anterior" present (an evanescence) over presence as the ontology of temporality itself. It is not (in the crudest of terms) a face-off between Temporality and Ontology, but rather between Temporality and *its own* Ontology. These are the terms in which Marinetti's rejection of Symbolism must be read, as a refusal to "go beyond" the "going beyond" of modernity, as a refusal to pass from the historical present of modernity to the historical and philosophical presence of full unfolding. Thus what seems like a regression, or a rootedness in the successive temporality of modernism—that is, Marinetti's system-immanent critique of Symbolism—is a refusal of modernity's own self-sublation.

To reframe the opposition of presence and the present: does Marinetti consistently inhabit the temporality of deferral implicit in his notion of the present, or are there moments when he falls back into the logic of presence itself? We have already seen, for example, the way in which his attempt to relocate the aesthetic critique to the realm of the political (in the critique of anarchism) obliged historical deferral to legitimate itself "representationally," that is, in the name of that which was deferred: in Man, in the history of becoming. But the question can also be situated at the level of a textual reading, at the level of the text's working, of its machinations.

The terminology of our investigation, whose importance will be examined in the next chapter, will focus upon the moment of *production* in Marinetti's work, as opposed to the moment of *representation*. Does the text produce or does it represent? And what, indeed, might either of these possibilities look like in literary form or in performance? Is the machinic process of literary production consistently privileged over the fixed and static representation? And what is the relationship of representation to production? This is the concern informing the textual analysis to follow. If representation is to be rejected as a form of re-collection, as slavery to the past, what would an aesthetics of production produce? In producing itself as text, what will it look like? And if it produces, what will be the *product* of production? Might representation, in fact, be the *excess* of production—a by-product—rather than an opposing moment of stasis and retrospection?

These questions raise important issues, which recontextualize much of the current debate on literary modernity. Thus, for instance, Marinetti's resistance to presence would constitute an apparently paradoxical extrapolation of the poetics of autonomy. The deferral of that moment of full unfolding, which Bürger takes to be possible only at the moment in which a discourse pretends to be itself and nothing more, is also a moment of self-negation of the aesthetic, a spilling over into the realm of conceptuality and philosophical truth. Likewise, the Jamesonian critique of spatialized modern form as intrinsically inimical to the historicity of progress could now be rethought as an opposition of a temporality figured spatially—and therefore sublated into the realm of cognition (presence)—and a temporality resistant to all such spatial mediation, in which the irreducibility of the discourse takes shape in the valorization of an unfixable, evanescent present. What has hitherto been thought in terms of a simple opposition of progressive temporality and reactionary spatialization might, then, be seen as a more fundamental confrontation of literature with its own sublation into philosophy.

Moreover, in this scenario, Marinetti—the avant-gardiste, the Fascist Modernist—is on the side of temporality, of the present, rather than of presence. Given Jameson's own preference for the temporal (as historical time), it is not surprising that he, for one, should alight almost despite himself on another Fascist Modernist writer: Wyndham Lewis. I would suggest that he thereby enters into a sublimated debate upon the autonomy of art; a debate in which writers such as Marinetti attempt to defer the moment of philosophization in order to bring about the long-awaited confrontation of art and life. Bürger's model implicitly philosophizes the aesthetic *before* the confrontation takes place, so that it is an already philosophized aesthetic ("fully unfolded") which finds itself in the arms of a prephilosophized life. "Politics" here would be nothing more than the name acquired by philosophy at the moment of its historical self-recognition.

We might begin upon a more concrete examination of these issues by identifying what it is, exactly, that Marinetti opposes within the *poetic* practice of Symbolism and by reconstructing the terms in which his opposition is couched. The treatment of Mallarmé in the 1913 manifesto "Destruction of Syntax–Imagination without Strings–Words-in-Freedom" is grounded in a critique of the Symbolists' use of the adjective: a critique which reads on the surface as a straightforward critique of linguistic preciosity.

> I oppose the decorative, precious aesthetic of Mallarmé and his search for the rare word, the one indispensable, elegant, suggestive, exquisite adjective. I do not want to suggest an idea or a sensation with passéist airs and graces. Instead I want to grasp them brutally and hurl them in the reader's face. Moreover, I combat Mallarmé's static ideal with this typographical revolution that allows me to impress on the words (already free, dynamic, and torpedo-like) every velocity of the stars, the clouds, the aeroplanes, trains, waves, explosives, globules of seafoam, molecules, and atoms.[5]

The adjective is presented here as ornamentation, as something extrinsic to the noun in all its immanent self-presence. And yet, though necessarily "decorative," the adjective nevertheless presents itself as "indispensable," as intrinsic to the very thing it decorates. The adjective is a necessary supplement.

Whereas the Mallarméan adjective *evokes* an experience, the futurist text *is* an experience, hurled in the face of the reader or the audience. Elsewhere, Marinetti explains, "Everywhere we tend to suppress the qualifying adjective because it presupposes an arrest in intuition, too minute a definition of the noun" (Marinetti, *FM*, p. 103). The decorative adjective is "an arrest in intuition," slowing down the noun, shading its brilliance—under the ornamentation, perhaps, of a filigreed brass mosque lamp. Implicitly, it would seem, the noun functions as intuition, as the unmediated presence of the thing itself; and by qualifying the noun, the adjective launches it into the realm of linguistic exchange. By "qualifying" the noun for linguistic use, in other words, the adjective both enables and distorts it. The adjective stands in a supplementary relationship to the noun, both defining and deforming, displaying and hiding its essence. In other words, the adjective both fixes and circulates the noun, fixes it qualitatively, yet draws it up into the play of language. Identity becomes systemic and dynamic—and yet, as intuition, as a force that resists any arrest, the noun is in and of itself naturally dynamic, and unthinkable in isolation. The adjective, then, does not really do anything alien to the nature of the noun itself, but rather facilitates and liberates the very essence of the noun.

The problem of the noun in Marinetti's work goes to the very heart of the problematic of presence. Is his celebration of the noun not a relapse into a metaphysics of immediacy and presence? To answer this question it is necessary to investigate the economic and historical subtext of Marinetti's critique of Mallarmé. The apparently straightforward critique of Symbolist preciosity opens up, by way of this consideration of a linguistic economy that both fixes and circulates the noun, to an examination of the status of poetics within the broader social context of high capitalism. This shift in register is marked by the critique of "preciosity," which draws its primary resonance from the critique of decadence and ornamentation: the noun should not be adorned precisely because it is itself reality unadorned. At first sight, Marinetti's attack on "preciosity" seems to offer no more than a conventional critique of mimesis as falsification, proposing instead an "intuitive" system of representation based on the noun, which would avoid falsification. To this extent, one might see in Marinetti's fetishism of the noun the makings of an essential poetics of presence, a poetics of the noun.

At the same time, however, he seems to be suggesting that this "decorative, precious aesthetic" operates on a second, economic level, where preciosity would be qualified not so much by the adjective "decorative," implying literary mannerism, but rather by its investment in the "rare word." Preciosity here seems, quite literally, to indicate the desire to uncover value in language, to manipulate and accumulate "precious" matter through a system of scarcity and "rarity." The rare adjective constitutes a monopolizing moment in the system of linguistic exchange, limiting and restricting the free exchange of noun against noun. Clearly, Marinetti is aligning the linguistic fetishism of the Mallarméan "precious" adjective—syntactically transferable, yet semantically fixated—with a capitalist fetishism of commodities. The suggestion is that the "precious" or "rare" adjective, like the fetishized commodity, presents a nexus of value at once arbitrary and absolute: it "affixes" qualities to the noun only in order that such value be liquidated in the flow of language. Aestheticism would be the adequate aesthetic expression of high capitalism.

But does this necessarily involve Marinetti in an alternative fetishism, the fetishism of the noun itself, the assertion of the immediate presence of value in the noun / name? On one level, the critique of supplementarity—of the adjective as ornament—would seem to point in this direction, and yet the recognition that the adjective also does the work of the noun by bringing it into circulation seems to suggest otherwise. In fact, Marinetti wishes to negate Mallarmé's poetics not in the name of the noun as plenitude, but rather by means of an acceleration of its exchange-oriented economy. For Marinetti, the problem with Mallarmé's adjectives is not that they operate within a specific commodity-economy, but that they *short-circuit* that system. Quite literally

in-dispensable (translation into English renders explicit the terminology of substitution in Marinetti's critique), the Mallarméan adjective cannot be spent; it withdraws from the system of expenditure that constitutes it and potentially forecloses the system of exchange within which value is created. This is the "stasis" Marinetti fears. Though seemingly propelling the noun into a system of linguistic exchange, the Mallarméan adjective simultaneously holds it back from that process.

Marinetti's fear of the precious and indispensable adjective is nothing less than capital's fear of itself. It is the recognition of the necessity of amassing capital—of situating value within one place—and of the hazards this presents to a concept of value predicated upon exchange. The critique of the Mallarméan adjective is not a critique of capitalism per se, but of capital's inalienable and alienating tendency toward fixation. There is something scandalous about a system in which value is realized only by exchange, yet which motivates exchange on the basis of the private accumulation of value—that is, on the basis of capital as a value no longer seeking to valorize itself through exchange but to withdraw itself from the general economy. The Mallarméan adjective qualifies and brings into play the noun, but threatens by its very preciosity and indispensability to collapse all value by withholding exchange, by setting the price too high. This is why the adjective is "too definite": at the same time as its very substitutionality is predicated upon the exchange-oriented nature of value, its fetishized fixation upon the noun endangers exchange. Exchange demands definitions that are precisely *not* definite, that are mutable and interdefining, and that allow the principle of metaphor fundamental to any economy of exchange, linguistic or otherwise.

At the ideological heart of capitalism, the fetishism of commodities inscribes within the dynamics of exchange a moment of ideological fixation. Momentarily, exchange supposes that value inheres in the objects being exchanged, that profit can be drawn from the acquisition of a commodity. At the same time, however, it must be understood that the commodity has no value outside the act of exchange, which supposedly postdates it. In the stage of full unfolding, capitalism would be forced to recognize that the ideology of inherent value is indeed an ideology, and that it is not the commodity but the process of commodification itself that must be fetishized. The unique, indispensable adjective of the Mallarméan poetics—as presented in Marinetti's critique—poeticizes the duping of capital by its own constitutive fetishism. By insisting upon the necessary relation of adjective and noun, Mallarmé imposes a false unity of object and value (noun and adjective), implying that the relation is somehow natural and real. Once relational value is taken to be inherent, however, the whole system of value formation collapses, for the process of exchange loses its function as the locus of *production* of value and (apparently) serves merely as the realization (or representation?) of a value supposed to be inherent. Once exchange becomes extrinsic to this fetishized value, it becomes redundant, and with the ideological denigration of exchange, the generator of all value, the system of values necessary to capitalism itself collapses.

As value ascends toward the absolute, the infinite, or at least the immeasurable, it loses value. The phenomenon might best be elucidated by the double entendre of the English terms "priceless" and "invaluable": the "absolute" of value, the "fixation" of value in a system in which value can be constituted only through a series of differences and in the act of exchange, is necessarily the negation of value. The absolute of value negates value: the highest price is no price at all. At its extreme, the Mallarméan aesthetic pushes the possibility of a capitalist representational system toward its null point. What Mallarmé represents (or rather, what he produces!) in the escalation of value toward the zero is the realization of that virtual goal that mediated representational systems must resist. In Mallarmé, *the system represents itself* (as nothingness), and thus all production is necessarily framed within representation. Aestheticism enacts a dialectical moment of self-negation within the representational ideology of capitalism.

The attempt to escape a poetics of presence, the attempt to offer a linguistic critique of capitalism, and the attempt to subvert the temporal dynamic of modernity all seem to turn on a certain

understanding of mimesis. But, as we have seen, there is in Marinetti's critique of adjectival preciosity at the very least a suggestion
of an alternative poetics of presence bodied forth in the noun, a
poetics in which "reality" threatens to enter, unmediated, into the
play of the text. However, it is important to supplement Marinetti's reading of the Mallarméan adjective with a reading of his
own prescriptions for the noun. He does not, in fact, propose the
noun as absolute value or plenitude, but rather as something intrinsically inessential and essentially relative—in short, as *analogia*.
Forced to deal with the way in which the adjective, despite its attempts to fix value to nouns, in some sense "does the work" of the
noun, by opening for it the dynamic field of linguistic exchange
which is its element, Marinetti develops a poetics of the "*sostantivo
doppio*." "Every noun should have its double," he proclaims, "that
is, the noun should be followed, with no conjunction, by the noun
to which it is related by analogy. Example: man-torpedo-boat.
woman-gulf, crowd-surf, piazza-funnel, door-faucet. Just as aerial
speed has multiplied our knowledge of the world, the percep-
tion of analogy becomes ever more natural for man" (Marinetti,
SW, pp. 84–85). The paradox of the "indispensable" Mallarméan
adjective is its attribution of essentiality to the noun, which exists
only within a system of interaction and interrelation. Whereas the
critique of the "precious" Mallarméan adjective seemed to imply
the operation within Marinetti's writing of a metaphysics of poetic
presence exemplified by the unmodified noun, this second passage stresses the way in which the noun necessarily modifies *itself*
and necessarily attaches *itself* to other nouns, thereby vitiating the
semblance of self-sufficiency and autonomous self-presence.

The *sostantivo doppio* redefines the noun beyond nomenclaturist
assumptions of identity. The noun as name is replaced by the process of differentiation and displacement inherent in the very *act*
of naming. Rather than an arrest in intuition, we have an interaction of nouns that, in their endless collision, suspend any final
meaning and manifest the *production* of meaning. Representation
is represented by its own production. The noun is characterized
both as an indissoluble unity of terms and as a naming of differ-

ence: for, though the noun or name might itself be arbitrary, the act of displacement and differentiation is essential, insofar as it adequately represents the dynamism of objects themselves. This, I would argue, would be the point at which one might begin to ascertain the reemergence of mimesis, of representational adequation, in Marinetti's work. The dynamism of the nouns enacts the dynamism of material objects. Analogia, classically, would not be the relation of one thing to another, but the relation of one set of relations to another; it is this relationship of relations that informs Marinetti's representationalism. The noun is not a name; nor is it in any sense an adequate representation of the thing itself. However, the action of noun upon noun in the *sostantivo doppio* does replay the actual dynamism of objects themselves.

Contrary to a traditional understanding of fetishism, Marinetti's poetics paradoxically fetishizes the relation itself *as* relation. It does not, at the primary level, freeze relations into things. What the *sostantivo doppio* articulates is the possibility of freezing the act of displacement inherent in substituting word for object, or word for word in the name itself. The maintenance of both terms in the analogy makes of it an "analogy-in-production." Thus the Futurist analogia suggests both a model of reference and representation, and also a model of production. No word or name is adequate as a representation of a "pre-textual" reality, but the process of linguistic displacements, foregrounded in the *sostantivo doppio*, comes to represent *itself*. The engine of the Futurist text is a machine for the production of representations, and what the representations represent is production. The text is a short-circuiting machine, representing and producing at once, representing production by producing representation. The important thing—the thing that the reified opposition of production and representation might lead us to neglect—is not to read representation necessarily as presence, but also as production.

If the critique of supplementarity, the critique of the ornamental and precious adjective does not exhaust itself in the assertion of linguistic plenitude in the noun, one might expect that it would also be necessary to reexamine the function of the adjective itself.

Rather than opposing noun with adjective, it might be necessary, in other words, to deconstruct a poetics grounded on the supposed polarity of adjective and noun. And indeed, the adjectival values of qualification, dispensability and displacement are, in fact, revived by Marinetti in an adjectival counterpart to the *sostantivo doppio*, the semaphoric adjective: "What I call a semaphoric adjective, lighthouse-adjective, or atmosphere-adjective is the adjective apart from nouns, isolated in parentheses. This makes it a kind of absolute noun, broader and more powerful than the noun proper" (Marinetti, *FM*, p. 103). To think the adjective as semaphor is to think it in a radically minimalist semiotic framework. As semaphor, the adjective might be expected to limit itself to the act of "flagging" or "signaling" the object: it would not define or modify the noun, but simply mark its presence. This act of marking is central to the Futurist adjective—but it is *not* the marking of a presence, not a simple flagging of what is already there. Marinetti goes beyond the notion of the semaphor to characterize such adjectives as "a kind of absolute noun, broader and more powerful than the noun proper." The original opposition of adjective and noun deconstructs itself. The adjective sequesters itself between parentheses and becomes a noun—but it is an "absolute" noun, more of a noun than the noun itself.

Whereas the noun offers little more than a static representation of the forces of language passing through it, the semaphoric adjective is not simply the *representation* of those forces of exchange, but the very medium whereby that exchange is enacted. At the same time as the noun reveals itself as a mere congealing of the adjectival function, however, the adjective is in turn "isolated in parentheses," sequestered from the process of linguistic exchange it enables. The presence it flags—semaphorically—is its *own* presence; that is, the presence of the system of exchange it mediates. Though set "apart from nouns," the adjective is itself a noun, a fixation of sorts. Consequently, at the same time as the Futurist poetic dissolves the fetish-noun, it creates the nominal adjective, thereby recontaining the forces of pure exchangeability it sought to liberate. Marinetti does not escape the static, fixative elements of the

Mallarméan adjective entirely; as signs of the process of signification itself, as objects caught in the process of commodification, the
semaphoric adjectives *do* present a momentary, nominal "arrest of
intuition."

Whereas Mallarmé (according to Marinetti) uses the adjective
to isolate and render absolute the value inherent in the noun, what
Marinetti seeks is an isolation of the function of the adjective itself
as a *principle* of evaluation and value creation. He does not celebrate the accruing of value in the noun, but rather the very system
of exchange whereby value can be created. What seems at first to
be an attack on the adjective (in Mallarmé) finally brings about a
fetishization of the relationality of the adjective (hence its fixation
as noun "in parentheses") and of the possibility of its displacement
from one noun to another. The freedom of the adjective to circu-
late is the essence of Marinetti's "words in freedom." The word
is free on one condition: that it be free! Thus the arbitrariness of
the linguistic fragment is not arbitrary at all, but motivated by the
system within which its exchange-value is established.

The collapse of the adjective-noun opposition further signals
the impossibility of segmenting the Futurist text along the lines
of production and representation. Representation is necessarily
produced: to think it merely as the denotation of something essentially other than itself is to think it within excessively constricting
mimetic confines. Representation is not simply the failure of production, but is itself a mode of production. At the same time as
he celebrates the pure productivity of the semaphoric adjective,
Marinetti nevertheless hypostatizes it as the referent of its own
semaphoric signaling. In parentheses, set aside from language—as
that moment making language possible as a system of exchange—
it congeals into a noun. Consequently, just as it is necessary to read
representation as production, to think the "static" noun in its radical relationality, as *sostantivo doppio*, so it must be recognized that
production can in turn be nominalized, producing for itself a sign
that is itself a representation, "a kind of absolute noun, broader
and more powerful than the noun proper." Whereas the collapse
of the noun into the modality of the adjectival shifter can be read

as a collapse of presence into difference, the parenthetical isolation of the adjectival function once again suggests the return of a metaphysic of presence. As the noun that signifies the system of exchange—which is itself alone constitutive of noun-values—the adjectival "absolute noun" signifies itself and its own coming into Being. It *is / signifies* absolute mimesis.

Recent work on Futurism has chosen to see in techniques such as onomatopoeia (or in the use of noise in the sound poem as a linguistic effect not mediated through rational meaning) the operation of an "absolute" mimetic impulse opposing bourgeois models of representation.[6] This would mean that Futurism denies the process of mediation and distantiation inherent in the relationship of signifier to signified and that the elision of the two represents an attempt to render language "material." Of course, what this argument serves to demonstrate is not so much an idiosyncrasy of Futurism as the virtual point of bourgeois models of representation—the point that must be invoked by such means as "natural language," and the point that must always be deferred if language is not itself to fall prey to presence understood in the most banal sense. For the virtual ideological goal of signification is the erasure of signification, the passage from signifier to signified without the former ever becoming visible. However, in order for a system of signification to be maintained, this virtual goal must be endlessly deferred and the conventionality of signification or the materiality of the signifier reaffirmed. The process of representation within an arbitrary sign system demands at least a minimal distance between signifier and signified. Once the sound *becomes* the noise it signifies (as in Futurist onomatopoeia and *bruitism*) it can no longer distantiate itself mimetically from the world it represents.

The "opposition" of Marinetti to Mallarmé must then be thought both in terms of the impossible attempt of mimesis to transcend itself, and in terms of the ideological self-sublation of capitalism. Representationally, the key question would be whether either Mallarmé or Marinetti places himself beyond the representational purview of mimesis itself—and if so, what they put in its place. It is precisely this question that forms the basis of Derrida's analysis of Mallarmé in "The Double Session," an essay that, with its consideration of the modalities of mimesis (or of the *mimique*), provides a frame of reference for our reconsideration of Marinetti's critique of Mallarmé.[7] In terms of my attempt to amplify the ambiguities of the relationship of production and representation (that is, the Futurist text as the representation of production or as the production of representation), the important element in Derrida's essay is his attempt to broaden the scope of the category of mimesis itself. Examining Mallarmé's apparent movement beyond mimesis, Derrida demonstrates the recontainment of that movement within a second form of the metaphysic:

> One can here foresee an objection: since the mime imitates nothing, reproduces nothing, opens up in its origin the very thing he is tracing out, presenting, or producing, he must be the very movement of truth. Not, of course, truth in the form of adequation between the representation and the present of the thing itself, or between the imitator and the imitated, but truth as the present unveiling of the present: monstration, manifestation, production, *aletheia*. The mime produces, that is to say makes appear *in praesentia*, manifests the very meaning of what he is presently writing: of what he *performs*. He enables the thing to be seen in person, in its true face. If one followed the thread of this objection, one would go back, beyond imitation, toward a more "originary" sense of *aletheia* and of *mimeisthai*. (Derrida, *Dissemination*, pp. 205–6)

Derrida's claim is that Mallarmé retains the differential structure of mimesis, thus escaping the metaphysic of present manifestation, but strips this structure of its Platonic interpretation. What I wish to retain from his analysis, however, is the isolation of *two* mimetic strategies, each of which feeds into a metaphysics of presence. There would be a "first stage" of mimesis, which would be the logocentric belief in the power of language to reveal Truth by adequation to its object. But beyond this there would be a second stage (or, in reality, a stage prior to the first stage, if an invocation of temporality were at all apposite here): the rejection of Truth as something referential, representational, or based in correspondence. Derrida refers here to a metaphysics of "the presence of the present," drawing its "truth-content" from the uniqueness and originary nature of the mimetic instance itself. Truth would manifest itself—"manifest," I think, being a key term here—precisely because it *is* itself.

In terms of the distinction between production and representation this would mean that the mimetic structure inherent in representation is nevertheless retained in the moment of production, as the moment of Truth's *self*-production. That the noun should so easily have revealed itself as dependent upon the adjective, that the adjective should have been so ready to parenthesize itself as noun—this is hardly surprising. For, as the principles of production and representation respectively, adjective and noun operate within the same mimetic economy. The thrust of Marinetti's critique against the fixated and cumulative nature of the Mallarméan adjective, which paradoxically serves both to define and fix the noun and to launch it into the realm of exchange, is essentially economic. By means of an overemphasis on the apposition of adjectives, Mallarmé succeeds (according to Marinetti) in privileging a particularly limited form of noun.

Marinetti's claim would be that Mallarmé's is a poetics of monopoly, fixation, and accumulation. Derrida complicates the interpretive paradigm, quoting from Mallarmé's "Or," by footnoting Mallarmé's text.

OR

. . . . . . The currency, that engine of terrible precision, clean to the conscience, smooth to consciousness, loses even a meaning.

. . . . . . a notion of what sums, by the hundreds and beyond, can be . . . The inability of numbers, whatever their grandiloquence, to translate, here arises from a case; one searches, with the indication that, when a number is raised and goes out of reach toward the improbable, it inscribes more and more zeros: signifying that its total is spiritually equivalent to nothing, almost.[62]

62. . . . . this page, less than thirty-two lines, seems at least to retain gold as its principal signified, its general theme. *Or*, through a clever exchange, it is rather the signifier that this page treats, the signifier

in the full range of its registers, whose orchestration Mallarmé illustrates here and elsewhere. For even the theme, were it present as such, is but another addition to the order of the signifier: not the metallic substance, the thing itself involved in "phraseless gold," but the metal as a monetary sign, the "currency," "signifying that its total is spiritually equivalent to nothing, almost," and which "loses even a meaning" (p. 398). (Derrida, *Dissemination*, pp. 262–63)

What Derrida points out is that disappearing point toward which Mallarmé's fixation of value tends. The addition of zeros, the accumulation of value, reveals its own affinity to the zero, to nothingness. Likewise, "Or"—as conjunction and value, as linguistic shifter—serves as a signifier of fixed and material value while enabling the flow of language as a shifting system of evaluation. Paradoxically, the fetish (the gold itself) is *not* a celebration of materiality, but the reduction of the "metallic substance" to "currency," to the amorphous liquidity of something that flows. Marinetti's problem with the reformulation of a poetics around the *sostantivo doppio* and the semaphoric adjective is precisely the problem of capitalism vis-à-vis commodification: namely, how to accept the fetishization of value to the extent that objects themselves remain worthy of exchange, without falling prey to the hypostatization of value that such a suspension of disbelief demands.

Thought of as performative, the project of mimesis sublates the opposition of production and representation. Production becomes a form of *theatrical* production—that is to say, a production that produces itself. In the performance, as in the avant-garde manifesto, there is no division of representation and production, precisely because mimesis reveals itself as something which is *not* necessarily fixed within a temporal sequentiality of primary reality and secondary (or parasitical) representation. Re-presentation is possible within the present itself, as the presence of the production (and the production of the representation). Derrida's text serves as a useful gloss on what I would call Marinetti's "politics of the manifest," which would be precisely that "present unveiling of the present."[8]

I would like now to take this notion of "the manifest" as

the scandal of both representation and production and see how (generically, for example, by means of the manifesto) it allows us to recast Marinetti's implicit critique of Mallarmé as a poet of monopoly capitalism. For it is not just the specific points of Marinetti's manifestos that should be read as the core of his rebuttal of the Symbolist aesthetic, but also the manifesto form itself, as an aesthetic response to the problem of the "manifest" and its relation to mimesis. The manifesto as a denotative and performative genre is Marinetti's attempt to articulate the representational ambiguities of mimesis in the presence of the present. The problematic can be identified as a working through of the implications of performance and textuality upon each other, and as an analysis of their implications for the legitimation of a particular literary form. What, if anything, is manifest in the manifesto?

In his use of the manifesto form, Marinetti is in many ways symptomatic of a general trend that marks the avant-garde. Whereas the manifesto had emerged at the end of the nineteenth century as a literary form precisely as a result of the exigencies of system-immanent criticism as an attempt to carve out the territory of modernism, at the hands of the avant-garde it serves the purposes of a discursive *Selbstkritik*. That is to say, the avant-garde manifesto seems to question the autonomy and the impermeability of discourses, the separability of, say, aesthetics and politics. In this respect, one might trace back to the avant-garde manifesto tendencies explicative both of fascism's aestheticization of politics and of the avant-garde's own attempted politicization of aesthetics. In the light of these historical developments, it has been claimed that the emergence of the manifesto as an art form reflects—and manifests—a rethinking of the relationship of theory to practice in the cultural realm. This implication of theory in practice—the instrumentalization of constative theory as polemical performance— would then constitute the specificity of the avant-garde manifesto in relation to its modernist predecessors: suddenly, theory itself begins to act within the field it had previously merely served to delineate.[9]

Such an assertion, while tempting, should be resisted, at least in this simplified form, for the manifesto's synsthesis of theory and practice leaves neither party untouched. Each is refashioned in the image of the other. Marinetti himself addresses the problem of the relation of theory to praxis in the address "Destruction of Syntax–Imagination without Strings–Words-in-Freedom" (1913). Far from asserting the synthetic nature of all discourses, he insists upon a distinction between poetic and nonpoetic discourses.

> My Technical Manifesto of Literature (May 11, 1912), with which I invented *essential and synthetic lyricism, imagination without strings*, and *words-in-freedom*, deals exclusively with poetic inspiration. Philosophy, the exact sciences, politics, journalism, education, business, however much they may seek synthetic forms of expression, will still need to use syntax and punctuation. I am obliged, for that matter, to use them myself in order to make myself clear to you. (Marinetti, *FM*, pp. 95–96)

Not only is Marinetti in fact proposing a radical separation of discourses (poetry, with its synthetic form of expression, from all those discourses that are obliged to use traditional grammar and syntax) but he is also drawing this distinction into the body of his own work. Is this address—presented, as it is, in a collection of "Futurist Manifestos"—a poetic work, or is it (since it is obliged itself to use traditional forms of address) nonpoetry? This is the question that the manifesto poses.

As a genre that blurs the distinctions between the historical field of enunciation and the representational field of its own textuality—as a text, that is, that inserts itself into the field of historical consciousness—the manifesto does not simply provide a vehicle for the Futurist intervention, but also points toward the sort of postrepresentational aesthetic Marinetti is eager to establish. The *practice* of the manifesto is the practice of the text itself. That is to say, aesthetics does not body itself forth into politics or vice versa; rather, the possibility of each is foreclosed in the moment of performance. Indeed, the moment of performance, the moment of physical presence, must be insisted upon as a temporality, as a resistance to presence understood in the metaphysical sense. The fusion of representation and production that I have termed "the manifest" serves in the performance to mark the temporal act of enunciation itself. Moreover, the physical presence of the declaimer in the Futurist manifesto is by no means sublated into a moment of plenitude: the persona of the performer, his presence, does not serve to legitimate the manifesto itself. Marinetti is quite clear on this point: the duty of the declaimer is to reduce himself to a signifying machine of the manifesto (gesticulating with all available limbs).[10]

In other words, Futurist performance refuses to situate any moment of plenitude either at the level of the performative or the constative. Each is present only as mediated through the other: the presence of the orator takes the text as its performative pre-text, and the text itself (a *written* text, a script, not simply ex-temporized or emptied out of historical contingency) depends upon the rhetor. The "address" / "manifesto" / "essay" quoted above is *performed* and yet consigns itself to the realm of the nonaesthetic. It neither manifests the aesthetic it proposes nor confines itself to the simple assertion of that aesthetic, but offers a critique, in the form of a performative contradiction, of the very possibility of propositional logic itself. In other words, the manifesto, when introduced into the repertoire of literary genres, serves to maintain a moment of externalizing self-consciousness and self-reflection that refuses to subjugate all rational discourse to the terms of the global aesthetic it proposes. Such philosophizing, however, should not be read as the "becoming-philosophy" of art or as the accession of art to a moment of reflective self-consciousness. On the contrary: a poetics of presence would consist not in the abdication of discursive autonomy in the face of an overarching philosophical discourse, but rather in the assertion of the possibility of discursive self-sublation.

By this I mean that the moment of full unfolding, possible only when art wishes to be art and nothing else, is caught within a dialectic of autonomy and sublation. By being nothing but art, art becomes nothing but philosophy. The value of the gesture made in the "Destruction of Syntax" address consists in the simultaneous (constative) assertion and (performative) negation of autonomy. Self-reflection does not mark the philosophy art shall (or has) become, but rather the art it has ceased to be. If "pure" art becomes philosophy, then art must be impure and philosophical in order to resist philosophy. Likewise, production, as "pure" production, must produce a representation, which will resist the sublation of production itself in the self-presence of immanent manifestation.

In Marinetti's manifesto, the synthetic rhetorical flourish, which undermines the grammar of propositional logic, modestly confines itself (at the level of assertion) to the realm of the poetic, and yet does so in a "grammatical," nonpoetic text, situated at the heart of the Futurist poetic canon. Rather than obliterating the division of art and life, and thereby rendering questions of discursive status immaterial, Marinetti's manifestos operate within and upon crucial discursive distinctions. What is manifested in Marinetti's work is the impossibility of and the desire for manifestation. What is "immediately present" is the act of mediation. Power in these texts is the power of production, and what is produced *is* power—or its representation. At the level of generic reading we return, it would seem, to the indivisible duality of production and representation.

Having problematized from the outset any simplistic opposition of production and representation, we have again and again found ourselves offering, against the charges of "presentism" as "presence," the defense that those moments in Marinetti's texts that lean toward an aesthetic of "absolute mimesis" nevertheless stave off notions of adequate representation by stressing the moment of production underlying that representation. The only things Marinetti can adequately represent, we have argued, are processes of production. Now, it would seem the defense must be read in reverse, in the face of the Futurist performance and of Derrida's reading of Mallarmé. Precisely *because* it produces representations—a residue that is not used up in the production and performance of representation itself—the Futurist text prevents the ontologization of production itself as the originary self-production of presence. There is never pure production, but always production and its (self-)representation, production *of* a representation and *as* a representation. No pure Art (and therefore, art). No pure History (and therefore, history). No pure Production (and therefore, production).

CHAPTER 5

Avant-Garde and Technology: Futurist Machines—Fascist Bodies

In his introduction to the Italian edition of Marinetti's collected works, De Maria summarizes many of the motives we have just examined in the previous chapter: "Nothing is more repugnant in Marinetti's eyes than that image of a pacified existence (one thinks of his continued attacks on the Kantian *pace perpetua*); hence his profound aversion to communism, which he sees as stagnation, levelling, deadly stasis, an arrest of the *élan vital*."[1] In this chapter, I wish to examine Marinetti's relationship to the sociophilosophical tradition of the *pace perpetua*, but also to the more immediate context of high capitalism in the advanced machine age. The possibility of examining these two elements in tandem is opened up by Marinetti's insistent use of the machine as a metaphor both of social order and of potential economic (dis)order. I wish to rework the notion of aestheticization, thinking it as a principle of *organization* of ideological material rather than as a substantive and coherent ideological position. Aestheticization will emerge as a productive (machinic) set of relations, rather than as the privileging of certain aesthetic concerns over political and ethical considerations.

In the previous chapter, I had commented on the way in which the translation of a historical perspective developed in Marinetti's critique of Aestheticism into a specifically political critique of anarchism involved a critical "falling away"; a fall, that is, into a form of ontology centered around Man as a historically self-constituting Subject. It would be timely now to move away from the figure of Man toward that more central figure in Marinetti's work, the machine. I wish to examine here the functioning of the Futurist machine in its specifically political implications, in order to understand whether, and how, a metaphysics of presence asserts itself in Marinetti's work at the political level.

Of course, given the model of the aestheticization of political life framing this work so far, it is impossible to isolate the political as a realm somehow sealed off from the aesthetic. However, before limiting our examination to the perspectives opened up by Benjamin's analysis, it is important that we situate aestheticization as a socially and culturally potent ideology. At face value, aestheticization might be taken to mean a displacement of social, political, and ethical concerns as the guidelines for political action and a replacement of these values by aesthetic criteria: for example, a political action is judged in terms of its beauty rather than its goodness or even efficacy. This displacement of the ethical by the aesthetic—if that is all that aestheticization might be taken to mean—begs the question of the constitution of "the beautiful" itself, as a category replacing "the good." If aestheticization is to be understood at a purely semantic level—that is, as the replacement of one set of values by another—then it is incumbent upon theorists of aestheticization to provide some content to the notion of the aesthetic itself.

Influenced, perhaps, by the fascist predilection for spectacle and its tendency toward cultural philistinism, those who work with this model—including Benjamin, as previously I argued—generally assume that "the beautiful" means what it had always meant in the nineteenth century; that it dictated a reliance upon falsified principles of harmony, organic totality, and unity.[2] On the one hand there would be decadence—the dark side of progress, as it were—and on the other simple philistinism. The fascist predilection for regimented spectacle, the adherence to nineteenth-century aesthetic standards that, in the light of the avant-garde, can resurface only as kitsch—all of these things tend to confirm the critical desire to equate fascism (as aestheticization) with cultural philistinism. This conflation of political and aesthetic tendencies might stress the importance of outmoded notions of aesthetic harmony and balance to fascist notions of the organicist State. Aesthetic resolutions would serve to paper over the cracks and fissures of an increasingly fragmented and noncohesive social totality. Thus from a broadly leftist perspective "the aestheticization of political life" comes to mean the masking of class struggle under a facade of aestheticized social unity.

But where does this leave us in the case of Marinetti, who insists from the very outset that "except in struggle there is no more beauty"? (Marinetti, *SW*, p. 41). To account for Marinetti, it would be necessary to broaden the terms of the model of aestheticization. Aestheticization, then, would be *either* the papering over of social divisions by imposing upon social organization an aesthetic ideology of harmony and unity; *or*, in the light of Benjamin's own specific references to Marinetti in the "Reproduction" essay, it would mean the ontologization of struggle as both an aesthetic and a political principle. But it begins to look, at this point, as if the aestheticization model abdicates in the face of such contradictions, lending itself to such varying interpretations that it loses any rigor as an analytic model.

It is necessary to read the Futurists' aesthetic of struggle not as a false reconciliation of specific social antagonisms, but, on the contrary, as the compensatory generation, within the aesthetic realm, of a semblance of struggle. If, within an increasingly reified and rationalized social and political sphere, revolutionary action is no longer possible, then art, which once had to assert a false unity in the face of social contradiction, is expected to create a realm of acceptable rebellion. (Although, of course, the one form of conflict Futurism never seriously invokes is class conflict.) Whereas models of affirmative culture tend to stress the importance of the classical aesthetic of harmonization or *schöner Schein*, thereby positioning the aesthetic sphere as the false reconciliation of social conflict, in Futurism the aesthetic realm functions as a form of *ersatz*-conflict in which the forces of opposition held in check in the social realm gain expression.

If, then, aestheticization is to be taken to imply the displacing of social and political concerns as guidelines for political action into the realm of the aesthetic, Marinetti's Fascist Modernism poses a second problem. Since "the beautiful," in this instance, is defined in terms of the machine, this "displacement" of the aesthetic into the political would serve merely to reaffirm judgments already displaced from the realm of the forces and relations of production: beauty, for Marinetti, is always already a technological and political category. In Futurism, the engine of capitalist mass production is functionalized as the basis of an aesthetic and it is *this* aesthetic, fundamentally economic and political, which is then subsequently reapplied to the political sphere. In this case, aestheticization would lead to little more than a form of technocracy, in which beauty and efficiency are mutually determining.

There is, however, one further way of understanding the relationship of reified harmony and ontologized violence, a way indicated by Marinetti. Rather than reading the process of modernization as a process of fragmentation and social division, it is possible—even necessary—to read it instead as a process of totalization and articulation. As the agent of production, the machine spills over into the realm of social organization, with the result that antagonisms centered around hierarchy and class become mere questions of technical functionality. In other words, advanced capitalism does not need fascism to "harmonize" it; it is itself already a coercive principle of harmonization. As an escape valve, then—as an essentially affirmative culture in the Marcusian sense—the aesthetic realm necessarily undergoes a change, for the nature of the society requiring affirmation has changed. Affirmative culture has traditionally been understood in terms of a tendentially aestheticizing harmonization, but if the process of socialization is itself coercively harmonizing, subsumed under the principle of machinic efficiency, then what must be offered in the aesthetic realm is an escape from harmony. In other words, whereas a more traditional analysis might stress the occultation and aesthetic resolution of class struggle under fascism, from a systemic point of view it might be more valuable to speak instead of the generation of depotentialized areas of struggle within the aesthetic. Only within such a framework of aestheticization is it possible to understand Marinetti and the Futurists.

Of particular interest in the case of the Futurists is the way in which it is the machine itself—the dynamic model for integrative totalization and functional harmonization—which figures as the locus of aesthetic struggle. Culture is no longer affirmative as something pristine and priggishly "other," as something that distantiates itself from the everyday; rather, it is affirmative as a specific experience *of* and *in* the everyday. With the supposed fusion of life and art in the avant-garde it is no longer a question, within the affirmative aesthetic of Futurism, of art *compensating* for life, but rather of art offering another way of living life. It is the same machine that operates in each "realm." Art ceases to be life's affirmative "other" and offers instead the possibility of affirming the totalizing negativity of the social machine itself.

I would like to argue that the example of Marinetti indicates that aestheticization must mean more than just the replacement of an ethical value by an aesthetic value. It must be seen as effecting a fundamental organizational and structural reworking of ideological material prestructured by the discursive system within which it originally operates—in this case, that of politics—in terms of the organizational media and principles of a second discourse—in this case, that of aesthetics. Aestheticization is not simply a subjugation of political discourse to the discourse of aesthetics, it entails the subjugation of *all* value to the dictates of a central organizing metaphor. This metaphor subsequently serves as the legitimation for both aesthetic and political systems. The central metaphor around which discourse is structured, with a mechanistic rigor, in the Futurist text is the metaphor of the machine. Subjugation to this metaphor amounts to a rationalization effected in terms of analogy, and metaphor, far from being "merely" a means of representation, becomes a means of ideological control.

The displacement of one set of values by another (ethical by aesthetic, for example) would not in and of itself suffice to propel an ideology outside the realms of traditional discursive organization, even if it does involve a seemingly radical rethinking of value systems. For to replace, say, politics with aesthetics as the principle of social action is nevertheless to retain both the notion of an integrative discourse, around and within which values can be articulated, and the centrality of the legitimate and legitimating grounding value itself. While the central values will necessarily vary, then, structurally the aesthetic or the political models of action still operate analogously. Where Marinetti departs from this liberal bourgeois organization of discourse is in the constant deferral of any central value in favor of the metaphoric system that creates value in the first place. Thus, to rethink aestheticization around the centrality of the metaphor is not to stress the displacement of one term by another, but to insist upon the *process* of metaphor as a compulsive binarism of terms in which value, as something fixed, is impossible.

The structure of ideological legitimation is such that the organization of social order around a central cohering value must go hand in hand with an occultation of the process of *production* of that value. A potentially fasticizing discourse that entails an "aestheticization of politics," on the other hand—Fascist Modernism—will valorize metaphoric production rather than the value itself. Production becomes the value, even when this value itself is nominalized in the absolute adjectival function, or in that by-product of production, representation. Given this reworking of the model, the question remains whether aestheticization marks a radical departure in the self-understanding of bourgeois political discourse (and the function of aesthetics in it) or whether Marinetti is in fact working with ideological material consonant with that discursive tradition. I hope to indicate that at a certain point Marinetti's valorization of production (of value) over value reveals itself as a contradiction. His writings rejoin the discursive tradition they oppose by presenting production itself as a value: and to valorize production is to reinstate the fetishized value that production was to replace.

At a purely pragmatic level, it is not difficult to trace instances of Marinetti's opposition to the political structures of democracy. The most obvious distinction to be drawn would be Marinetti's opposition to any model of social checks and balances. Marinetti's proposed social machine certainly does not run like clockwork. He consistently finds himself in opposition to a strain of sociological thought traceable back to Kant and the ideal of *pace perpetua.* Certainly, Marinetti's excoriation of the parliamentary two-chamber system, for example (which he characterizes as an attempt to rein in the already clapped-out old nag of democracy), his proposal of an activist *eccitatorio* as a second chamber to incite rather than temper change, and his critique of anarchism and its pacifist ideals are obvious ways in which this opposition manifests itself.[3] At the same time, however, there are many ways in which Futurism actually arrogates to itself and repotentializes latent tensions inherent in the Kantian social model. In what follows, I certainly do not seek to give a coherent account of a Kantian sociology or politics, but only to reconstruct the values Kant came to represent for Marinetti. I contend that to read Marinetti through and against Kant is to open up the discussion of the machine to the broader considerations of society and its relation to the natural order, to open the debate between fascist organicism and fascist technocracy.

For Marinetti, Kant would be readily assimilable into that tradition of liberalism that—by virtue of its origin in (and pragmatic reconciliation with) absolutism—views the state as a mediating instance within the social construct, as the arbiter for competing individual desires. Within such a tradition, Kant would at best be accorded the position of the Enlightenment optimist, giving a new twist to Hobbes's ultimately pessimistic and defensive analysis in *Leviathan.* To understand Kant purely in terms of a social contract, however, is to miss the crucial modification of liberal models that takes place in his writing, and to miss precisely that strain of thought which begins to make comprehensible the emergence of fascism within and against the liberal political discourse of modernity.

In the essay "Idea for a Universal History with a Cosmopolitan Intent" Kant sets the terms for his subsequent thinking about the relations of Man to Man.[4] Here, social or interpersonal relations are consistently thought in terms of a broader relationality; in terms, that is, of their relation to those relations pertaining between Man and Nature. Whereas the State might be thought of as an instance of arbitration for conflicting and potentially divisive social forces—that is, it can represent specific power interests and yet subdue competing powers and ensure peace—Nature, for Kant, works on quite the opposite principle. It both grounds and exists within a set of *antagonisms*: "The means that nature uses to bring about the development of all of man's capacities is the **antagonism** among them in society, as far as in the end this antagonism is the cause of law-governed order in society. In this context, I understand antagonism to mean men's *unsocial sociability*, i.e., their tendency to enter into society, combined, however, with a thoroughgoing resistance that constantly threatens to sunder this society" (Kant, pp. 31–32). To this extent, Kant's model does not seem startling or unusual, but within the social and historical economy he establishes, antagonisms are not simply natural imperfections to be abolished by the social construct. Progress itself depends upon antagonisms. Crudely stated, this assertion might seem to offer little more than a philosophical legitimation of a form of enlightened self-interest. However, it is not to Man—at least, not to Man as a *social* animal—that Kant attributes this principle of antagonism, but to Nature itself: "Thus, thanks be to nature for the incompatibilities, for the distasteful, competitive vanity, for the insatiable desire to possess and also to rule. Without them, all of humanity's excellent natural capacities would have lain eternally dormant. Man wills concord; but nature better knows what is good for the species: she wills discord" (Kant, p. 32). The social order is at once an order between men and women as human beings and an order established between Man and Nature. Discord is no longer the threat to be held at bay, but rather the impetus toward interaction and the accommodation of needs. Moreover, any political assumption on the social level that human "nature" is essentially antagonistic overlooks the very real sense in which, for Kant at least, discord is framed by harmony. By acting in accord with human nature, people would create social discord. At this stage, Kant's thought would not be at odds with the assumption that nature, in the guise of "human nature," enters into the social equation as a bothersome, discordant principle. But by theorizing human nature as itself a relation—the relation of human beings to nature, or of humans to themselves through nature—Kant opens up the possibility of a legitimation of social discord.

Although Kant is writing of the discord motivating both social relations and historical progress, there is nevertheless a more categorical antagonism built into his model: namely, the antagonism that exists between "human" and "natural" modalities, the differend of concord and discord itself. The utopian project of social concord finds itself as a dyadic term within a broader opposition to the natural discord that impels it. The Kantian *pace perpetua*, therefore, far from resulting in the stagnation of eternal peace, establishes a double bind that necessitates a relentless social dynamic. To be at peace with one's fellow humans is to be at odds with nature, which craves antagonism: to be at one with nature, then, is to be in a state of antagonism to one's fellow human beings. More fundamentally, however, one cannot "be at one with" nature at all. If nature is established upon a principle of discord, how is one to be at one with it? To be at one with it is to project a harmonious relationship of Man and Nature that is at odds with Nature itself. Thus, to oppose Nature is, paradoxically, to be at one with it, to take its principle as one's own.

It is this double bind that conditions the ambiguity of Marinetti's relationship to both nature and the machine—to organicism and technocracy. With Futurism and the advent of the avant-garde, the ambiguous antagonism that divides/unites Man and Nature finds its expression in the figure of the machine. In order for the simultaneous processes of opposition and reconciliation to be possible within the same relationship it is necessary that the principle of antagonism itself be ontologized. In this ontologization, the machine, as a social symbol of a natural antagonism, becomes crucially important as a figure for the unification of natural and social orders. The machine, which represents a struggle without protagonists, becomes the central organizing metaphor for Marinetti's social vision; it is with reference to this overarching figure that one must read the political ideologies embedded in the Futurist texts. As a figure of both conflict and resolution, the machine offers a symbolic resolution of specific social tensions. To understand the political importance of Marinetti's metaphoric configurations, then, it is necessary that one rethink the machine as a form of "translation"—a translation of one set of realities (political life) into another (aesthetic order).

The machine serves both to displace existing social tensions and to generate new antagonisms of its own. As a displacement of specific class antagonisms the figure of the machine institutes a new form of humanism by locating struggle in the interaction of Man and Nature, rather than in the confrontation of class with class. The worker acts as the representative of Man, rather than of a class, and the mechanized "multiplied man" functions as the subject of this neo-humanism.[5] Notably, it is not the worker as the protagonist of struggle, but rather the machine itself, as the disembodied meeting point of antagonistic forces, that Futurism celebrates. The machine ontologizes struggle itself, rather than any specific struggle. It also serves a second function as a *generator* of antagonism. In so functioning, it effects (with reference to the Kantian double bind) a broader reconciliation. The principle of antagonism, in whose name Marinetti causes the factory worker to wage war on nature, is itself a "natural" rather than a "social" principle; that is to say, it flies in the face of what Kant takes to be the human tendency to social collectivism. In turning this principle of antagonism against nature itself, by means of a rhetoric of industrial exploitation, Marinetti opposes—and by opposing is at one with—nature. In other words, the machine as a figure of conflict reconciles itself with the antagonisms of nature that it confronts. Paradoxically, the machine is conciliatory precisely insofar as it is antagonistic. In this respect, then, it is still possible to read the Futurist machine in terms of the nineteenth-century model of harmonization and reconciliation; but now as the reconciliation of discord with discord.

Reified harmony and ontologized violence—those apparently contradictory moments of aestheticization—are not only reconcilable with the tradition of a bourgeois sociology but intrinsic to it. Rather than opposing the Kantian *pace perpetua*, Marinetti's particular brand of Fascist Modernism seems to be working through some of its complexities at the philosophical level. And it is the machine, as a model of the State and as a model of aesthetic resolution, which performs that work. Although the celebration of machinic domination over nature can be read on one level as a championing of the forces of human industry over and against the arbitrary power of nature—in short, as a cornerstone of fascist technocracy—it can be argued that the machine that "opposes" nature is simply obeying the oppositional, antagonistic principle of nature itself. In its most brutal, industrialized attacks on nature, Fascist Modernism nevertheless bears witness, then, to a perverted form of organicism, in which harmony has become the conceptual harmony of two antagonisms. The victory over nature celebrated in the fascist text is at the same time a surrender to nature and its principle of antagonism.

Thus it would not be enough to claim that Fascist Modernists merely ontologize the oppositional psychical structures specific to capitalism, for they do so not in the name of "human nature"—which craves concord—but in the name of that inhuman nature which Kant takes as his principle of progress. Marinetti's insistence, over and against the threat of stagnation posed by anarchism, on "the continuous development of man" should not, therefore, be reduced to a form of humanism. History does not play itself out as the actualization of a humanist ontology, but as the oscillation between contradictory imperatives, the social and the natural, in which the double bind of those imperatives is manifested. It is the energy generated by this oscillation that serves as the motor for the fascist State.

The theory of aestheticization as harmonization and false reconciliation, which only *seems* problematic in the case of the Futurist celebration of the machine, is actually inextricable from the machine aesthetic. It is not only Marinetti who pursues the project of an aestheticized politics through an aesthetics of the machine, but bourgeois State theory itself.[6] It is within this machine aesthetic—the State as a machine, the machine as a model of aesthetic order—that fascism subsequently works. In its various forms, fascism is perfectly capable both of celebrating the organic unity of the *Volk* and of imposing this ideology with all the force at the disposal of the modern State bureaucracy.

It would not, I feel, be necessary to engage in a detailed reading of Hobbes to note the insistence of a tropological nexus: the State–the Body–the Machine. It is in terms of these images that we must seek now to understand the phenomenon of Fascist Modernism, and more specifically the aesthetico-political project of Marinetti. For Marinetti and the Italian Futurists, the State *is* a body, and the project of any politics must consist in the "liberation" of that body. "Italian democracy is for us a body which must be liberated," proclaims Marinetti. This liberation, however, is envisaged as a form of technological advancement, as an increase in the performance potential of the machine and as an augmentation and acceleration of its essential functions: "liberate, unleash, lighten, in order to accelerate its speed and multiply a hundredfold its productivity."[7] The liberation of the human body, the liberation of Italian democracy, and the efficient reworking of the machine are one project for Marinetti. To understand the State one must understand the body, and to understand the body one must understand the machine.

A problem arises, however, when one wishes to examine the project of "liberation" itself as a principle oriented to the notion of machinic efficiency. It should be stressed from the outset that the intention is not simply to equate mechanization with control and dehumanization. The point, rather, is to take seriously the machinic function of the body as a libidinal prototype of the fascist State. With the mechanization of the anthropological model of early liberalism, I do not intend simply to examine a certain tropology of alienation, whereby human beings are "mechanized." I wish, instead, to take seriously the possibility that the bourgeois individual, like the bourgeois State, is radically machinic, that his or her desires are not, per se, incompatible with a machinic form of gratification, and that, indeed, they are constituted according to a machinic ideology insofar as they are theorized within an economy of need, fulfillment, and its deferral. It is not, moreover, in relation to fascist theories of the State that I wish to pursue this line of thinking, but rather with reference to that strain of the avant-garde that seems—at least superficially—to consist of a celebration of the project of technological modernization.

The political project of Fascist Modernism appears inconsistent only when judged from a traditional political perspective oriented toward categories of progress and reaction. The consistency of Marinetti's politics is *metaphoric*—it is the working through of a metaphor (which, if Carl Schmitt's analysis of the bourgeois State is to be believed, is *not* a metaphor) in ways which may appear progressive in certain cases, reactionary in others, but which are not tailored to fit any such terms.

The centrality of the machine in Futurist writing has been dismissed by certain critics as only the most superficial element of the Futurists' work.[8] Insofar as it is understood to be nothing more or less than the paradigmatic figure for the victory of science, the machine might have been overemphasized in writings on Futurism and its influence. The originally enthusiastic international response to Futurism, moreover, was tempered by a more skeptical attitude to the machine, which—though seemingly offering a way out of the calculated rationality of human logic—served merely to impose a super-individual "irrational" rationality of its own. There was also a rejection of Marinetti's celebration of the machine as a passéist remnant of decadent modernism. Wyndham Lewis's turn against the Futurists, for example, was motivated by contempt for the provinciality of Marinetti's obsession with the machine.[9] At best, then, the machine's importance to Futurism seems to reflect nothing more or less than the economic underdevelopment of Italy and an understandable fascination with industrialization on the part of Italian modernists.

If later critics have tended to downplay or recontextualize those celebrations of the machine that seem now to date Futurism, such a move is not without justification from within Marinetti's own work. He himself argues:

> It is not my intention as a poet to offer up a lyric eulogy of the machine, which would be childish and unimportant: with the machine, I intend to signify rhythm and futurity; the machine gives lessons in order, discipline, force, precision and continuity. . . . With the machine I mean to leave behind all that is languorous, shadowy, nebulous, indecisive, imprecise, unsuccessful, sad and melancholy in order to return to order, precision, will, strict necessity, the essential, the synthesis.[10]

The figure of the machine, then, is not a synecdoche for the process of industrial modernization (and therefore should not be used to range Marinetti alongside the modernists) but rather the symbol of a specific social and political organization. It is the figure both for a philosophical position, and given its control over discussion of the State and the body, for a political project oriented toward the liberation of the body. The machine legitimates an organization stressing "order, precision, will, strict necessity, the essential, the synthesis." In other words, the machine can be situated squarely in the camp of technocratic and bureaucratic political ideologies.

Written in the twenties, this assessment by Marinetti of the importance of the machine in his work is, in fact, already a revisionist reading of his own oeuvre. Although the metaphor of the machine forms a focus for Marinetti's aesthetic and political visions, it is a shifting focus. Rather than constituting a coherent ideological unit, the machine occurs in Marinetti's work in two quite distinct forms that seem to mirror the two sides of the machine's ambiguous reconciliation of organicist and technocratic positions. The machine is not simply a metaphor for order and regulation but also a vehicle of liberation on both the macro- (national) and micro- (biological) levels. It is in the earlier works that the machine represents all those energies that render capitalism so curiously self-transgressive and productive. It is the symbol of the productive antagonisms that pit Man against Nature and fuel historical progress. In these terms, the machine is valued for its productivity, for its regeneration of natural resources and energies, and for the material objects it produces. The machine functions as a figure for a progressive ends-oriented rationalization, and the machine celebrated in the early essay "Multiplied Man and the Reign of the Machine," for example, is essentially *productive*: "your machine of fused iron and steel, this motor built to exact specifications, will give you back not only what you put into it, but double or triple, much more and much better than the calculations of its builder—its father!—made provision for" (Marinetti, *SW*, p. 91). Productivity seems, here, to overstep the mark of mere purposive calculation, for it is defined precisely in terms of an excess, a beyond of calculation. The machine is essentially self-transgressive in its ability to produce more than any calculation might have foreseen. It is disordered, both the result of a calculation of "exact specifications" (a form of mathematical rationality) and the negation of any such principle of accountability. It is quantity become quality, rationalism become suprarational. This machine, then, is a machine of both expansion and negation—but above all a machine of productivity.

The second imagistic strain characterizing the machine in Marinetti's writings is typified by that passage from the twenties quoted above. Notable in this reworking of the metaphor is the new importance of "order," "discipline," "precision," and "strict necessity." It would appear that the machine can be celebrated not only as a productive force but also as a model of organization. Although the metaphoric virtue of the machine is rooted in its functionalism, the espousing of a *principle* of functionality divorces the machine from a concern with any actual production. In this sense, the machine becomes not an instrument of control over nature, but rather the end product of that control expressed as a control over human nature (as labor). The machine is not just a tool, but rather itself the paradigmatic expression of control in its disposition of natural resources and its concrete expression of human potential. In this second sense, in which the machine serves not as a figure of proliferation but of binding and constraint, we see developed a model of totalitarianism.

In speaking of "the Machine" in Marinetti's work, then, it is necessary to distinguish between these two types of machine, or rather, between two possibilities latent within the same machine: order and transgression, function and proliferation, organization and productivity, rationality and *élan vital*, technocracy and organicism. Insofar as the "productive" machine bears within itself the germs of the other "totalitarian" machine, it is always politically ambiguous. By the same token, however, the totalitarian machine must also be read as a reworking of the transgressive and vital energies of the "productive" machine.

While it is important, given the centrality of the machine metaphor to the theories of State briefly outlined above, to stress the inherence of one sort of machine in the other, it is also possible to observe in the course of Marinetti's career a gradual shift toward the model of order. This shift seems to take place in the early twenties—that is, in the period of Italian Fascism's ascendance to power and of the movement's entrenchment as a regime. It is not my intention to chart here the history of Marinetti's relationship to Mussolini, but it is clear that the vicissitudes of the machine metaphor are related to his attempts at this time to reestablish a more positive relationship to the newly established regime. Moreover, the development of the machine metaphor in the direction of order and "strict necessity," as well as the resulting shift in those ideological spheres determined by the metaphor, would seem to mark a return to a more traditional model of aesthetic value. If, as seems likely, the function of the machine as metaphor changes with the changing political climate, how might one begin to employ a metaphoric reading (that is, a reading of political content through the organizing principles of the figure of the machine) to resolve some of the contradictions in Marinetti's political and social pronouncements? Where do those contradictions lie?

Political contradictions, as we observed earlier, are not difficult to locate in Marinetti's work. De Maria, for example, isolates some such "contradictions" (or, I would argue, overdeterminations):

> Marinetti wavers several times between these two conceptions of poetry. At times he seems to be arguing—*à la* Lautréamont—that *La poésie doit être faite par tous. Non par un.* In this he is a forerunner of the Surrealists. At other times he seems to cling to the idea of art as a consolation and superhuman distraction from a life which, however hard they try, men cannot rescue from the hell of society and economics. The formulations are even ambiguous and wavering in *Beyond Communism*; in the same way, in the two Tactilism manifestos Marinetti seems at times to embrace a notion which—beyond the genital organization of sexuality—results in the eroticization of the entire body. In the same way, in the Inequality manifesto, Marinetti rejoins—perhaps unwittingly—the Marxian utopia of an end to the division of labor in a general accommodation of the classes.[11]

It is only when read in terms of the central metaphor of the machine that these "contradictions" begin to make sense. In this passage De Maria touches upon several discourses: a poetics, politics, and a sexualized discourse of the body. He clearly feels all are linked, yet he is perturbed that the unity linking them all should not be a unity of "tendency" or of progressive (or even reactionary) convictions. He encounters difficulties precisely because the discourses subjugated to the central machinic metaphor cannot simply be repoliticized without reference to that metaphor and to their own analogous relationship to that metaphor. There is no central *value* system, be it ethical, political, or aesthetic.

The particular problematic of the body and the State foregrounds itself precisely because the project of bourgeois State theory as Marinetti reads it consists in reconciling a discourse of the body with its own sublation in the Body Politic. The ambiguity of centering and decentering—the movement beyond subjectivity to a notion of the mediated *Körperschaft*, and the retroactive reconstruction of subjectivity as the basic unit of the collective—*must* be read (and not by way of a merely metaphoric similitude) in and through a critique of genital and degenitalized sexuality. In other words, the body is not simply a trope for political organization in Marinetti's Fascist Modernism: the body is itself the micropolitical unit.

At face value, the move toward a more ordered, rigorous model of the machine would seem to be at odds with what De Maria sees as the development of a more "liberated," degenitalized and tactile sensuality. If we are to observe Marinetti's movement toward a more constraining "totalitarian" model of the machine, it will be necessary to reconcile that development with the apparently contradictory liberalization and degenitalization of human sexuality that takes place within the same time-frame. In the earlier writings such as "Let's Murder the Moonshine" and "Against *Amore* and Parliamentarism"[12] Marinetti's attitude to sexuality was colored to a great extent by his critique of the aestheticization and effeminization of democracy. The thrust of his attack on "lussuria" would seem to be that the phenomena of love and romance exert an effeminizing influence within democracy. Consequently, he opposes any inflation of sexuality beyond the merely procreative and espouses a cause of national fecundity of which his archenemy, the Vatican, might have been proud: "There is nothing natural and important except coitus," he proclaims, "whose purpose is the futurism of the species. . . . The carnal life will be reduced to the conservation of the species, and that will be so much gain for the growing stature of man" (Marinetti, *SW*, pp. 72–73). Likewise, works written at this time—most notably, *Mafarka Le Futuriste*—abound with images of nonsexual procreation, consistently eliminating the figure of the effeminizing mother. This tendency is expressed programmatically in Marinetti's railings "Against *Amore* and Parliamentarism" in "War, the World's Only Hygiene": "Well then: I confess that before so intoxicating a spectacle we strong Futurists have felt ourselves suddenly detached from women, who have suddenly become too earthly, or to express it better, have become a symbol of the earth that we ought to abandon. We have even dreamed of one day being able to create a mechanical son, the fruit of pure will, a synthesis of all the laws that science is on the brink of discovering" (Marinetti, *SW*, p. 75). The antifeminism (perversely expressed in this piece as prosuffragism, based on the belief that women will only serve to hasten the internal decay of parliamentary democracy) is not entirely unreflective here. Whereas in the passage on the productivity of coitus there was a valorization of procreation as something "natural," the identification of women with "the earth" in this passage is modified: "or to express it better . . . a *symbol* of the earth" (my italics). There is a desire not only to go beyond women as something "natural"—as the very principle both of nature and of a naturalized parliamentarianism—but also to go beyond the oppositional terms in which such a symbol is practicable. Clearly, though, there is a privileging of (re-)production as an essentially masculine activity which by some biological freak has fallen to the lot of women.

Viewed in terms of the controlling figure of the machine, the coexistence of Marinetti's early transgressive, productive expansionism and this rather doctrinaire regulation of sexual desire becomes understandable. The application of the principle of productivity to the realm of sexuality originates (at least in this instance) not in the reactionary utopianism of organicist ideology, but in the modern technocratic impulse, and necessarily results in a celebration of industrialized fecundity. The body as a machine is a body for (re-)production. Birth becomes an issue of industrial efficiency and all nonprocreative sexuality is prohibited by the dictates of a self-transgressing, productive machinery. The contradictions of a political ideology—the coexistence of "progressive" and "reactionary" ideologies—resolve themselves when read at the level of figurative organization. The regulation of sexuality envisaged in this early work, written in the heyday of the productive model of the machine metaphor, is extremely strict: sex serves the function of procreation. Desire is machinic precisely insofar as it motivates (re-)production.

The text best expressing the move toward a more diffuse model of sexual and sensual organization is the Tactilism manifesto of 1924 (Marinetti, *SW*, pp. 109–12), to which De Maria makes reference in his introduction. The basic argument of this manifesto is that the organization of human sensuality reflects a constraining centralization of power and that the sensual potential of the human body should be given greater expression by uncoupling the senses from this tyranny. Marinetti argues that "the distinction between the five senses is arbitrary. Today one can uncover and catalog many other senses. Tactilism promotes this discovery" (Marinetti, *SW*, p. III). Pending the discovery of these alternative human senses, however, Marinetti proposes an "*educazione del tatto*" as a means of developing the least privileged of human senses: touch. The intention of the manifesto is the reestablishing of a sensual relationship to matter by means of a resensualization of the body itself as the mediation of all matter. We should refrain from referring to a "re-eroticization" of the body, however, since Marinetti takes his project to be directly opposed to "morbid erotomania" (Marinetti, *SW*, p. III). The erotic is not, then, something that can simply be spread a little thinner, or diffused around the body; it is the name for precisely that form of sensual channeling that focuses sensations genitally.

Again, it is with reference to the organizing metaphor of the machine that one can begin to understand the shift to a celebration of a degenitalized sensuality. If the early machine concentrates sexual energies on the act of procreation, then the dissociation of the machine from the act of production—its utilization as a model of order rather than as a principle of proliferation—results in a celebration of the *technology* of creation and necessarily dissociates sexuality from the act of procreation. Sexuality itself becomes the exercising of a power rather than the creation or regeneration of a power in the act of procreation. Thus the "dispersed" sexuality of the Tactilism manifesto—though subversive or progressive when viewed purely in terms of discursive divisions that take no account of the subjugation of ideology to the machine metaphor—corresponds to a shift in Marinetti's understanding of the function of the machine and gives expression not to liberational impulses but to an ideology of control at the level of the body. The "efficiency" of the body as machine does not consist, here, in its productivity, but in its full utilization, its functioning at full capacity, every orifice plugged and every inch of the epidermis aroused.

In this form of desublimated control through liberation the degenitalization of sexuality effects a depoliticization, or rather the distancing of a politicized erotics from the intentionality of the centered subject. For Marinetti, on the other hand, this control is envisaged as something that postdates any such phallocentric sexuality. "Desiring-control" consists precisely in a degenitalization of power, in a dispersal of erotic energies that opposes phallocentrism. In Marinetti's career it is, in fact, the earlier works such as *Mafarka Le Futuriste*—those works that are generally taken to be typical of the early "heroic" or prefascist Futurism—that quite overtly envisage power as centered upon the phallus. However, though the earlier works articulate a more centralized phallocratic power as opposed to the local operation of power through self-regulation (or systemic self-gratification) in the later texts, they nevertheless still work with a model of democracy.

Despite the critique of parliamentarianism and of the effeminization of the political sphere, Marinetti's earlier writings are not antidemocratic. In the essay "The Futurist Concept of Democracy," for example, he proposes a specifically Italian form of democracy: "We are therefore able to give the directions to create and to dismantle to *numbers, to quantity, to the mass*, for with us *number, quantity and mass* will never be—as they are in Germany and Russia—the number, quantity and mass of mediocre men, incapable and indecisive" (Marinetti, *FF*, p. 125). The similarity of this defense to his earlier praise for the machine is self-evident. Just as the machine inaugurates (in the "productive" phase) an ideology of proliferation in which quantity effects a dialectical *Umschlag* into quality and a transcendence of mere quantity, of the mass, so the Italian people exist as a machine, whose products can be calculated, but whose actual production will surpass all calculation. The subsequent development of strong antidemocratic elements in Marinetti's work is directly linked, once again, to the shift in function of the machine metaphor, for it is only by way of analogy to the productive machine that democracy—a concept one might otherwise have expected to be profoundly distasteful to Marinetti—is legitimated. With the move away from this particular metaphoric function of the machine toward a model of technocratic functionalism the democratic impulse in Marinetti's work dwindles accordingly.

While it serves to reestablish a logic of sorts in Marinetti's texts and in his political development, the methodological import of this examination of specific political contradictions in terms of figurative overdeterminations demands a questioning of the political and ideological assumptions that commonly inform our own readings of Fascist Modernism. Thus, for example, Marinetti's shift from a phallocentric notion of power toward a degenitalized configuration coincides with a shift from a broadly democratic to an overtly authoritarian model of the State. In other words, the assumption that fascist power is necessarily a phallocratic, fixated power would not seem to be supported by the evidence of those texts that mark Marinetti's development toward a more conformist fascism. However, the move beyond the productive machine—which heralds the move toward the totalitarian machine—also marks a move beyond a machine that delivers "not only what you put into it, but double or triple, much more and much better than the calculations of its builder—its father!—made provision for." With the shift to the organizational model of the machine one would expect that the father, the guarantor of the machine's functioning, might reassert himself (and of course in the figure of the *Duce* he does). This patriarchalism, however, cannot simply be termed "phallocratic," for it is in the machine and not in the father that power is located. Thus while Italian Fascism presents a structural organization that appears phallocratic, the fascist patriarch is actually no more than a technician of the State machine.

In terms of a poetics, meanwhile, Marinetti's move away from phallocratic power constructs is paralleled by a move away from logocentric discourses and toward that discourse of metaphoricity which I take to be the essence of aestheticization. The word and the phallus form a powerful unity within his oeuvre and the aim of the later poetics is to move away from the power of both. In other words, the degenitalization of sexuality is at the same time an attack on the word as the privileged signifying medium. The

Tactilism manifesto, for example, offers a perfect example of the ideological deconstruction of phallo-logocentrism, since it sees the project of a diffused eroticism and of a rethinking of communicative processes as one and the same. However, the linguistic renewal envisaged in the Tactilist manifesto is in no way linked to what would conventionally be considered a liberational or progressive political project, but rather to a gradual process of fascisticization. Faced with the example of Marinetti, then, one is forced to conclude that neither an attack on phallocratic models of power nor an attack upon logocentric discursive organizations is by any means necessarily linked to a broader political project of liberation.

How, then, are we to read the Futurist project of liberation? If texts such as the Tactilism manifesto are not necessarily to be read along a trajectory leading away from reactionary regimentation toward a political liberation of the human subject, how exactly are they to be read? It would seem that for Marinetti the very notion of "liberation" necessarily goes beyond, and eventually negates, traditional political understandings of liberation. What is to be liberated in the Futurist text is energy itself, an energy that runs through the human body, that helps constitute the subject, but that nevertheless cannot be fixed upon that subject or be said to originate in it. This project of dissemination of both libidinal and textual power negates the materiality of its own manifestation, denies the moment of its own appearance. Within its economy, the body becomes a medium, a process, and enters into a system of energetic exchange that will necessarily destroy it as an autonomous entity. What Marinetti resists is an ontologization of the body as an origin of desire. The body becomes passage and flow, constituted in and through desire rather than as the generator of such desire.

Again and again—in the realm of representation, in the realm of economics, in the realm of the libidinal—Marinetti privileges the act of deferral (or, similarly, the act of exchange) over the terms of that deferral. In this case, the body as entity faces the same fate as the fetishes Marinetti opposes elsewhere. At the same time as it constitutes a programmatic textual strategy, the valorization of deferral and exchange articulates a specific model of libidinally mediated political and ideological control. The sexual fascination of fascism stems from the same organizational principles as its political fascination. The encoding of sexuality is not subliminal, that is; it does not function hermeneutically, through a process of interpretation in which the libidinal content is recognized and rescued from beneath its representation. The displacement itself is sexually potent. Just as the fetish is refetishized *because* it is a simulacrum, *because* it both fixes and refuses to fix the system of exchange passing through it which constitutes and valorizes it, so the sexual fetish is eroticized for its *failure* to exhaust the libidinal charge running through it. Power is not read libidinally nor libido as a manifestation of power—it is the momentary conjunction of the two that is experienced as a powerfully erotic fascination.[13]

Futurist discourse, like the rhetoric of the fascist spectacle, does not aim at an affective displacement that might be termed "sublimation," but rather fetishizes the act of displacement itself. In the dynamic materialism characterizing Marinetti's texts, power does not inhere in an object and therefore cannot simply be transferred to another object along the lines of a simple sublimation. Power is generated by the act of transference itself, by the action of object upon object, by the interaction and overlaying of words. At the same time as it unbinds the power of desire from the name that fixes it in language (the noun), the Futurist text aims to affix that desire, not to another noun, but to the very process of displacement and naming itself. In this respect, the power of analogy—conventionally understood as a power of sublimation and displacement, in which an origin is hypostatized—is challenged by Marinetti in favor of a principle of desublimation, which recognizes and affirms the creation of desire only through displacement, the generation of power through confrontation and collision.

This system of confrontation and collision, political and physical, also provides the basis for Marinetti's analysis of capitalism— and it is the body itself that will provide for him the most fundamental paradigm of the commodity. In his narrative of the birth of the Futurist aesthetic, for example, he quite explicitly conflates the negation of the embodied subject by death and the negation of fixed value by the endless chain of exchange. Commodification sets in action that ultimate effacement of materiality, which consumes even the body. In this macabre parable, Marinetti takes the businessman rather than the poet or artist as the champion of the Futurist aesthetic, but a businessman who deals in an unusual commodity:

> But the plainest, the most violent of Futurist symbols comes to us from the Far East.
>
> In Japan they carry on the strangest of trades: the sale of coal made from human bones. All their powderworks are engaged in producing a new explosive substance more lethal than any yet known. This terrible new mixture has as its principal element coal made from human bones with the property of violently absorbing gases and liquids. For this reason countless Japanese merchants are thoroughly exploring the corpse-stuffed Manchurian battlefields. In great excitement they make huge excavations, and enormous piles of skeletons multiply in every direction on those broad bellicose horizons. One hundred *tsin* (7 kilograms) of human bones bring in 92 kopeks. (Marinetti, *SW*, p. 82)

The business exchange—which itself entails a privileging of exchange over materiality—results in the destruction of the body. In the gruesome parable of the Manchurian war, Marinetti chooses as an emblem for his own aesthetic project "the sale of coal made from human bones," for at the absolute point, Futurism abhors even that minimal fixation of value that is the human body.

The invocation in the Manchurian passage of commodification as the most fundamental systemic negation of materiality is of great importance, for it marks a third stage in the development of the machine metaphor. Neither productive energy nor model of order, the machine is now primarily an economy for the generation of *value*. Perhaps most interesting, however, is the way in which the negation of materiality in that act of exchange, which is both commodification and death, nevertheless leaves a measurable evaluative residual: the equivalence of 7 kilograms and 92 kopeks. The exchange does not entirely consume itself, for while the body itself becomes explosive, the inert mass of money remains—to pass, perhaps, into another exchange, an ineradicable marker of the body's materiality. Could it be that Marinetti's centralization of exchange and value *production* nevertheless falls prey to the inescapability of value itself and thereby replays that organization around value typical of bourgeois liberal discourse? By eliminating even that minimal fixation that constitutes the body as a locus of the libidinal energies passing through it, Marinetti already places himself beyond that postmodern deconstruction of the subject which results only in the subject's surreptitious reconstitution as body. But can the same be said of his relation to capital? Is his valorization of exchange itself enough to eradicate the last traces of capital—or do the 92 kopeks remain long after the body has been burned?

The central machine (the nonmetaphoric machine grounding a metaphoric system) is now no longer the machine as such but the *commodity*. It is through the process of commodification that the Futurist dynamic is expanded across the entire socius. Marinetti's shift from a model of production to a model of (exchange) value as the organizing metaphor of the Futurist text serves to elide the system of metaphoricity typical of the aestheticization of politics into the value-oriented system that informs bourgeois political rationalizations.

At the outset, by way of a broad and rather crude opposition, I offered the polarity of a liberal political discourse oriented around values (whether those values be political or aesthetic) and a fascisticized (aestheticized) discourse subject to the whim of a central metaphor. For Futurism, this metaphor was originally the machine, but now it is the commodity, or rather the process of commodification itself, that serves as metaphor. By offering in the figure of the commodity (as the principle of exchange and deferral) a metaphor of *value*, Marinetti finally merges "liberal" (value-oriented) and "fascistic" (or metaphoric) political discourses. The play upon "value" effects this elision, for what Marinetti parodies is the ethical organization of liberal politics founded upon values. By taking value as its new central metaphor, however, this later strain of Futurist discourse seeks to effect a seamless discursive passage from liberal capitalism into fascism. Moreover, this elision of capitalism into fascism—which I offer here *not* as a historical or economic observation but as a rhetorical analysis—foregrounds that value which is, in reality, the ethical center of capitalism: the commodity itself. The commodity is not simply fetishized, for, at some point, effective fetishization must suspend disbelief and deny its own willful constitution of the fetish. The commodity is valorized *as* a fetish. That is to say, the false consciousness of fetishization has been surpassed: the commodity is itself only a metaphor of value, a residual of that real process of actualization which is exchange itself. By organizing his discourse around this metaphor of value, Marinetti both incorporates (in self-consciously fetishized form) the traditional notion of value-oriented discourse, and distantiates himself from it by presenting value as *mere* metaphor.

At the same time he compromises the aesthetic of production to an aesthetic of value (in the move from the model of production to a model of production of values / signs), Marinetti also compromises the radical project of his early fascistic politics in favor of more conventional models of political action. The metaphoric displacement that constitutes *economic* value as an all-pervasive *ethical* value in the logic of late capitalist social organization (that is, the process of rationalization) allows for a rapprochement of the "fascisticized" or "aestheticized" discourse of metaphoricity and traditional bourgeois value systems, precisely because bourgeois ethical systems thereby also reveal themselves as metaphoric. Once a value system—even if it is only the figure or image of value offered by the commodity—occupies the central position previously held by the metaphor in Futurism's discursive organization, the movement ceases to be avant-garde in quite the same sense as it was. Likewise, once a metaphor of value (the commodity) displaces rationally legitimated, discursively encoded values at the heart of bourgeois ideology, that ideology in turn lowers its defenses against Futurist / fascist political discourse.

Marinetti's attack upon the principle of fixation of value is figured as an attack upon the materiality of the human body, which must be reduced to ashes before it can realize its full potential, both as a commodity and as an explosive. To understand the ideological background of such an attack, it is perhaps necessary to read within a capitalist tropological tradition most clearly articulated by Marx in the *Communist Manifesto*. Commenting upon the merciless de-auraticization of the commodity, which is necessary in capitalist relations of exchange if the commodity is not to regress to the status of the precapitalist use-value, Marx and Engels characterize the iconoclasm of the bourgeoisie: "All fixed fast-frozen relations, with their train of ancient and venerable prejudices and opinions are swept away, all new-formed ones become antiquated before they can ossify."[14] In its most radical form, capitalism negates all fixed values "before they can ossify." In Marinetti, however, the ideological subject—and the investment of that subject in the materiality of the body—already marks just such an "ossification." The project of the Futurist aesthetic, exemplified no less in the commerce of this Japanese businessman than it is in the critique of Mallarméan preciosity, is to reverse the tendency of late capitalism to fix, monopolize, and ontologize value in specific forms. What Marinetti represents is an attempt to thwart the powers of ossification inherent in the monopolization of value, which takes place under the cartels of monopoly capitalism. Yet discursively, Marinetti rejoins the ideology he seeks to surpass. Futurism espouses the cause of an earlier, more radical and self-destructive capitalism—the capitalism Marx describes in the manifesto—against the self-preserving forces of monopoly. Historically and politically, it is this that constitutes the specificity of the Futurist/fascist avant-garde: the recognition that the project of modernism, entailing the parallel progress of an aesthetic and a political project under capitalism, has been betrayed by capitalism's ossification. The only way out lies in a radicalization of the processes of exchange—in a burning of bones.

CHAPTER 6

Fascist Modernism and
the Theater of Power

In this final chapter, I wish to return to the terms
of Benjamin's treatment of fascism in order to work
through more fully the implications of his analysis of the aestheticization of political life. The implications I seek to chart are those
that impact both upon the possibility of thinking the avant-garde
in the present, and upon the political position from which we
seek to historicize both the avant-garde and fascism. I return to
"aestheticization" not simply to assess its applicability to the historical phenomenon of fascism, but rather to understand the ways
in which it has influenced postwar theories of the relationship of
aesthetics to politics.

Any postwar, "postfascist" theory will necessarily also be a
theory constructed in the wake of the failure—or sublation?—of
the avant-garde, and the analysis here will therefore tangentially
raise questions of modernism and postmodernism about which
much—too much, perhaps—has already been written. The intention is decidedly not to work through that debate once again, but
merely to insist upon fascism as well as the avant-garde as a framework for understanding the so-called postmodernism debate. In
other words, I will be taking the avant-garde and fascism as analo-

gous moments of ideological *Selbstkritik* within—and necessarily across—discursive parameters. I do so in order to understand what critical, philosophical, and aesthetic discourses have arisen in response to the phenomena of fascism and the avant-garde— phenomena which, in their respective scramblings of the political and the aesthetic, threaten the traditional discursive organization of the public sphere.

I commented at the outset of this work on the emergence of theories of the avant-garde at precisely that moment when the *élan* of the movements seemed to have exhausted itself, bringing the very possibility of the avant-garde into question. This sense of crisis was captured in its most lapidary form by Enzensberger's assertion that "the avant-garde has become its opposite: anachronism."[1] One begins to theorize the avant-garde at precisely that point where it has become anachronism. Theory itself (or so it would seem) is the very stigma of anachronism. Nevertheless, it is important to examine the philosophy of history that alone makes Enzensberger's analysis possible. What, after all, might it mean to declare the avant-garde "anachronistic"? What notion of temporality ascribes value and meaning to the category "anachronism"?

The answer is close at hand. If the avant-garde is to be understood as a liberation of cultural history from the linearity of progress, from the tradition of innovation, then it must surely debunk the evaluative pretensions of "anachronism" as a category. The reemergence of the category as a historicizing and evaluative judgment *upon* the avant-garde is itself evidence of the reemergence of a modernist vocabulary—or, one might argue, of an attempt to relegitimate ("anachronistically") the category of modernism. The avant-garde would thus function as the scapegoat of modernity, sacrificed in the name of a more comforting "progressive" philosophy of history. The "crisis" of the avant-garde would thus function ideologically, as the reassertion of an earlier or more fundamental project of modernity.

There is, in Enzensberger's judgment, a curious and forceful conjunction of the performative and the constative. The proclamation of the judgment—that "the avant-garde has become its opposite: anachronism"—serves at the same time as proof of the validity of that judgment. If the judgment, with its dependence upon the imperative category of anachronism, is to have any meaning, then the temporality of progress, the temporality of modernity, must be assumed to have reestablished itself. If, as Bürger asserts, the avant-garde's "simultaneity of the radically disparate" disempowers the charge of anachronism; and if, as Bloch argues, fascism obliges us to rethink political analysis in terms of the coexistence of nonsynchronous social forces, how is it possible to historicize both fascism and the avant-garde in terms of a category of anachronism, which in light of the very phenomena it seeks to judge is itself paradoxically anachronistic? For Enzensberger to be able to make the statement, and for the statement to have any meaning whatsoever, the statement must be true. It is, in fact, a truism. If the avant-garde can meaningfully be said to be anachronistic, then we surely *have* passed beyond the temporal self-understanding of the avant-garde—it really *is* anachronistic.

The suspicion arises that in the apparent lamentation over the loss of the avant-garde impulse a more conservative postwar modernism is seeking to reassert itself. The conflation of avant-garde and modernism in critical terminology is, in fact, undone—explicitly, of course, in Bürger's analysis, but implicitly also, in the very notion of "crisis" exemplified by Enzensberger. The avant-garde is sacrificed at the altar of modernism. But why? What, with the exorcism of the avant-garde, is achieved in this modernist lamentation over modernism? Could it be that the critical imperative expressed by the "crisis of the avant-garde" is an imperative of historical distantiation, motivated by the philosophical affinities of the avant-garde and fascism? A discourse about that which we seek to escape but cannot—fascism—is carried on in terms of a lamentation over that which we seek to retain but cannot—the avant-garde. In historicizing the avant-garde as anachronism we at least effect a break with that nonsimultaneity so central to our understanding of both the avant-garde and fascism.

Enzensberger might be said only to begin a debate that will subsequently be played out as a confrontation of and with the

avant-garde and fascism. His reinscription of a modernist temporality—a temporality of anachronism—will subsequently be problematized. This veiling of the actual debate, this substitution of
the avant-garde for fascism, of lamentation for relief, can, I think,
be traced back to Benjamin's original analysis of aestheticization.
It is an ideological move Benjamin himself will ultimately resist,
but which his analysis of aestheticization will make possible. In
the context of postwar debate "The Work of Art in the Age of Mechanical Reproduction" will be vulgarized as an attempt to rescue
the project of modernity from the stigma of fascism, as an attempt
to insist upon political literacy in the face of theatrical depoliticization. And Benjamin, it must be said, is not altogether a passive
victim of this reappropriation. Though he harbors doubts about
his own analysis, he consigns them to the footnotes of his text.
To understand fully the breadth of the analysis of aestheticization, it is necessary to read Benjamin against the grain, through
the doubts his essay seeks to marginalize, but bravely confronts.

Benjamin concludes his analysis of fascism's aestheticization
of politics with a polemical flourish: taking Brecht as his model,
he proposes instead the politicization of aesthetics. It is interesting to note that, just as Benjamin invokes Brecht as a response
to the problem of aestheticized politics, Bürger too will invoke
him as a resolution to the aporias of the avant-garde. Already, it
seems clear that the discussion of fascism and the discussion of
the avant-garde will run parallel, within the same parameters. Implicitly, what Benjamin is proposing is the playing off of a quite
specifically defined avant-garde against fascist aestheticization. I
would like to frame this chapter by looking at the ways in which
critical thought has reacted to and adapted Benjamin's proposal
in ways Benjamin himself might not have sanctioned, but which
are ultimately necessitated by the realization that the avant-garde
and fascism cannot, in fact, be played off against each other in any
unmediated fashion; necessitated, that is, by the realization that
both fascism and the avant-garde—insofar as there is any "truth"
to them—partake of a similar logic.

In response to Benjamin's rhetorical opposition of "aestheticization" and "politicization," Philippe Lacoue-Labarthe has had the following to say: "Now it is true that 'politicization' is the starting point of 'totalitarian logic' from which no one seems to have been immune during this period. However, as regards Nazism, the verdict was incontestably exact: the 'aestheticization of politics' was, indeed, in its essence, the programme of National Socialism. Or its project."[2] Lacoue-Labarthe is both affirming the value of Benjamin's analysis and questioning the implications of that analysis for the construction of a counterdiscourse. Benjamin's analysis, so suggestive in its characterization of fascism, carries within it the risk of an alternative totalitarianism. The underlying suspicion, then, which I wish to examine in this chapter, is that the totalizing claims of aesthetics and the totalizing claims of politics cannot be clearly differentiated. We have already seen with regard to Marinetti that it is necessary to complicate the model of aestheticization beyond any simple analysis of the substitution of aesthetic "value" for political and ethical "value." Fascist aestheticization would be the movement beyond *any* systematic encoding of values into the realm of metaphor. The challenge, then, must be to work within Benjamin's "incontestably exact" model of aestheticization while resisting that temptation of the simple rhetorical inversion that he offers. Indeed, in the wake of fascism's irreversible confusion of discourses, is Benjamin's proposal even thinkable in the present?

If, as an alternative to the aestheticization of politics, Benjamin offers the politicization of aesthetics, it is in terms of a politics of representation that he offers his analysis. However, rather than doing battle for control of the means of production of representation, we must recognize how any such battle for representational hegemony will leave untouched the philosophical hegemony of representation itself as a way of understanding the world—a world supposedly split into realities and their representations. It is precisely the Fascist Modernism of a Marinetti, with his deconstruction of the dyad of production and representation, which forces us to reject this terminology as a means of understanding fascism. What must be resisted in order for a more radical politicization to be possible—a politicization, that is, which calls into question the category of the political itself as a privileged empirical discourse, predating representation—is the de-realization of representation. "De-realization" would be the consignment of representation to a secondary mode, to a position of dependence vis-à-vis the hypostatized Real. It is necessary, then, to take into account the reality of representation, without reducing reality itself to a representation.[3]

Within any postmodern theory, fascism will become both an explicit and an implicit testing ground for the rethinking of representation. Indeed, it is possible to trace a strain of analysis conducted in this vein back to Benjamin's "Reproduction" essay, which moves beyond a vulgar materialist celebration of technological progress by virtue of its insistence upon technical *reproducibility* and not upon simple reproduction.[4] By insisting upon the retroaction of the possibility of reproduction (reproducibility) upon the object of reproduction itself, Benjamin builds upon an essentially economistic analysis of the logic of mass production to suggest a phenomenological mutation of the concept of origin. Benjamin's inscription of reproduction within the original aesthetic artifact—the object's orientation toward its own doubling, the possibility of a representation that is essential and primary, rather than incidental and secondary—opens up the simulacral space of what has since been termed the "hyperreal," a space in which "the very definition of the real becomes that of which it is possible to give an exact representation."[5] This is the space in which postfascist, post–avant-garde theory moves. Despite the rhetoric of theatricality (which I will examine more closely later) which seems to suggest a reading of aestheticization as theatricalization and misrepresentation, Benjamin nevertheless problematizes its attempt to establish any such theatrical criterion for reifying the real.[6] Benjamin refrains from stigmatizing "the aesthetic" as a category and attempts to direct his critique against a specific understanding of theatricality. At the same time, the attack on theatricality will serve to legitimate an alternative project of political literacy.

The argument of the "Reproduction" essay hardly needs reiteration. What does require further elucidation, however, is the subtext of that analysis. This is quite literally a sub-text, confined largely to a series of footnotes in which Benjamin examines precisely the ways in which fascism has been empowered by technological advances, making use of the very reproductive techniques that supposedly oppose it. The baldest statement of this counterposition to the main argument of the essay occurs in the following footnote:

> Mass reproduction is aided especially by the reproduction of masses. In big parades and monster rallies, in sports events, and in war, all of which nowadays are captured by camera and sound recording, the masses are brought face to face with themselves. This process, whose significance need not be stressed, is intimately connected with the development of techniques of reproduction and photography. Mass movements are usually discerned more clearly by a camera than by the naked eye. . . . This means that mass movements, including war, constitute a form of human behavior which particularly favors mechanical equipment. (Benjamin, *Illuminations*, p. 253)

Since Benjamin emphasizes *reproducibility* as something inherent to the reproducible object, rather than *reproduction* as a secondary and accidental process to which the object is subjected, he will be constrained, in the political arena, to take into account the reproducibility of the proletariat itself as an objective historical agent. Since reproduction reduces the specific to the reproducible, the proletariat to the amorphous mass, technological advances potentially lead into a depoliticization which runs counter to Benjamin's argument. The very process of liberating reproduction, which Benjamin celebrates, nevertheless feeds directly into the fascist spectacles, the marches and the wars that he condemns.

The ambiguity of mass reproduction—the reproduction of masses—is reflected in the fundamental ambiguity of fascism itself, as Benjamin notes in his critique of expression, or *"Ausdruck."* He claims that fascism meets a desire for self-expression, which it offers to the masses in place of the fulfillment politics demands: "Fascism attempts to organize the newly created proletarian masses without affecting the property structure which the masses strive to eliminate. Fascism sees its salvation in giving the masses not their right, but instead a chance to express themselves. . . . The logical result of Fascism is the introduction of aesthetics into political life" (Benjamin, *Illuminations*, p. 243). Implicitly, a play is being made upon the complementary and compensatory relationship pertaining between political and aesthetic senses of "representation." At the same time that he criticizes fascism for offering mimetic instead of political representation, however, Benjamin is obliged to see this displacement as itself "*Ausdruck*"—as an adequate expression, in other words, of the "truth" of the *essentially* reproducible masses. Indeed, elsewhere he insists upon "Man's legitimate claim to being reproduced" as one of the basic demands of the proletariat (Benjamin, *Illuminations*, p. 234). Hereby, he effaces the crucial distinction of "*Ausdruck*" and "*Recht*," upon which his critique of representation is based. The "truth" of fascism is that representation is not a lie—that it is, quite to the contrary, the precondition of a certain mimetological model of truth, which is central to political discourse.

What Benjamin chooses to overlook is the way in which the loss of specificity of the aesthetic moment implicit in the process of the art work's loss of aura encourages the process of the aestheticization of politics by liberating aesthetic experience from the institutional constraints that held it in check. Reproducible art is not only an alternative *to* fascistic social practice, but also a potential tool *for* it. It is not this aspect of Benjamin's analysis that I wish to pursue here, however. Instead, I wish to concentrate upon his characterization of the bourgeois and fascist public spheres.

Also in a footnote, Benjamin examines the impact of techniques of technological reproduction upon the very structure of parliamentary democracy.

> Since the innovations of camera and recording equipment make it possible for the actor to become audible and visible to an unlimited number of persons, the presentation of the man of politics, before cameras and recording equipment becomes paramount. Parliaments, as much as theaters, are deserted. . . . Though their tasks may be different, the change affects equally the actor and the ruler. . . . This results in a new selection, a selection before the equipment from which

the star and the dictator emerge victorious. (Benjamin, *Illuminations*, p. 249)

A certain reproductive escalation becomes discernible here, problematizing the celebrated process of de-auraticization. Bourgeois parliamentarism is implicitly linked with the theater and its decadence is shadowed by the demise of theater. Likewise, Benjamin suggests that we think the relationship of fascism to democracy as analogous to the relationship of film to theater. But what is that relation? At the most basic level, both theater and film share certain representational presuppositions: fundamentally, that there is a reality that is subsequently to be represented, acted, filmed. At the same time, however, the emphasis in Benjamin's essay upon reproducibility and upon the retroaction of reproductive techniques upon that which is reproduced moves against so simple a presupposition. Theater and film are not just two ways of representing the same thing; they necessarily reconstitute the thing itself.

It is strange, then, that in an essay that celebrates the liberational potential of technologies of reproduction it should be film—the medium deprived of aura—that creates both stars and dictators. How can it be that the charismatic dictator and the Hollywood star are produced by precisely that medium that is most inimical to aura? Clearly, it is necessary to rethink the aura of the dictator and the star in this context. The aura of the dictator is predicated upon his lack of specificity and intrinsic reproducibility. In other words, the aura attacked by the filmic medium and the charisma of the dictator are not one and the same; indeed, charismatic authority seems to be created precisely by virtue of the effacement of aura.[7] For charisma is *not* created—as vulgar usage would have it—by an act of individual volition, but rather by a collective act of faith. The aura of the dictator consists in the recognition of a certain arbitrariness: in the awareness that he could be anyone. More than this, as an always already reproducible representation of individual, antidemocratic authority, the Führer already *is* anyone.

The representational degeneration Benjamin traces from theater to film in this footnote involves a recognition of the charismatic leader as something *less*—rather than more—than the individual. Charismatic individuality must be understood as a form of contradiction in terms, for it involves the collective investment in the category of the individual. It is possible, then, to extract from Benjamin's analysis of the liberating potential of filmic representation a critique of the totalitarian potential of the medium of film. It is in the context of these totalitarian possibilities, already uncovered in Benjamin's own analysis, that one might place responses such as that of Lacoue-Labarthe quoted above.

This differentiation of film and theater should certainly not be mistaken for a nostalgia for the theater, however, for it is the intrinsic theatricality of bourgeois democracy that first opens it up to the deformations of filmic representation. "The present crisis of the bourgeois democracies," argues Benjamin, "comprises a crisis of the conditions which determine the public presentation of the rulers. Democracies exhibit a member of government directly and personally before the nation's representatives. Parliament is his public" (Benjamin, *Illuminations*, p. 249). What Benjamin is outlining here is the conflation of the political and the mimetic in the category of representation. The institutions of bourgeois democracy (in this case, parliament) structure a political form of representation and serve also to frame a specific form of "*Repräsentation*" of the leader. The parliamentary audience of the leader—who represents the people—are themselves representatives. Democracy, Benjamin seems to be arguing, is a veritable orgy of representation, a meeting point for seemingly incompatible models of power.

The degeneration of democracy is thus likened to a form of theatricalization, in which the immediate power of the people is fixed upon a leader and in which parliament is reduced to a mere audience. This critique, oriented around the model of the theater, contains several important elements. I would ultimately argue that it is built upon a repression of the theatrical organization of both political and philosophical thought within modernity, but for now I will limit myself to outlining some of the implications of the model. On the most obvious level, the critique might be taken as aimed against the double distantiation of the electorate from power. As the representatives of the power of the people, both leader and parliament are simulacra—at once the real origin of power and yet its mere representation. Within this theatrical model of power the process would be as follows: first, the people surrenders its power to elected "representatives," then those representatives, in turn, fail to represent, and become mere spectators. The disempowering of the people, then, is synonymous with the reduction of their mode of representation to the status of specularity. The political and the mimetic meet in this critique of parliamentary representation.

However, to read the escalation of representation in this way—as a process of distantiation of the people from power—is to misunderstand or underestimate both the participatory imperative of charismatic authority and the historicity of the simulacrum as a model of power. In short, there are two diametrically opposed ways to develop the argumentation in Benjamin's essay. The first would seek to understand aestheticization as the reduction of the real to its mere representation, and the disempowering of the spectator as mere onlooker. The second would examine the loss of critical distance inherent in fascism's *integration* of the spectator as an integral legitimating instance within the political performance itself. In subsequent attempts to rethink social specularity, these opposing tendencies have generally been conflated.

The first interpretation would insist upon the theatricality of fascism as a radical instance of the alienation of the audience from power.[8] In other words, the distinction of life and representation is resurrected as a way of reconstituting a simplistic model of ideology in which "real" (lived) contradictions are resolved at the "unreal" (ideological or representational) level. By contrasting life and its representation, however, this interpretation of Benjamin nevertheless remains within the mimetic terminology of the theatrical model he seeks to oppose. By hypostatizing the "real" and "representation," one fails to take into account the fundamentally simulacral nature of the reproducible original.

One major difficulty of fascism, which ushered in the simulacral representational episteme in which we still live, consists in the impossibility of differentiating the real from its representation. One critic has argued that the politically affirmative nature of fascism's false resolution of contradictions, though different from the problematic of German Idealist aesthetics, must be approached in similar terms. Fascism is aestheticization, and yet:

> The fascist public sphere should be understood as a "beautiful illusion" which is, however, different from the "beautiful illusion" of art which serves as a means for private psychic flight from reality. The fascist illusion is the factual result of a flight from reality by the petty bourgeois masses, who are socio-economically and sociopsychologically most disposed to such a flight. German fascism can therefore be understood as a false, perverted, merely formal fulfillment of the ideals and intentions of classical aesthetics for which bourgeois society had no use, i.e. as a pseudo-socialist changeling.[9]

Fascism is not ideological in quite the same way that an aesthetic can be·said (to use Marcuse's term more properly) to be affirmative. In order to resolve contradictions transplanted from the political realm, the aesthetic must somehow exempt itself from that realm, thereby insisting upon a traditional bourgeois system of discursive differentiation. The resolution offered by fascism, on the other hand, is—or at least *becomes*—the real, rather than an affirmative compensation *for* the real. What Stollmann characterizes as a "flight from reality by the petty bourgeois masses" might better be understood as a flight *of* reality itself. The petty bourgeoisie does not find itself in some elsewhere of reality— in representation, for example, or in ideology. Reality itself has shifted ground. The socioeconomic marginalization of the petty bourgeois masses—or rather the reaction of the petty bourgeoisie to that marginalization—leads in turn to a marginalization of the socioeconomic itself, to a marginalization of that way of thinking which Stollmann identifies with "the real."

Significantly, then, the sense in which Stollmann is able to present fascism as falsification and distortion is limited to the charge of a "false, perverted, merely formal fulfillment of the ideals and intentions of classical aesthetics." Fascism is not "real" classical aesthetics. But is, then, an aesthetic project to be cited as a criterion for the definition of the "real"? Moreover, in terms of this critique, classical aesthetics was itself never quite "real" anyway, since it was constituted precisely by virtue of a certain exemption *from* the real. As the negation of the aesthetic negation, fascism seems to reconcile aesthetics and politics, reality and representation. The paradox of aesthetic autonomy, of course, is its articulation—within a rationalized discursive system—of a move beyond rationalization. As a negation of rationalized and reified social conditions, the aesthetic at the same time tendentially negates the conditions of its own possibility. The realization of the autonomous aesthetic is therefore profoundly ambiguous, for it offers a critique oriented toward the ideal suspension of critique, as Bürger recognizes in judging the avant-garde a failure and in suspending the demand for the reintegration of art and life. Something of this ambiguity is retained in Stollmann's analysis, when he argues that "the fears of classical aesthetic theory that the spread of capitalism would mean the end of all art—meaning the end of humanity as well, of liberated man, of his ideal image preserved in autonomous art— these ideas were fulfilled in fascism" (p. 53). Aestheticization paradoxically means the end of art, in the sense of its completion and of its demise. If, as Benjamin insists in the "Reproduction" essay, one of the characteristics of the fascist mentality is its ability to experience its own death as an aesthetic pleasure, then the project of a totalizing aesthetic judgment partakes of that mentality, for it too is oriented toward its own demise as category.[10]

These are, as I have pointed out, the problems raised by only one of two dominant interpretive models which have served to maintain the potency of Benjamin's analysis. The second model is likewise centered around the question of theatricality, but understands the theatrical experience of the audience very differently. Paradigmatic here would be Brecht, for whom the theater alienates precisely by virtue of offering a false community and a mechanism of identification. In this model, the problem would not be too *much* distance between spectacular power and passive audience, but too *little*: theatrical alienation would constitute rather than annihilate identity. If Benjamin offers the paradigm of aestheticization, it is Brecht who—in a passage from the *Messingkauf* entitled "Concerning the Theatricality of Fascism"—makes explicit that critique as a critique of theatricalization: "What results is that empathy of the public with the actor, which is normally taken to be the essential achievement of art. Here we have that excitement, that transformation of all the spectators into one unified mass, which is demanded of art."[11] It is not, for Brecht, a problem of specularity as distantiation, but rather of the collapse of the critical *Publikum*. Implicitly, he reads distantiation as an empowering critical distance, whereas in the first interpretive model it was understood as a disempowerment. Here the theatrical space is privileged precisely by virtue of the critical separation it potentializes and fascism would be the displacement of critique by coerced participation.

Where these two interpretations meet is in their critique of the absence of any critical space in fascism. For the first set of analysts, the masses are silenced, or their voices left unperceived thanks to the distance placed between them and the instantiation of power; and for the second, the masses are ventriloquized. Brecht's critique of Hitler's emotional rhetoric, however, raises the question as to whether a specifically fascist public sphere exists.[12] For what Brecht brings to light is the ambiguity of the model of the theater as a way of understanding the degeneration of the bourgeois public sphere. Conservative cultural critics such as Daniel Bell have even reworked a position not dissimilar to Brecht's and reapplied those arguments in a premodern critique of the aesthetic itself, arguing that "in the classical pre-modern view, art was essentially contemplative: the viewer or spectator held 'power' over the experience by keeping his aesthetic distance from it. In modernism, the intention is to 'overwhelm' the spectator so that the art product itself . . . imposes itself on the spectator in its own terms."[13] In other words, if fascism is to be understood in terms of this model of theatricality, then it is with modernism—according to Bell—that theater begins to function as an experience of being overwhelmed. Once again, the avant-garde's implication in the process of fascisticization cannot be glossed over: if fascism owes something to the theater, it is to a specifically modernist theatricality rather than to the classical, critical proscenium that it appeals.

It is not difficult to appreciate how the avant-garde desire to *épater le bourgeois*, with its ostensible disregard for the audience or *Publikum* as a philistine moment of economic control, might feed into a critique of the very existence of any critical public sphere.[14] The category of *Publikum*—a category inhabiting a realm between the aesthetic and the political, as a model both of consuming audience and of public sphere—offers an important insight into the possible points of convergence of avant-garde and fascism. Avant-garde opposition to the dictates of the public can be interpreted in many ways: for Brecht, as for Benjamin, it would entail an opposition to a certain subject-position forced upon the audience, the position of passive consumer. For the early avant-garde—and Expressionism, against which Brecht himself polemicized, would be typical here—the audience is rejected as a moment of control, as the instantiation of bourgeois philistinism. For the fascist, meanwhile, rejection of the *Publikum* is based upon a lack of respect for the institutions of the democratic public sphere.[15]

At a certain historical point, it becomes extremely difficult to disentangle some of these diverse ideological moments that convene in the opposition to the *Publikum*; fascism and the avant-garde rejoin in their opposition to the audience. The logic behind this opposition differs, of course, in each case. The protofascist opposes the theatrical staging of a potentially intellectualizing critique; the avant-garde opposes the potential for passive receptivity. What Benjamin articulates, however, albeit against himself, is the necessity of reading the fascist spectacle in terms which map themselves onto the bourgeois model of literate "*Räsonnieren*," but which must be distinguished from it. Thus he observes that "fascist art is executed not only *for* the masses, but *by* the masses.

Consequently it is tempting to conclude that in this art the masses are concerned with themselves, that they are reaching an agreement among themselves. . . . Everyone knows that this is not the case."[16] The problem is not just that the spectacle is intrinsically inimical to democratic *Räsonnieren* or to rational *Verständigung*, nor that it is identical with them: the problem is that both these models potentially legitimate the actual disempowerment in the spectacle. The self-alienation of the *"repräsentativ"* masses can be mistaken for the critical distance of self-reflection. The issue, of course, is whether—in light of the similarity in the construction of the spectacle and the logic of democratic discussion—it is possible to insist upon the strict divisibility of the two.

In order to understand the political ambiguity of any opposition to the *Publikum*, it is important to grasp the centrality of the term to the bourgeois public sphere. Is the theatricality of fascist spectacle in any way prefigured in the bourgeois public sphere? The obvious answer—the answer that fascist and antifascist alike seem to agree on, and the answer, therefore, which must remain unsatisfactory—is that theater and critique, aesthetics and politics, inhabit entirely different planes.[17] It cannot be ignored, however, that the Enlightenment understanding of the public sphere as a collection of *private* individuals gathered as a public or audience itself invokes one of the categories of theatricality—the *Publikum*—which is central to fascism's refashioning of the political. Although the bourgeois public sphere is clearly (at least in theory) dialogic and depends upon the exercise of critical reason within a self-emancipating society, we should still take seriously the ambiguous theatricality of the *Publikum*.

The Kantian model of Enlightenment *Räsonnieren* allows us to pursue the ambiguities of theatricality even further and complicates even more that distinction between the solitude of reflection and the collectivity of drama. It cannot be ignored that Kant, when called to answer the question: What is Enlightenment?, criticizes the "self-imposed immaturity" of the timorous bourgeoisie in terms of an experience of *reading*: "It is so easy to be immature. If I have a book to serve as my understanding, a pastor to serve as my conscience, a physician to determine my diet for me, and so on, I need not exert myself at all."[18] In other words, it is not simply a question of the topos of the *Publikum* coincidentally carrying certain theatrical connotations. Any critique of fascist aestheticization must take into account the intrinsic ambiguity of the bourgeois public sphere toward the power relations encoded in reading itself. Contrary to subsequent rationalizing attempts to critique political theatricalization from the position of literacy, it is precisely to an experience of *reading*, rather than of theatricality, that Kant traces the problem.

Could it be, then, that beneath the traditionally antispecular, antitheatrical ideology of the bourgeois public sphere, there is a more deep-seated theatricality to which fascism merely gives expression? What such an assertion would boil down to is a confusion of the public and the private spheres so central to Kant's establishing of the Enlightenment political project.[19] Does fascism, then, attempt a radical reprivatization of the public sphere (I tend to think not), or does it merely refashion the affective possibilities latent within Enlightenment models of publicly exercised reason?

Curiously, the most schematic attempt to trace out this whole problematic area—Habermas's seminal study *The Structural Transformation of the Public Sphere*—is of little assistance in answering this question. Originally published in the early sixties, this work historicizes the notion of the public sphere and articulates a more or less explicit opposition of literacy and specularity, writing and theater. This study insists upon the literary sphere as the realm in which the bourgeoisie begins to constitute itself as a political and critical instance within the antagonistic parameters of eighteenth-century absolutism.

Arguing that the public sphere cannot be isolated as an autonomous sphere of feudal society, Habermas traces its emergence to the emergence of a bourgeois reading public in the eighteenth century. In so doing, he attempts to establish an opposition of specularity and critique, which he subsequently presents as an implicit opposition of theatricality and literacy. In order to explain the two notable lacunae in his study—namely, the absence of any consideration of Robespierre's Jacobinism or of the twentieth-century Western dictatorships—Habermas is obliged to invoke the criterion of literacy. The grounds he offers in *The Structural Transformation of the Public Sphere* for these omissions are twofold: first, that Jacobinism is "illiterate," and second, that the Western dictatorships of the twentieth century are "post-literary":

> In the stage of the French Revolution associated with Robespierre, for just one moment, a public sphere stripped of its literary garb began to function—its subject was no longer the "educated strata" but the uneducated "people" . . . it must be strictly distinguished from the plebiscitary-acclamatory form of regimented public sphere characterizing dictatorships in highly developed industrial societies. Formally they have certain traits in common; but each differs in its own way from the literary character of a public sphere constituted by private people putting reason to use—one is illiterate, the other, after a fashion, post-literary. (p. xviii)

As a category, the bourgeois public sphere is constituted not only upon the criterion of literacy, but, it would seem, within a certain trope of reading. Read from within this tradition, then, the deformation of the public sphere in fascism—the process of aestheticization—would be understood as a displacement of the paradigm of reading by the paradigm of theater.

In its putative opposition to the specularity of feudal (and fascist) *"Repräsentation,"* the bourgeois public sphere is dependent upon a notion of literacy. It is through the invocation of literacy—the reading of a writing—that Habermas seeks to forestall the culmination and collapse of the mediational semiotic in fascism. Historically, the insistence upon literacy follows from the argument that the politicized public sphere of a fully developed bourgeois democracy originates in the depoliticized realm of a literary public sphere. It is in and through the autonomy granted critical thought and exchange within the literary public sphere, argues Habermas, that the bourgeoisie constitutes itself as a political force. Emerging from within the power relations of absolutism, which severely limit its freedom to exercise its economic strength in the political sphere, the bourgeoisie, gathering in salons and coffeehouses, first comes into being as a collection of literary critics, practicing their free judgment in the process of "*Räsonnement*."

There is, however, a subtext to Habermas's narrative of the origins of the bourgeois public sphere. This subtext radically undercuts his elision of "*Räsonnieren*" into literacy. One can see how the bourgeois public sphere in fact emerges as an *audience* from a dialectic encoded within the feudal public sphere. Although instantiated purely in and through the bodies of its rulers, the absolutism of feudal power does not exclude the masses; it accords them a quite specific function. Tied as it is to the manifestation of its sovereign body—to the specular literality of the body politic—the theatricality of feudal power demands an audience. Tracing the development of what he calls a "representative" ("*repräsentativ*") public sphere through the Middle Ages into the eighteenth century, Habermas makes the following point: "The common people, content to look on, had the most fun. Thus, even here the people were not completely excluded; they were ever present in the streets. Representation was still dependent on the presence of people before whom it was displayed" (Habermas, *Structural Transformation*, p. 10). What this passage clarifies is the doubly constitutive function of the theatrical model. First, theater is only theater *because* the audience is present: the presence of the audience is not accidental but essential. In terms of Benjamin's model of reproducibility, it is only the presence of an audience that marks representation as representation. It is only *because*, in other words, fascism stages the spectacle that it can wield its simulacral power. More important, however—at least for the argument I wish to make here—the exclusion of the "people" is precisely that which marks and collectivizes them *as* people. It is not a question of a certain class being excluded, but rather of the constitution of a certain class on the basis of its exclusion. In this particular case, the bourgeoisie is constituted within the confines of the theater; it is not simply a case of the consignment of an already constituted class to the position of mere spectator. The common people—so Habermas's argument seems to run, in spite of itself—are precisely those who are content to look on.

At first sight, this specular instantiation of feudal power might seem to support the division of the literate public sphere of the bourgeoisie from the specular sphere of feudalism (and, indeed, an analysis of specular and spectacular fascism—as well as of the mass media—in terms of "refeudalization"). However, the divisive theatrical model presented here by Habermas contains the moment of its own negation. Precisely by virtue of its dependence upon an audience that it must nevertheless exclude from the dramatic unfolding of power—in its insistence, in other words, upon a classical, proscenium model of social interaction—the feudal public sphere creates a unified and alienated bourgeois body: the audience. What this implies, I think, is that the bourgeois public sphere is predicated *not* upon literacy, but quite specifically upon the specular relationship that renders it an *audience*. The bourgeois public—*"das Publikum"*—constitutes itself as an audience, and critique is grounded in a specifically *specular* set of relations. Critique does not, then, necessarily depend upon a notion of literacy, and Habermas's elimination of Jacobinism and fascism is illegitimate.

Fascist theatricality—and, I would contend, the performative shift in the avant-garde toward the aesthetics and politics of the manifest—might, indeed, be taken as an attack on the bourgeois system of mediated representation. Its particular form of totalitarianism might be understood as an immanentism, an absolutism, in which the conflation of signifier and signified, the conflation of power and its representation has been completed. While this movement would be explicable, within Habermas's model, as a simple historical regression, it should not be forgotten that the bourgeois representational semiotic is itself oriented—putatively, at least—toward an unrealized and unrealizable project of absolute mimesis. *"Repräsentation"*—the immanence of fascist representation—marks the virtual point at which the semiotic project both fulfills and annuls itself. This collapsing of the distinction of power and its representation is, in fact, a charismatic phantasm of democracy—of the people, for the people, by the people. The fascist mutation of this ideology into the dogma of *Volk* offers a literalistic and impossible realization of that ideal. It should be stressed that to make such an assertion is not, of course, to collapse the distinction between fascism and democracy in any way, but to show how fascism articulates a certain "truth" about democracy, a truth that nevertheless becomes a lie in its articulation—precisely because it is the silent center of bourgeois ideology.

We have arrived at, then—and rejected as illegitimate—the critical division of the specular and the literate, theatricality and literality: it would seem that the Enlightenment model of the public sphere has depended all along upon a certain theatricality. At the same time, however (and the confrontation with the fascist spectacle would be paradigmatic here) a certain impulse seems to be in operation to repress this theatricality and to normalize a certain model of reading. It is this tendency that must be resisted as a simplification and as an attempt to exonerate the bourgeois public sphere from any involvement in fascism. The political and philosophical confrontation with fascism is itself staged as a confrontation with a certain conceptual mode, a confrontation with theatricality—and this confrontation will play itself out in seemingly aesthetic terms.

The apparent escalation of aestheticization that fascism seems to invite at the level of critique is in fact necessitated by the ineradicable historical slippage of terms effected in fascism. At this point, it is possible to return to Benjamin; for this tendency within criticism is, I think, directly attributable to him and to his critique of aestheticization. One might gloss the model of theatricality by supplementing Benjamin's original analysis of fascist specularity with one of those rare essays in which he does offer an example of what the politicization of aesthetics might look like. I have in mind the treatment of Tretyakov in "The Author as Producer." The model of literary production presented here is a model of reversibility—a model the theater seems to foreclose. What Benjamin is suggesting is that if we might, for a moment, characterize as "theatrical" that mode of literary production in which a dialogue across the footlights is impossible, then the very institution of the bourgeois literary sphere is also "theatrical."

In a long self-quotation Benjamin details the difference between the experiments of Tretyakov and the bourgeois literary tradition: "The reader is always prepared to become a writer, in the sense of being one who describes or prescribes. . . . In a word, the literarization of living conditions becomes a way of surmounting otherwise insoluble antinomies, and the place [*Schauplatz*] where the words [are] most debased—that is to say, the newspaper—becomes the very place where a rescue operation can be mounted."[20] What opposes fascist "*Ästhetisierung*" here is a "*Literarisierung*" of life. In other words, having problematized traditional aesthetic production as a nonreciprocal disempowerment, Benjamin somewhat perversely characterizes the deconstruction of that productive model as a "literarization." And yet—as in the "Reproduction" essay—Benjamin seems to problematize the ostensible celebration of literacy. For the newspaper (Tretyakov's model for literary production) is also a speculative and specular locus (*Schauplatz*) in which critical language is debased. The literary and the theatrical have already merged historically in the newspaper and it can no longer be a question of extricating a purely "literate" verbal culture from the onslaught of theatricalization. The opposition of the so-called verbal and the so-called visual has become a debate internal to the terms of the overarching philosophy of the specular categories themselves. Mass reproduction—in this case, the mass dissemination of news through the newspaper—is the "*Schauplatz*" of the confusion of theatricality and literacy.

Aestheticization, then, should not be understood primarily in literary terms—as the false literalization, for example, of metaphors of race, purity, and so on. If aestheticization can be equated with a form of theatricality, and if that theatricality can itself be taken to be implicated within a whole nexus of specular relations extending far beyond the aesthetic, through philosophy, and into the political, as it constitutes itself as a discursive realm, the question for a "postfascist" praxis must be a question of rethinking the specular. However, if thought is itself conceptually framed by the theatrical, it becomes highly questionable whether the specular can be rethought at all—outside of the specular structures under discussion. This crisis of thinking specularity outside the specular is a crisis of philosophy.[21] Contemporary theory must confront the aestheticization model by attempting not simply to politicize a preexistent aesthetic, but to question the construction of the aesthetic itself. In other words: contemporary thought takes up the challenge of politicizing the aesthetic not in the sense of a simple sublation of aesthetics into politics but by questioning the construction of the categories.

The question, then, is: How to think the spectacle as the real, rather than as its degenerate representation? What this question opens up is less an opposition of visible and invisible, theater and reading, iconic and semiotic, than it is the possibility of a critique of the visible as an organizing epistemological category. In this vein, Debord has argued: "The Spectacle inherits all the *weaknesses* of the Western philosophical project which undertook to comprehend activity in terms of the categories of *seeing*; furthermore, it is based on the incessant spread of the precise technical rationality which grew out of this thought. The spectacle does not realize philosophy, it philosophizes reality. The concrete life of everyone has been degraded into a *speculative* universe."[22] Aestheticization and philosophization become thinkable within the same paradigm of the specular, and it is in this sense, perhaps, that one needs to understand that strange coincidence of aestheticization and the death of aesthetics. Aestheticization would consist both in the constitution of the object of experience as an alienated (aestheticized) object of disinterest (the traditional reading of aestheticization) and in the very organization of a discourse as an autonomous specular, or theatrical, totality. Aestheticization has become philosophization.

But how? Where in the aesthetic is that opening up to a philosophy of history? Where in history that orientation toward the aesthetic? In this chapter we have examined the nexus of avant-garde and fascism—aesthetics and politics—from the perspective of a synchronic analysis of the constitution of the public sphere. But how does the reconfiguration of those discourses manifest itself historically, and how is history manifested in and through this reconfiguration? This is not the place to enter into a discussion of the historical dynamic of Idealist aesthetics, but I would like to suggest (by way of introduction to what will be my concluding comments on "postfascist" and "postmodern" theory) a model within which the state of the current debate might be understood.

In his essay on "The Sublime and the Avant-Garde" Jean-François Lyotard moves at one crucial point beyond the strict purview of the avant-garde to suggest (and ultimately to deny) possible affinities with fascism. "The aesthetics of the sublime," he suggests, "this neutralized and converted into a politics of myth, was able to come and build its architectures of human 'formations' on the Zeppelin Feld in Nuremberg."[23] It is in its commitment to an aesthetic of the sublime that the avant-garde seems to open up the possibility of an aestheticization of politics—or through a distorted manipulation of the sublime, in other words, that fascism renders the political aesthetic. Lyotard's inference is that the deferral of aesthetic resolution in avant-garde works of art expresses a historical reality against which fascism reacts by reasserting a reified, and ultimately conciliatory, model of the sublime. To simplify somewhat, Lyotard argues that the avant-garde reworks the notion of the sublime as a "beyond within," that is, as an inexpressible residue of praxis, of expression *as* praxis. Thus in the avant-garde sublime, "the inexpressible does not reside in an over there, in another words, or in another time, but in this: in that (something) happens. In the determination of pictorial art, the indeterminate, the 'it happens,' is the paint, the picture. The paint, the picture as occurrence or event, is not expressible, and it is to this that it has to witness" (Lyotard, "Sublime," p. 4). Fascism, meanwhile—according to Lyotard—insists upon a sublime of the "over there," a messianic sublime in which the inexpressible is projected into the realm of history as an expectation and anticipation: "*Is the pure people coming? Is the Führer coming? Is Siegfried coming?*" (Lyotard, "Sublime," p. 16).

The aestheticization of politics, then, would be the aestheticization (indeed, the construction) of history through the sublime. This process, according to Lyotard, would occur in reaction to the avant-garde's troubling reevaluation of the sublime. The violence done to political history through the aesthetic is replicated by the violence done to the sublime through its false historicization. Fascism's neutralization and mythification of the sublime would consist in refashioning the sublime as a form of negative theology, wherein the absence in the sublime is projected historically as the absence of a pure presence, rather than as the impossibility of such a presence, as the inherence of that absence in the materiality of the work itself. The avant-garde resists (so the argument would run) its own sublation into the Idea: fascism, on the other hand, would be precisely that sublation thought historically and politically.

Lyotard's argument is suggestive, compelling—but ultimately problematic. I suspect that there is more of a collusion between avant-garde and fascistic renderings of the sublime than he is prepared to acknowledge, and that it is precisely in the spectacular politics of the Zeppelin Feld that this collusion becomes apparent. For it is in the spectacle that the question "*Is the pure people coming?*" finds its answer, but not its resolution. The *Volk* is *both* the anticipated presence—mythified, as Lyotard points out, historicized within a form of messianism—*and* the subject posing the question. In other words, the *Volk* is constituted by the myth of presence articulated in its anticipation and yet this constitution through anticipation constantly defers the constitution of the *Volk* in the present as the subject of anticipation. The *Volk* becomes the collective of those who anticipate the *Volk* and thus the *Volk* itself cannot be reduced (as Lyotard suggests) to the mythic referent of the question (which is a constitutive performative) but must be understood as suspended in a state of anticipation. The *Volk* is here—here on the Zeppelin Feld—constituted by the question ("*Is the pure people coming?*") which must constantly mythify yet defer its ostensible presence, and which must problematize the category of presence itself.

It is in these terms that we must understand the logic of fascist representation; the logic of the manifest that legitimates both a certain avant-garde aesthetic (of the manifest) and a certain fascistic politics. But how are we to think this form of political representation logically or rhetorically? The *Volk* is here not a metaphoric construct or a metonymy: the individual is not a part of a whole, but (to use a term coined by Hitler) a "representative form of Being" of the *Volk*.[24] Whereas rhetoric names relations of representation, the political structure enacted on the Zeppelin Feld is not a model of representation; it is beyond mimetic representation. And beyond representation is *Repräsentation*.

Once again, it is Benjamin who helps make the links here between the avant-garde (as characterized by Lyotard) and fascism. In the analysis of the fascist spectacle in the first "Pariser Brief" Benjamin offers a scenario that translates into sociopolitical terms that model of the avant-garde sublime—that "beyond within"— which Lyotard identifies with "the indeterminate" of "the paint, the picture." Thus what for Lyotard constituted the inexpressibility of art—the paint, the picture as occurrence or event— becomes, in the spectacle, the masses themselves: "The material from which Fascism creates its monuments—which it considers to be like iron—is above all so-called human material. And it is thanks only to these monuments that this human material finds any form."[25] The materiality of the masses and the materiality of the work are not vitiated by the monumentalism and transhistoricism of fascism, for even the Thousand Year Reich, precisely *as* myth, consistently defers the presence it seems to assert. The "beyond within" of fascism consists in the processual nature of the spectacle—in the self-constituting, self-negating unity of the *Volk* as both subject and referent of its own anticipatory question: "*Is the pure people coming?*" History thus becomes the modality of the sublime—rather than its reified myth.

If this is true, if both history and the sublime have been thus compromised, how might we—"postfascists," "postmoderns"— position ourselves historically in regard to fascism and the avant-garde? This was the question we began with in this chapter, a question we can now understand in both its political and its aesthetic context. Perhaps we might return to Enzensberger as a means of sketching out an answer. Does the current situation of theory truly reflect the avant-garde's failure, or is it not a logical emanation of that failure? In other words, does the "postmodern" end of history—the end, that is, of the great idea of history's end—mark the death of the avant-garde as a vehicle for that idea, or, in its very contingency, a more radical and paradoxical form of that "end" articulated by the avant-garde itself? The question will touch upon the sense in which it may or may not be possible to break with the temporality of breakage, to innovate *against* the tradition of innovation. The question will necessarily touch upon the postmodern.

As Enzensberger points out, the avant-garde does not exhaust itself in the collapsing of the historical past. The historical deformation it brings about is oriented against the very notion of any history in which even a *future* is thinkable.

> To be sure, the avant-garde metaphor does not exclude the dull and inferior view that whatever came earlier can, for that very reason, be thrown on the junk heap. But it cannot be reduced to vulgar worship of the latest thing. Included in this concept is the non-simultaneity of the simultaneous: precursors and stragglers are, at every moment of the process, simultaneously present. External and internal contemporaneity fall apart. The *en avant* of the avant-garde would, as it were, realize the future in the present, anticipate the course of history. (Enzensberger, p. 23)

In a sense, the avant-garde finds itself in the same position vis-à-vis modernism as do those discourses more recently labeled "postmodern." If modernity is a logic of the "post-," an ontologization of fashion, it can but find its most radical form in the "post-" of that "post-"—in a "postmodernity," which, as the beyond of modernity, is at the same time its *ne plus ultra*. (It is in this sense that we must understand Lyotard's invocation of the past-anterior as a model for understanding postmodernism. Modernity is always already postmodern).[26] This philosophical observation is borne out empirically by the experience of the historical avant-garde, which can be seen at one and the same time as a form of high modernism and as a deconstruction of the sequential temporal modality of modernism.

But there is more to Enzensberger's observation. The *en avant* of the avant-garde not only liquidates the sequentiality of the past; it liquidates the sequentiality of the future also. Its millennarianism is bodied forth as apocalypse. In other words, while I think it is possible to speak of the avant-garde rethinking history, that rethinking does not simply consist of a displacement of time by space, an arbitrary and reactionary opposition to historical progress. Instead, history is thought as an impossible presence, as the concentration of history in the present, as the presence, so to speak, of the present. This would mean that the avant-garde realizes rather than rejects the project of modernity, but that in doing so it necessarily liquidates modernity. Enzensberger—in terms we have traced back to Bloch's analysis of fascism, and forward to Bürger's analysis of the avant-garde—characterizes this gesture as a nonsimultaneity of the simultaneous.

This analogy of terms—in Bürger, Bloch, and Enzensberger, in analyses of fascism and of the avant-garde—helps to elucidate the ways in which (subsequent to the avant-garde, and subsequent to fascism) it is impossible to return to conventional (economistic) models of historical causality. Fascism is not an ideological interlude in which economic concerns were sidelined only to return in the wake of Hitler's defeat. There can be no question of simply restoring the categories of critical analysis operative before the emergence of fascism. Once, as Reich argues, the economy begins to function without the active participation of numerically and ideologically significant groups—the impoverished peasantry, the unemployed, and so on—then ideology (or Reich's "character-structure") acquires immediate political value. With the concentration of capital and the rationalization of labor, the rapid expansion in economically marginalized groups can no longer be accompanied by political marginalization. Consequently, politics must be managed with an eye to ideological rather than only economic determinants. But how might this process shed any light on the avant-garde?

Obviously, it would be foolish to propose any causal relation between the emergence of fascism and the emergence of the avant-garde—one is not responsible for the other. Both, however, take root among marginalized groups otherwise disenfranchised, politically or culturally, by the rationalization of economic production and social reproduction. Both, in other words, display a certain "nonsimultaneity of the simultaneous," which will be reflected in the aesthetic of the avant-garde as theorized by Bürger. The argument at least bears examination that the same process of centralization—of capital and of culture—potentializes both the fascist and the avant-garde impulses. Both acquire a certain compensatory value that overthrows dominant cultural and political structures.

The danger, however, is that this argument, with its invocation of economic marginalization, simply be used to legitimate a return to the economistic analysis it seemed to render anachronistic. The return to such an analysis would be in the political realm the ideological counterpart of Enzensberger's assertion of the anachronism of the avant-garde. It would be tantamount to an anachronistic and self-defeating reassertion of a modernist temporality, which is itself constituted upon the abhorrence of anachronism. If theory's return to a certain discourse of modernity can no longer be stigmatized as outmoded (after the avant-garde, after fascism, nothing is "outmoded," not even those discourses in which the idea of being "outmoded" can be articulated), theories of fascism must nevertheless eschew any totalizing, causally explicative value.

If both avant-garde and fascism emerge from and exemplify a certain "nonsimultaneity of the simultaneous" (or, conversely, a simultaneity of the nonsimultaneous), their difference consists in the ways in which they project that nonsimultaneity into a vision of the future. One might do worse than to invoke Bloch's notion of the objective and the subjective to illustrate how fascism exemplifies nonsimultaneity "subjectively," whereas the avant-garde attests "objectively" to that same nonsimultaneity inherent in the modern. This would mean that whereas fascism expresses itself in a nonsimultaneous desire for historical simultaneity—that is, for a normalization of historical conditions and for a paradoxical liquidation of that "nonsimultaneous" moment of the modernist avant-garde from which fascism itself emerges—the avant-garde faces the radical consequences of nonsimultaneity and thereby also risks self-liquidation. Fascist nonsimultaneity gives rise to certain anachronistic ideological formations, which subsequently seek to stabilize themselves, to reorient history around themselves, and, in turn, to stigmatize modernity itself as anachronistic. Fascism would, in other words, constitute a "postmodernity" in the most vulgar sense: an ideological break with the progressive temporality of modernity, but a break that, through the charge of anachronism leveled at modernity, secretly reasserts a normative temporality.[27]

The avant-garde, on the other hand, is obliged to face the paradoxical anachronism inherent in any charge of anachronism. It accepts the impossibility of passing beyond that temporality from whose perspective its own *en avant* is anachronism. If, as Bürger argues, the avant-garde brings about a certain synchronicity of the radically disparate, then one of the disparate "styles" it liberates is modernism itself. Precisely *because* the avant-garde wishes to position itself as a self-reflexive *Selbstkritik*, it must refuse the passage "beyond" modernism. What this means (and this is why the avant-garde and its apparent failure has necessitated a move beyond any historical dialectic in which *Selbstkritik* can be hypostatized) is that a separation can no longer be effected between a radical *Selbstkritik* and system-immanent criticism. The avant-garde work "quotes" modernism, just as it quotes any other style—but it is deprived of the means to mark that quote as a quote. This is a classic double bind: to pass beyond modernity is to remain within the temporality of the modern, whereas to remain within the modern—albeit provisionally, as one possibility among others—is to pass "beyond" it. The political and historical problematic of postmodernism is thus traced out in the avant-garde, as that sublime "beyond within" of modernity itself.

In concluding my consideration of the questions raised here, I would like to indicate the position of Fascist Modernism between and in relation to the twin possibilities of fascism and avant-garde. I can do no better than to begin, by way of marker, with a comment by Philippe Lacoue-Labarthe that seems to me one of the sanest assessments of our fascination with both fascism and the avant-garde.

> However necessary the political study may be, as has frequently been proved, it can obscure the analysis. This in no way means that one should become involved in any "rehabilitation" or "re-evaluation" of fascism. It simply means that it would be better to learn to stop considering fascism a "pathological" phenomenon (from what extra-social position, asked Freud, might one make such a diagnosis?) and recognize in it not only (at least) one of the age's political forms—and one no more aberrant or inadequate than any other—but the political form that is perhaps best able to bring us enlightenment regarding the essence of modern politics. (Lacoue-Labarthe, p. 107)

Lacoue-Labarthe's assessment helps move analysis beyond the sterile debate over rationality and irrationality, a debate that sets, for example, Lukács against the first generation of the Frankfurt School and that has led at least one critic of technological fascism to experience his own engagement with the issue of Fascist Modernism as a "conversion" of sorts: away from the pessimistic analysis of a "dialectic of Enlightenment" to a belief that fascism suffered from too little rather than too much Enlightenment.[28] While sympathizing with such objections to the oversimplification of the Enlightenment project, I believe it is necessary to go beyond the quantitative analysis of "too much" or "too little" Enlightenment. Fascism is, as Lacoue-Labarthe insists, "*the political form that is perhaps best able to bring us enlightenment regarding the essence of modern politics*"—but this does not make it a historically necessary development of the Enlightenment.

It is only at the risk of serious simplification that the relationship of fascism to the Enlightenment—and its notion of political democracy—can be thought in terms of a "dark" and an "enlightened" side of reason. First, there can be no question of pathologizing fascism, as Lacoue-Labarthe points out (or of pathologizing the avant-garde, as becomes clear in the failure of Poggioli's invocation of psychologistic taxonomies). Fascism is not a hidden malady. At the same time, it would also be wrong to resort to a vulgarized political unconscious in which fascism would function as a wish fulfillment, as the "real" desire of civilized society, held in check, but somehow given free rein in the historical sleep of the interwar years. The "truth" about politics manifested in fascism is not a determinate content-related truth, and cannot be reconstructed by raiding the ideological store of fascism. It is instead a "structural" truth, ineradicable and nonpathologizable because, I would contend, incurable. One does not "cure" history of fascism, any more than one "cures" a patient of the unconscious. Fascism's "truth," the "truth of politics," is that there *is* a truth of politics: that politics, despite its self-effacing modesty, is not simply a ragbag of contingencies, a domain of the hopelessly empirical, but an aesthetic—a discourse for the staging of history.

An analysis of fascism framed by the model of aestheticization need not pass through an analysis of the historical unconscious of bourgeois politics. The problematic is not simply one of repression. Indeed, the real repression lies in the insistence upon such a terminology, in the reversion to a modernist temporality of anachronism, which has itself been rendered anachronistic. If the critique of high modernism is to be oriented around the notion of a "repression of History," we must take into account that access to reality is necessarily mediated by the political unconscious; and the action of this unconscious is always a process of textualization, or narrativization. Thus if it is by way of a "political unconscious" that we have access to history, then a "repression" of *some* sort is implicit in the creation of that unconscious. All access to history is necessarily effected by way of a repression, which is at the same time a narrativization. The repression and the construction of history in the political unconscious begin to merge.

Consequently, the charge that modernism functions as a "repression of History" means nothing more than that modernism mediates history through specific narrative techniques. It is important to note the dangers of reducing history to text, but the value of invoking categories of repression or distortion to characterize undesirable reformulations of history is unclear when such repression seems to be the modality of *any* historical mediation. The question we need to ask is: What narrative of history—what *petit récit*—shall position us with respect to the avant-garde? For just as fascism seems to scramble our spatio-temporal understanding of the political to the extent that we can no longer tell left from right or progress from reaction, so the avant-garde seems to effect a similar disorientation in the cultural realm. As culture at the stage of *Selbstkritik*, the avant-garde does seem to offer a momentary stasis, a self-reflection, in which spatial and temporal trajectories become indeterminate. The question, then, is where the phenomena under analysis leave theory itself (spatio-temporally).

My reasons for returning in this conclusion to the paradigm of aestheticization emanate from a desire to understand why both cultural and political theory since the war have been preoccupied with the problematic of aesthetic incursions into the so-called political realm. It is not enough to trace the obsession of postwar theory back to the experience of the war or of fascism. Quite to the contrary, the confrontation with fascism seems, in its most interesting forms, to consist in the attempts to come to terms with a *loss* of experience—the loss, that is, not only of the war and the extermination *as* an experience, but the loss of the very possibility of *experience* itself.[29]

In a sense, of course, the movement beyond a dialectical understanding of experience will take us right back to our starting point—back to Benjamin. To the Benjamin, that is, of the "Theories of German Fascism," to the Benjamin who analyzes the German war experience and the subsequent emergence of fascism in terms of a similar loss. We stand in a historical relationship to the horrors of fascism that is not altogether dissimilar to the historical perspective of the fascists themselves upon the horrors of World War I. Benjamin argues that the loss of the war mutates historically from the original experience of losing the war into a subsequent loss of the experience of the war. Fascism, for Benjamin, would then be the historical reaction to this loss of experience, this loss of history. National Socialism names an attempt to regain experience, to sublate it as an *experience* of loss (of experience), to ontologize loss itself as the essential German experience. Losing the war— thereby losing the *experience* of the war—and then regaining the experience of loss in compensation for the loss of experience: such would be the spiral toward fascism traced in Benjamin's analysis. The implications for our own position vis-à-vis both fascism and the avant-garde must lead us to question the value of ever attempting to retrieve either experience. A utopian avant-garde and a murderous fascism must remain irretrievable.

Within the specific context of the avant-garde's relationship to fascism, my own concern in this work has not been the attempt to articulate philosophy's dilemma in the face of the loss of experience, but rather the attempt to think the fascination of the political for the aesthetic and vice versa. Benjamin's call for the "politicization of art" obliges us not to a simple subsuming of one discourse (aesthetics) under another (politics), but rather to a rethinking of the aesthetic as both discourse and metadiscourse. I wish to suggest that the "politicization of art" today *necessitates* a certain "aestheticization of politics," necessitates at the very least a recognition of the intrinsic, "aesthetic" formulation of that which we designate the political.

It is possible, I think, to differentiate the modern from the so-called postmodern by means of their respective assessments of the possibility of an "end" both of art and of history (an "end," that is, in the sense both of completion and of annihilation). The *Selbstkritik* of the avant-garde and the transhistorical historicity of the Thousand Year Reich both depend upon a notion of historical self-completion in the eventual annihilation of history. That "postmodern condition," however, which is caricatured (and which caricatures itself) as an incredulity toward metanarrative —and toward historiography as the paradigmatic metanarrative— will be less apocalyptic than either fascism or the avant-garde. Postmodernism's "end of history" (if one may use the term) would not be an end *as* history, but rather the *humiliation* of history. For it is only within the parameters of a dialectical notion of historical development that an "end of history" would be thinkable. Both fascism and the avant-garde, albeit from very different perspectives, had a sense of such an end. The false sublation of the avant-garde, no less than the demise of the Thousand Year Reich, has meant the end of the end of history.

Reference Matter

Notes

Introduction

Note on Abbreviations: All references to Marinetti will be cited—where possible—from Marinetti, *Selected Writings (SW)*. Texts not in this collection will be cited from one of the following: *Futurist Manifestos (FM)*; *Teoria e Invenzione Futurista (TI)*; *Futurismo e Fascismo (FF)*. In-text quotations will be accompanied by the abbreviation of the book title. English translations from the Italian editions are my own.

1. See P. Bürger, *Theory of the Avant-Garde*.

2. See Lyotard, *Differend: Phrases in Dispute*.

3. In "The Politics of Theory," Jameson writes: "Indeed, when we make some initial inventory of the varied cultural artifacts that might plausibly be characterized as postmodern, the temptation is to seek the 'family resemblance' of such heterogeneous styles and products, not in themselves, but in some common high modernist impulse and aesthetic against which they all, in one way or another, stand in reaction" (p. 103).

4. For a consideration of the career and ideological development of Hanns Johst, see Pfanner, *Hanns Johst*.

5. Benjamin's analysis is elaborated in "The Work of Art in the Age of Mechanical Reproduction." Perhaps the best consideration and elaboration of Benjamin's paradigm with reference to the political and aesthetic conjuncture to be examined here is to be found in R. Berman, "Aestheticization of Politics."

6. The study of patriarchy as an analytic category on fascism is an interesting addition to this analysis. See J. Benjamin, "Authority and the Family Revisited"; Koonz, *Mothers in the Fatherland*; and Macchiochi, *Jungfrauen, Mütter und ein Führer*. Of course, perhaps the most useful recent research in this area is Theweleit's *Male Fantasies*.

7. Marx and Engels, "Manifesto of the Communist Party."

8. See Bloch, "Non-Synchronism and the Obligation to Its Dialectics."

9. While it might be argued that fascism itself—specifically, National Socialism—attempts to invoke that moment of plenitude, I will take issue (in the final chapter) with Lyotard's attempt, on this basis, to effect a recuperation of the avant-garde from the clutches of fascism.

10. On the topic of the political implications of the construction of the modernist canon, see Hermand, "Das Konzept 'Avantgarde.'"

11. I feel I must legitimate the choice of Marinetti as a means to critically focus on Fascist Modernism, less because of what Marinetti will lead me to say about modernism than as a result of what he *will not* lead me to say about fascism. Specifically, concentrating on the Italian context has led me to neglect the question of anti-Semitism in the analysis of fascism. Italian Fascism was not as resolutely or consistently anti-Semitic as German National Socialism. I do not, however, wish to excuse the failure to confront the question of anti-Semitism as the unfortunate by-product of certain literary-historical choices. On the contrary, if I spoke in the opening pages of my discomfort at dealing with fascism as a form of aestheticization, it was primarily the impossibility of speaking of genocide in such terms that led me to make those limiting choices in the first place. When, in chapter 5, I deal with Marinetti's paradigmatic presentation of the Futurist aesthetic in the burning of bodies, the historical and political resonance of that aesthetic must be all too clear. Thus, while I can conceive of extending the analysis of aestheticization into a consideration of genocide, the enormity of the question obliges me to hold in reserve the potentially simplistic and ahistorical explicative claims implicit in any such analysis.

12. This development is most clear in manifestos in which Marinetti explicitly invokes the Symbolists as his "former masters," and abjures them. The influences, however, are apparent from the Founding Manifesto on.

Chapter 1

1. Typical of the spirit of the times is an article to be cited at greater length in the final chapter, Enzensberger's "The Aporia of the Avant-Garde."

2. In conclusion to his consideration of the category of autonomy and its fate in the "post-" avant-garde era, Bürger's *Theory* concludes that: "Given the experience of the false sublation of autonomy, one will need to ask whether a sublation of the autonomy status can be desirable at all, whether the distance between art and the praxis of life is not requisite for that free space within which alternatives to what exists become conceivable" (p. 54).

3. On the category of "the new," see Bürger's critique of Adorno in *Theory*: "If we sought to understand a change in the means of artistic representation, the category of the new would be applicable. But since the historical avant-garde movements cause a break with tradition and a subsequent change in the representational system, the category is not suitable for a description of how things are" (pp. 62–63).

4. It has also been argued quite convincingly that the rhetorical opposition between "aestheticization" and "politicization" is *not* intended to be so clear-cut. See Alexander Garcia-Düttmann, "Tradition and Destruction."

5. It is this insistence upon radical "*Selbstkritik*" as opposed to a limited "system-immanent" critique that differentiates Bürger's *Theory of the Avant-Garde* from other such works and allows him to locate both Adorno and Lukács—otherwise antagonists in the modernism debate—within the same ideological and institutional space.

6. See Hermand, "Das Konzept 'Avant-Garde.'" A variation on this history of canon formation is provided by P. Bürger, "Vorbemerkung," *Postmoderne*, pp. 7–12. Bürger argues that the subsequent canonization of a modernism built on categories of formal asceticism actually runs counter to the project of the avant-garde itself and represents a form of anti-avant-garde. For an examination of the phenomenon of postwar canon formation—albeit from an opposing political slant—see Kenner, "The Making of the Modernist Canon."

7. See Jameson, *Fables of Aggression*. The best consideration of Fascist Modernism outside the Anglo-American canon is the analysis of French Fascist Modernists in Kaplan, *Reproductions of Banality*.

8. Among the most important analyses for understanding the phenomenon of political reaction in the English context are Kenner, *The Pound Era*; Dasenbrock, *The Literary Vorticism of Ezra Pound and Wyndham Lewis: Towards the Condition of Painting*; Casillo, *The Genealogy of Demons: Anti-Semitism, Fascism and the Myths of Ezra Pound*; Chace, *The Political Identities of Ezra Pound and T. S. Eliot*.

9. Jameson, *The Prison-House of Language*, p. 45.

10. Jameson, *The Political Unconscious*, p. 280.

11. Jameson's invocation of the category of "heterogeneity" as a resistance to the spatializing reaction of high modernism is particularly curious when examined in the light of Fascist Modernism. For it is precisely the incorporation of the heterogeneous that Bataille's analysis of fascism takes as constitutive in fascist ideology. See Bataille, "The Psychological Structure of Fascism."

12. For an application of politically coded models of spatiality and temporality to the criticism of modernism, see Lodge, *Modes of Modern Writing*.

13. In this sense, it is still possible to locate Jameson within the broad tradition of formalist readings traceable back to Josef Frank's seminal analysis of modernist spatialization. See Frank, "Spatial Form."

14. "Artistic means is undoubtedly the most general category by which works of art can be described. But that the various techniques and procedures can be *recognized* as artistic means has been possible only since the historical avant-garde movements" (P. Bürger, *Theory*, p. 18).

15. This particular position is taken in Libby, "Conceptual Space, the Politics of Modernism." Libby proposes, in opposition to the time-space / progressive-reactionary equation, that it is not only impossible to disentangle time and space, but impossible also to valorize that crude opposition in any consistent sense: "The relation between aesthetic shape and political implication is too complex and variable to be described so reductively; eventually, I will argue that to the extent (after the popularization of Einstein's visions) that 'spatial' can be distinguished from 'temporal' form, it can be seen as supportive of liberal or progressive political visions" (p. 12).

16. Irigaray, *This Sex Which Is Not One*, p. 80.

17. In his introduction to Bürger's *Theory*, Jochen Schulte-Sasse cites, as just two examples of the confusion of modernism and avant-garde in Anglo-American scholarship, Weightman, *The Concept of the Avant-Garde: Explorations in Modernism*, and Howe, *Decline of the New*.

18. Calinescu, *Faces of Modernity*, p. 96. (Subsequently revised and enlarged

as *Five Faces of Modernity: Modernism, Avant-Garde, Decadence, Kitsch, Post-modernism.*) All quotations here are from the earlier text.

19. Koselleck, "Neuzeit," p. 279.

20. Bloch's notion of nonsynchronism will be invoked at several points in this work—most evidently, in the final chapter—as a way of expanding Bürger's analysis of the avant-garde to the broader political spectrum.

21. Herf, *Reactionary Modernism*, p. 1.

Chapter 2

1. I think Bürger is guilty of such an oversimplification in a rather more troubling sense. The general thesis on the separation of art and life and the subsequent attempt of the avant-garde to reintegrate the two not only rests upon a simplistic view of the nineteenth century but also legitimates a certain philosophical paradigm in which the avant-garde marks a moment of historical presence.

2. Thus in Germany, for example, *Grimms Deutsches Wörterbuch* of 1889 notes the first use—twenty years earlier—of the term *"Neuzeit"* as a compound noun describing the present not only as something that follows upon the past, but as something qualitatively different from the past. *Grimms Deutsches Wörterbuch*, vol. 7 (Leipzig, 1889), p. 689, in Koselleck, " 'Neuzeit.' "

3. Lukács develops this position in various works, such as *Studies in European Realism*; *Realism in Our Time: Literature and the Class Struggle*; *Writer and Critic and Other Essays*; and *Essays in Realism*.

4. In *Le avanguardie artistiche del Novecento*, De Micheli attempts to retain a more programmatic model of historical development, arguing that in the post-Napoleonic period the collaboration of cultural and political avant-gardes was close. In keeping with the "formalist" tradition, but disregarding the formalist conflation of political and formal progressiveness, he traces the origins of the avant-garde proper back to that group of *"déclassés,"* epitomized by Baudelaire, for whom direct political action no longer seemed feasible.

5. The following accounts of the emergence of the cultural avant-garde in the nineteenth century are drawn in large part from Egbert, "The Idea of Avant-Garde in Art and Politics"; Calinescu, *Faces*; and Poggioli, *Theory*.

6. This position is ably argued by Lohner, "Die Problematik des Begriffes der Avantgarde."

7. See Henri Saint-Simon, "The Artist, the Scientist and the Industrial."

8. See, for example, Crispolti, "Appunti sui materiali riguardanti rapporti tra Futurismo e Fascismo"; De Felice, *Mussolini il Rivoluzionario*; De Micheli, *La matrice ideologico-letteraria dell'eversione fascista*; Lista, "Marinetti et les anarcho-syndicalistes"; Mariani, *Il primo Marinetti*; and Schilirò, *Dall'anarchia all'accademia*.

9. Sauer, "National Socialism: Totalitarianism or Fascism?" The startling claim that the Nazis rather than the socialist labor movement trod the "true revolutionary way" also implies a critique of the avant-garde. As a movement of *déclassés* Nazism asserts social *ressentiment* in the political sphere, whereas the formation of a subculture institutionalizes and subjugates that *ressentiment* as a structural possibility of the status quo. Of course, by referring to socialism

as a "subculture" Sauer overlooks the fact that socialism also asserts itself in the political sphere.

10. For a convincing presentation of an argument based on this idea see R. Berman, *The Rise of the German Novel.*

11. Bürger isolates three major historical periods—the sacral, the courtly, and the bourgeois—on the basis of the categories of purpose, mode of production, and mode of reception. These periodizations are by no means absolute and allow of certain anachronisms precisely because the development across categories is not synchronous. Important to note, however, is the way in which the development of the institution is a development toward individualization—not only in terms of production and reception but also in terms of the work's function as a confirmation of bourgeois notions of subjectivity. One might say, then, that in Bürger's model, the process of modernization is implicitly a process of privatization. Bürger goes on to argue that the avant-garde marks a definitive break with the institution of art as it has been developed throughout these three periods. Avant-garde artists effect this break not by proposing a new development *within* the terms of the categories of production, consumption and function, but by questioning the validity of the categories themselves. This is the shift from "system-immanent" critique to "*Selbstkritik.*"

12. Within German studies, a considerable body of work has been dedicated to the reformulation and historicization of the notion of the autonomy of art, and it is largely in the light of these studies that a model of autonomy will be reconstructed here as a means of reexamining theories of the collapse of autonomous aesthetic discourse, which is often held to be at the root of literary modernism. See, for example, P. Bürger, ed., *Zum Funktionswandel der Literatur*; Müller, ed., *Autonomie der Kunst*; Schlichting and Seiverth, "Autonomie der Kunst"; Freier, "Ästhetik und Autonomie"; Warneken, "Autonomie und Indienstnahme"; Winckler, "Entstehung und Funktion des literarischen Marktes"; Hauser, *Sozialgeschichte der Kunst und Literatur*. The autonomy question is raised with specific reference to the avant-garde in P. Bürger, *Theorie.*

13. C. Bürger, "Philosophische Ästhetik und Populärästhetik." Quotes from this essay are in my translation.

14. For an elaboration of the notion of "affirmative art," see Marcuse, "The Affirmative Character of Culture."

15. On the function of literature as a pre-form of the bourgeois political sphere and for a consideration of the shift from a "representative" to a bourgeois mediation of power, see Habermas, *Structural Transformation*; and Koselleck, *Critique and Crisis.*

16. This case is argued in Lindner, "Aufhebung der Kunst in Lebenspraxis?"

17. Bürger is convincing in his presentation of Schiller as the key figure in the political and ideological valorization of art *as* art; that is, as a discourse whose truth value is immanent and oppositional in respect both to everyday life and to reified philosophical discourse.

18. Goebel, in "'Literatur' und Aufklärung," avoids simplistic valorizations by distinguishing between *Autonomie* and *Autonomismus* as a means of ex-

plaining how political engagement and literary autonomy can coexist in the nineteenth century.

19. See Lukács, "Expressionism: Its Significance and Decline."

20. Lukács's essay provided the ideological framework for the subsequent "*Expressionismusdebatte*" which took place in the exile journal *Das Wort* in the years 1937–38 and which was concerned precisely with the implication of literary modernism in the project of political reaction. The contributions to this debate have been collected (along with other pertinent materials) in Schmitt, ed., *Die Expressionismusdebatte.* A similar but lesser-known debate took place at exactly the same time *within* Germany: for details, see Schonauer, "Expressionismus und Faschismus."

21. In his analysis of the origins of German fascism in the ontologizing of loss and antinomies of the war experience, Benjamin argues along similar lines. See Benjamin, "Theories of German Fascism."

22. See Bloch, "Discussing Expressionism."

23. Lukács will prove vital in any critical reading of the rise of "conservative revolutionary" ideologies. Specifically, he helps in the rereading of critical reconstructions of those ideologies, such as those offered in Mohler, *Die konservative Revolution*; and Sontheimer, *Anti-demokratisches Denken in der Weimarer Republik.* The project of recuperating a "conservative" from a fascistic form of reaction in the interwar periods is criticized in Petzold, *Wegbereiter des deutschen Faschismus.*

24. This notion of a shift in legitimation strategies and principles of discursive organization is examined in greater detail in chapter 5, which deals with Marinetti's celebration of the machine and which attempts to see in the principle of a metaphorically organized political discourse the basis of a more complex and more specific understanding of the aestheticization of political life.

Chapter 3

1. Benjamin's argument is ill-served by the translation of "*Reproduzierbarkeit*" (reproducibility) as "reproduction." Throughout the essay, he insists that it is not simply the *mediation* of a given object that he is dealing with, but rather the retroactive power of mediation in the structuration of the object itself: "For the first time in world history, mechanical reproduction emancipates the work of art from its parasitical dependence on ritual. To an ever greater degree the work of art reproduced becomes the work of art designed for reproducibility" (*Illuminations*, p. 226).

2. See Benjamin, *Understanding Brecht.*

3. P. Bürger, *Theory*, p. 27.

4. In Bürger's *Theory* the isolation of the aesthetic discourse is a precondition of its passage into "*Selbstkritik*": "The self-criticism of the social subsystem that is art can become possible only when the contents also lose their political character and art wants to be nothing other than art. This stage is reached at the end of the nineteenth century, in Aestheticism" (pp. 26–27).

5. Benjamin, *Gesammelte Schriften*, 3: 488 (my translation).

6. "In bourgeois society, it is only with aestheticism that the full unfolding of the phenomenon of art became a fact, and it is to aestheticism that the historical avant-garde movements respond" (P. Bürger, *Theory*, p. 17).

7. Bürger has been criticized for this revisionist heresy in the collection of essays edited by Lüdke.

8. This, again, is a central thesis of Bürger's *Theory*: "It is, on the other hand, a distinguishing feature of the historical avant-garde movements that they did not develop a style. There is no such thing as a dadaist or a surrealist style. What did happen is that these movements liquidated the possibility of a period style when they raised to a principle the availability of the artistic means of past periods. Not until there is universal availability does the category of artistic means become a general one" (p. 18).

9. Calinescu, *Faces*, p. 151.

10. Terms outlined by Schulte-Sasse in his introduction to the English translation: "Bürger's historical view proves, when closely examined, to be pessimistic as well. He is convinced that the avant-garde's intention of reintegrating art into life praxis cannot occur in bourgeois society, except in the form of a false sublation or overcoming of autonomous art" (Schulte-Sasse, p. xli).

11. For an explanation of this dichotomy, see the preceding chapter.

12. The assessment of Marinetti's political development is a model case in the instrumentalization of anarchism to explain some of the more compromising manifestations of the avant-garde. Anarchism seems to function in such cases as an essentially dilettantish and decadent travesty of modernism. De Maria, for example, has the following to say in his introduction to Marinetti's works: "As for the socialist element (Sorelian in its derivation, supplemented by Mazzinian influences and therefore alien in substance to Marxism) this is complicated by the presence of extremely vital anarchic and libertarian strains culled by Marinetti from the milieu of the French Symbolists, which held him back—in opposition to Fascism—from the cult of the State and bureaucratic authority" (Marinetti, *TI*; De Maria's introduction, p. xlii; my translation). The need to cite anarchist or anarcho-syndicalist precedents for Futurist cultural innovation reflects the inability of literary criticism to conceive of the cultural avant-garde as emanating from anything other than a revolutionary political impulse or to portray capitalism as anything other than an unendurable stasis.

13. "If in symbolism there was a duality of art and life, the ideal of the dandy represents neither pure art nor pure life, but rather their unification. It is a unity born of inversion, which aestheticism [*estetismo*] realized from the perspective of the aesthetic as *Vita Estetica*. It will be Art Nouveau [*Liberty*]—more homogeneous with the imperialistic phase of capitalism—which attempts this unification (of art and life, art and the commodity) from the perspective of the commodity. Art Nouveau gives form to the function, beautifying the functional object. It is an affirmative beauty. It is the beauty of the new, technical beauty; it is industrial art, the ultimate in substitution. The avant-garde will reject all this, for the avant-garde is the death of art in the

bourgeois sense of the word. In the period of imperialism art can but die as art. It cannot survive in some substitute form" (Franci, *Il Sistema del Dandy*, pp. 220–21; my translation).

14. See Sontag, "Fascinating Fascism."

15. Baudelaire, "The Painter of Modern Life," p. 28.

16. Valesio, "The Beautiful Lie," pp. 173–74.

17. For a convincing interpretation of capitalism in these terms, effected through a rereading of Marx, see M. Berman, *All That Is Solid Melts Into Air*.

18. More specifically, I have in mind the treatment of Rousseau and Lévi-Strauss in Derrida, *Of Grammatology*; the periodizations offered in Foucault, *The Order of Things*; and the treatment of savage, barbarian, and civilized modes of representation in Deleuze and Guattari, *Anti-Oedipus*.

19. Deleuze and Guattari, *Anti-Oedipus*, p. 261. One might schematize the representational modes of *Anti-Oedipus* as follows:

	Savage	Barbarian	Civilized
Full Body	Earth	Despot / Urstaat	Money-Capital
Territory	Territorializes	Deterritorializes	Deterritorializes
Code	(Pre-)Coding	Over-Coding	De-Coding
Representation	Connotation / Connection	Subordination / Disjunctive	Coordination / Conjunction
System of Power	Affiliation (Group)	Filiation (Hierarchy)	Axiomatic (Diffused)

The **full body** is described by Deleuze and Guattari as a "recording surface" and is not necessarily related to the body itself. In effect, it is the key to the "code" of a given representational system, in that it offers an imaginary model of the symbolic itself as something which is *not* symbolic. In the reading of Marinetti's imperialism that follows, I understand Deleuze and Guattari's notion of **territory** somewhat literally: not simply as the system (or "code") of meaning, but as its material representability. However, it should be noted that the categories of "territorialization" and "deterritorialization" are themselves relativized by Deleuze and Guattari's assertion that "it may be all but impossible to distinguish deterritorialization from reterritorialization, since they are mutually enmeshed, or like opposite faces of one and the same process" (*Anti-Oedipus*, p. 258).

20. "While de-coding doubtless means understanding and translating a code, it also means destroying the code as such, assigning it archaic, folkloric or residual function" (*Anti-Oedipus*, p. 245).

21. Marinetti, "Primo manifesto politico futurista per le elezioni generali del 1909," *FF*, p. 22.

22. Marinetti, *FF*, p. 74.

23. Marinetti, *SW*, p. 87.

Chapter 4

1. Egbert, "The Idea of Avant-Garde," p. 344.

2. Mallarmé, "Crisis in Poetry," pp. 42–43.

3. Marinetti, *SW*, p. 67. Subsequent citations in this chapter will be made in text as *SW*.

4. Marinetti, "Trieste, nostra bella polveriera," *FF*, p. 27. Subsequent citations in this chapter will be made in text as *FF*.

5. Marinetti, "Destruction of Syntax—Imagination without Strings—Words-in-Freedom," *FM*, p. 105. Subsequent citations in this chapter will be made in text as *FM*.

6. See, for example, Schnapp, "Politics and Poetics in Marinetti's *Zang Tumb Tuuum*."

7. In Derrida, *Dissemination*, pp. 172–285.

8. Bürger insists that the status of the avant-garde "manifestation" as opposed to the neo–avant-garde "work" constitutes one of its defining moments.

9. This argument is most coherently argued in Perloff, *The Futurist Moment*. This vein of analysis is further exemplified by several journal editions dedicated to the question of the manifesto: *Etudes littéraires* 11, 2 (1978); *Littérature* 39 (1980); and *Etudes françaises* 16, 3–4 (1980).

10. See, for example, Marinetti, "Dynamic and Synoptic Declamation," *SW*, pp. 142–47.

Chapter 5

1. De Maria, "Introduzione," *TI*, p. xlv (my translation).

2. This position is belied by more differentiated studies such as Peschken, "Klassizistische und ästhetizistische Tendenzen in der Literatur der faschistischen Periode," which shows how the inheritance of the nineteenth century actually allows the coexistence of disparate elements—both "*völkisch*" and classicizing—within Nazi aesthetics. This fundamental disparity is developed even further in Schäfer, *Das gespaltene Bewußtsein*, where it is argued at the level of mass culture that Nazism actually permitted of a real cultural pluralism.

3. The political essays collected in *Futurismo e Fascismo* manifest a consistent concern with the *dynamics* of government. Marinetti attempts to develop a model of democracy based not upon the reining in of oppositional forces but upon the unleashing of antagonistic powers and the construction of confrontation even at the level of government.

4. Kant, *Perpetual Peace*, pp. 29–40.

5. Marinetti, "Multiplied Man and the Reign of the Machine," *SW*, pp. 90–93.

6. **"As an autonomous realm of pure functionality the bourgeois State appears to be the objectively adequate and essential projection of the technical forces of reproduction—of the machine**. 'One could even see it,' according to Schmitt, 'as the first product of the technical age . . . as the *machina machinarum*.' This work of art—based on a contract resulting from a fear of the anarchic state of nature—is, historically, not only 'the pre-condition for the subsequent technical and industrial era' but also a typical—a prototypical, even—work of the new technical age" (Jürgens, "Bemerkungen zur Ästhetisierung der Politik," p. 16). Jürgens deals specifically with Carl Schmitt's *Der Leviathan in der Staatslehre des Thomas Hobbes*. Jürgens's citation is from the 1938 Hamburg edition, p. 60.

7. Marinetti, "Concezione futurista della Democrazia," *FF*, pp. 124–27.

8. See, for example, Nazzaro, *Introduzione al Futurismo*.

9. Lewis, originally extremely receptive to the ideas of Marinetti, later has the following to say: "AUTOMOBILISM (Marinettism) bores us, We don't want to go about making a hullo-bulloo about motor cars, any more than about knives and forks, elephants or gas pipes. . . . The futurist is a sensational and sentimental mixture of the aesthete of 1890 and the realist of 1870" ("Long Live the Vortex," p. 8).

10. Marinetti, "Il Futurismo mondiale—Conferenza di Marinetti alla Sorbona." Quoted in De Maria, "Introduzione," *TI*, p. xxix (my translation).

11. De Maria, "Introduzione," *TI*, p. lxiii (my translation).

12. Marinetti, *SW*, pp. 45–54; and *SW*, pp. 72–75, respectively.

13. See Finter, *Semiotik des Avantgardetextes*, where, in a comment upon fascist ceremonial, she makes the following comment which might equally well apply to the textual practice of Marinetti and the Futurists: "Fascist discourse does not bind by means of the more or less latent sexual symbols, but rather by means of the relationships which these historically changing symbols enter into with the symbols of power. It does not produce any replacement for satisfaction but makes a much more subtle appeal to the experience of the relationship of eroticism and power" (p. 80, my translation).

14. Marx and Engels, "Manifesto of the Communist Party," p. 338.

Chapter 6

1. Enzensberger, "Aporias," p. 41.

2. Lacoue-Labarthe, *Heidegger, Art and Politics*, p. 61.

3. Jameson approaches this issue from one side when he argues in *The Political Unconscious* "that history is *not* a text, not a narrative, master or otherwise, but that, as an absent cause, it is inaccessible to us except in textual form, and that our approach to it and to the Real itself necessarily passes through its prior textualization, its narrativization in the political unconscious" (p. 35). In this chapter, I approach the problem from a complementary position, stressing not the ideological construction of the Real, but the reality of ideology itself; not the mediation of forces of production by representation, but the productive value of representation itself.

4. See note 1, chapter 3, above. Subsequent references to Benjamin in this chapter will be made in text.

5. "The very definition of the real becomes that of which it is possible to give an exact reproduction. . . . At the limit of this process of reproducibility, the real is not only what can be reproduced but that which is always already reproduced: the *hyperreal*" (Baudrillard, *Simulations*, p. 11).

6. One of the most detailed and complex accounts of the "theatrical" paradigm in the construction of a metaphysics is to be found in Lyotard, *Des dispositifs pulsionnels*.

7. Benjamin, in the body of the text, presents this phenomenon as extrinsic to the technological apparatus itself, as a compensatory effect of the system of distribution. "The film responds to the shrivelling of the aura with an artificial build-up of the 'personality' outside the studio. The cult of the movie star,

fostered by the money of the film industry, preserves not the unique aura of the person, but the 'spell of the personality,' the phony spell of a commodity" (*Illuminations*, p. 233). The idea of an "artificial build-up of the 'personality'" is particularly problematic in an essay whose analysis of reproducibility radically questions the division of original and artifice.

8. One would arrive, thereby, at a critique of the "Society of the Spectacle" as a form of ideological distortion, at Debord's assertion that "in societies where modern conditions of production prevail, all of life presents itself as an immense accumulation of *spectacles*. Everything that was directly lived has moved away into a representation" (Debord, *Society of the Spectacle*, p. 1).

9. Stollmann, "Fascist Politics as a Total Work of Art," p. 59.

10. "Mankind, which in Homer's time was an object of contemplation for the Olympian gods, is now one for itself. Its self-alienation has reached such a degree that it can experience its own destruction as an aesthetic pleasure of the first order" (*Illuminations*, p. 244).

11. Brecht, "Über die Theatralik des Faschismus," p. 563.

12. Habermas makes no attempt to characterize a public sphere in fascism and indeed exempts it from the terms of his analysis. The rudiments of an approach to the fascist public sphere are sketched out in P. Brückner et al., "Perspectives on the Fascist Public Sphere." Here, Oskar Negt—the theorist who attempts to theorize precisely those alternative forms of the public sphere left unarticulated in Habermas's essentially bourgeois, liberal model—characterizes the fascist public sphere: "If I would have to define the public sphere in fascism according to the construct which we worked out in our book *Öffentlichkeit und Erfahrung*, then we are dealing with forms of a representational and demonstrative public sphere and, in any case, not with a public sphere in the transcendental sense of a mediation of politics and morality, as Kant thought of it" (p. 96). I would argue that Kant's model leaves more room for ambiguity than Negt implies, and that fascism responds to some of those ambiguities.

13. Bell, *Cultural Contradictions*, p. 48.

14. See, for example, the antibourgeois, antipublic rhetoric of the Expressionist and subsequent fascist, Hanns Johst: "Who is this *publicus* which always has the final word? This species of *homo sapiens* is a consistent danger to any culture" ("Vom Geschmack des Publikums," p. 419, my translation).

15. At the same time as fascist and protofascist dramaturges rejected traditional theatrical models, they nevertheless wished to rework the theater itself as an alternative—postpolitical—model of the public sphere. This tendency becomes apparent even in the earlier experimental works of Fascist Modernists such as Johst in Germany. For example: "In the theater we see the final place of worship of a threatened and scattered popular [*völkisch*] community, a final pedagogical possibility to save the people from the materialization of an immanent here and now [*einer rein aktuellen Zeit*]. In the living theater we experience a final asylum for popular [*völkisch*] discussion and popular edification . . . We believe in the stage, and serve it, because we hope to save the people from politics as the only possible way of achieving happiness" (Johst, "Bekenntnis zur Bühne," p. 682, my translation).

16. Benjamin, *Gesammelte Schriften*, 3: 488 (my translation).

17. A recent theorist of performance poses the question well when he asks, rhetorically, "What, at first glance, could be less close, less akin than drama and reflection? Drama demands a stage, actors, a heightened atmosphere, spectators, the roar of a crowd, the smell of the grease-paint. Reflection is at least one of the things one does with one's solitude. But to counter this opposition an anthropologist tends to think in terms not of solitary, but of plural reflection, or, much better, plural reflexivity, the ways in which a group or community seeks to portray, understand, and then act on itself. Essentially, public reflexivity takes the form of performance" (Turner, "Frame, Flow, and Reflection," p. 33). Lacoue-Labarthe reworks a similar position in an analysis of Bayreuth as a German Dionysia, concluding: "[This] does not merely mean that the work of art (tragedy, movie, drama) offers the truth of the *polis* or the State, but that the political itself is instituted and constituted (and regularly re-grounds itself) in and as work of art" (Lacoue-Labarthe, p. 64).

18. Kant, "An Answer to the Question: What Is Enlightenment?" *Perpetual Peace*, p. 41.

19. We would do well to remember, with Brecht, that "the Painter [i.e. Hitler]—in order to be able to feel more deeply—speaks as a private individual to private individuals" (Brecht, "Theatralik," my translation).

20. Benjamin, "The Author as Producer," p. 90.

21. Lacoue-Labarthe articulates a similar problem in his philosophical confrontation with fascism: "Philosophy is finished / finite [La philosophie est finie]; its limit is uncrossable. This means we can no longer—and we can only—do philosophy, possessing as we do no other language and having not the slightest notion of what 'thinking' might mean outside of 'philosophizing'" (Lacoue-Labarthe, p. 4).

22. Debord, p. 20.

23. Lyotard, "The Sublime and the Avant-Garde," p. 16. Subsequent references in this chapter will be made in text as "Sublime."

24. "In my opinion there is not the slightest room for the unpolitical man. Every German—whether he wishes it or not—is, by virtue of his birth into the German destiny, by his very existence, a representative form of Being of that Germany" (Hitler, quoted in Johst, "Begriff des Bürgers: Ein Gespräch zwischen Adolf Hitler und Hanns Johst," p. 55, my translation).

25. Benjamin, *Gesammelte Schriften*, 3: 489 (my translation).

26. See Lyotard, *The Postmodern Condition*.

27. This is where I would locate the distinction made between fascism as project and fascism as program. As project, fascism is born of the same "critical" impulses as the avant-garde, but as program it rejects them in favor of self-normalization. Thus to reject as "vulgar" the postmodernity of National Socialism as an empirical historical event is not to deny the radical postmodernity it might share with the avant-garde. Lacoue-Labarthe writes: "The distress (*Not*) which underlies the National Socialist insurrection . . . is also, and perhaps even principally, the anxiety and even the dread arising from the

acknowledged exhaustion of the modern project in which the catastrophic Being of that project stands revealed" (Lacoue-Labarthe, p. 20).

28. "Enlightenment reason meant more and other than the means-ends rationality of bureaucratic terror. It is not the Enlightenment, but its inadequate and partial incorporation into German society that should be condemned—and understood" (Herf, "Preface," p. ix).

29. What seems to be at stake—in treatments such as Lyotard's *Differend*, for example—is the movement beyond a certain dialectical notion of history, and with it a movement beyond traditional models of historical experience. For if, as Lyotard points out, quoting Hegel, experience is the "dialectical process which consciousness executes on itself," if it "endures death and in death maintains its being," we are obliged—in the light of the impossibility of "phrasing" anything so monstrous as the holocaust—to ask ourselves: "Can one still speak of experience in the case of the 'Auschwitz' model? Is that not to presuppose that the 'magical force' is intact? Is the death named (or unnamed) 'Auschwitz' thus an 'abode' where the reversal, the old paradox of the affirmation of non-Being can take place?" (Lyotard, *Differend*, p. 89).

Bibliography

Apollonio, Umbro, ed. *Futurist Manifestos*. London: Thames and Hudson, 1973.

Bataille, Georges. "The Psychological Structure of Fascism," trans. Carl Lovitt. In *Visions of Excess: Selected Writings 1927–39*, ed. Allan Stoekl. Minneapolis: University of Minnesota Press, 1985.

Baudelaire, Charles. "The Painter of Modern Life." In *The Painter of Modern Life and Other Essays*, trans. and ed. Jonathan Mayne, 1–40. London: Phaidon, 1964.

Baudrillard, Jean. *Simulations*. New York: Semiotext(e), 1983.

Bell, Daniel. *The Cultural Contradictions of Capitalism*. New York: Basic Books, 1976.

Benjamin, Jessica. "Authority and the Family Revisited: Or, a World Without Fathers?" *New German Critique* 13 (Winter, 1978): 35–57.

Benjamin, Walter. "The Author as Producer." In *Understanding Brecht*, trans. Anna Bostock, introduction by Stanley Mitchell, 85–103. London: Verso, 1983.

———. "Pariser Brief ‹1›." In *Gesammelte Schriften*, vol. 3, ed. Hella Tiedemann Bartels, 482–95. Frankfurt: Suhrkamp, 1972.

———. "Theories of German Fascism: On the Collection of Essays, *War and Warrior* edited by Ernst Jünger." Trans. Jerolf Wikoff. *New German Critique* 17 (Spring, 1979): 120–28.

———. "The Work of Art in the Age of Mechanical Reproduction." In *Illuminations*, ed. with an introduction by Hannah Arendt; trans. Harry Zohn, 219–53. New York: Harcourt, Brace and World, 1968.

Berman, Marshall. *All That Is Solid Melts Into Air: The Experience of Modernity*. New York: Simon and Schuster, 1982.

Berman, Russell A. "Aestheticization of Politics: Walter Benjamin on Fascism and the Avant-Garde." In *Modern Culture and Critical Theory*. Madison: University of Wisconsin Press, 1989.

———. *The Rise of the German Novel: Crisis and Charisma*. Cambridge, Mass.: Harvard University Press, 1986.

Bloch, Ernst. "Discussing Expressionism," trans. Rodney Livingstone. In *Aesthetics and Politics*, 16–27. London: New Left Books, 1977.

————. "Non-Synchronism and the Obligation to its Dialectics." Trans. Mark Ritter. *New German Critique* 11 (Spring, 1977): 22–38.

Brecht, Berthold. "Über die Theatralik des Faschismus." In *Gesammelte Werke*, vol. 16, 558–68. Frankfurt: Suhrkamp, 1967.

Brückner, Peter, Wilfried Gottschalch, Eberhard Knoedler-Bunte, Olav Münzberg, and Oskar Negt. "Perspectives on the Fascist Public Sphere: A Discussion with Peter Brückner, Wilfried Gottschalch, Eberhard Knoedler-Bunte, Olav Münzberg, and Oskar Negt." Trans. Ted Gundel. *New German Critique* 11 (Spring, 1977): 94–132.

Bürger, Christa. "Philosophische Ästhetik und Populärästhetik. Vorläufige Überlegungen zu den Ungleichzeitigkeiten im Prozeß der Institutionalisierung der Kunstautonomie." In *Funktionswandel*, ed. Peter Bürger, 107–22.

Bürger, Christa, and Peter Bürger, eds. *Postmoderne. Alltag, Allegorie und Avantgarde*. Frankfurt: Suhrkamp, 1987.

Bürger, Peter. *Theory of the Avant-Garde*. Trans. Michael Shaw. Minneapolis: University of Minnesota Press, 1984.

————, ed. *Zum Funktionswandel der Literatur*. Frankfurt: Suhrkamp, 1983.

Calinescu, Matei. *The Faces of Modernity: Avant-Garde, Decadence, Kitsch*. Bloomington: Indiana University Press, 1977.

————. *Five Faces of Modernity: Modernism, Avant-Garde, Decadence, Kitsch, Postmodernism*. Durham, N.C.: Duke University Press, 1987.

Casillo, Robert. *The Genealogy of Demons: Anti-Semitism, Fascism and the Myths of Ezra Pound*. Evanston, Ill.: Northwestern University Press, 1988.

Chace, William M. *The Political Identities of Ezra Pound and T. S. Eliot*. Stanford: Stanford University Press, 1973.

Crispolti, Enrico, ed. *Arte e Fascismo in Italia e in Germania*. Milan: Feltrinelli, 1974.

Dasenbrock, Reed Way. *The Literary Vorticism of Ezra Pound and Wyndham Lewis: Towards the Condition of Painting*. Baltimore: Johns Hopkins University Press, 1985.

Debord, Guy. *Society of the Spectacle*. Detroit: Black and Red, 1983.

De Felice, Renzo. *Mussolini il Rivoluzionario*. Turin: Einaudi, 1965.

Deleuze, Gilles, and Félix Guattari. *Anti-Oedipus: Capitalism and Schizophrenia*. Trans. Robert Hurley, Mark Seem, Helen R. Lane. Minneapolis: University of Minnesota Press, 1983.

————. *A Thousand Plateaus: Capitalism and Schizophrenia*. Trans. and with foreword by Brian Massumi. Minneapolis: University of Minnesota Press, 1987.

De Micheli, Mario. *Le avanguardie artistiche de novecento*. Milan: Feltrinelli, 1966.

————. *La matrice ideologico-letteraria dell'eversione fascista*. Milan: Feltrinelli, 1976.

Derrida, Jacques. *Dissemination*. Trans. and with introduction by Barbara Johnson. Chicago: University of Chicago Press, 1981.

————. *Of Grammatology*. Trans. and with introduction by Gayatri Chakravorty Spivak. Baltimore: Johns Hopkins University Press, 1976.

Egbert, Donald D. "The Idea of Avant-Garde in Art and Politics." *American Historical Review* 73, 2 (1967): 339–66.

Enzensberger, Hans-Magnus. "The Aporia of the Avant-Garde," trans. John Simon. In Michael Roloff, ed., *The Consciousness Industry: On Literature, Politics and the Media*, 16–41. New York: Continuum, 1974.

Etudes françaises 16, 3–4 (1980).

Etudes littéraires 11, 2 (1978).

Finter, Helga. *Semiotik des Avantgardetextes: Gesellschaftliche und poetische Erfahrung im italienischen Futurismus*. Stuttgart: Metzler, 1980.

Foucault, Michel. *The Order of Things: An Archaeology of the Human Sciences*. New York: Vintage, 1973.

Franci, Giovanna. *Il sistema del Dandy: Wilde, Beardsley, Beerbohm (arte e artificio nell'Inghilterra fin de siècle)*. Bologna: Patron, 1977.

Frank, Josef. "Spatial Form in Modern Literature." In *The Widening Gyre: Crisis and Mastery in Modern Literature*, 3–62. New Brunswick, N.J.: Rutgers University Press, 1963.

Freier, Hans. "Ästhetik und Autonomie. Ein Beitrag zur idealistischen Entfremdungskritik." In Bernd Lutz, ed., *Literaturwissenschaft und Sozialwissenschaften III: Deutsches Bürgertum und literarische Intelligenz 1750–1800*, 329–84. Stuttgart: Metzler, 1979.

Garcia-Düttmann, Alexander. "Tradition and Destruction: Benjamin's Politics of Language." Paper presented at the 2d Annual International Colloquium on Comparative Literature, Buffalo, N.Y., April 20, 1990.

Goebel, Gerhard. " 'Literatur' und Aufklärung." In Peter Bürger, ed., *Funktionswandel*, 79–93.

Grimm, Reinhold, and Jost Hermand, eds. *Faschismus und Avantgarde*. Königstein: Athenäum, 1980.

Habermas, Jürgen. "Modernity: An Incomplete Project," trans. Seyla Ben-Habib. In Hal Foster, ed., *The Anti-Aesthetic: Essays on Postmodern Culture*. Port Townsend, Wash.: Bay Press, 1983.

———. *The Structural Transformation of the Public Sphere: An Inquiry into a Category of Bourgeois Society*. Trans. Thomas Bürger with the assistance of Frederick Lawrence. Cambridge, Mass.: MIT Press, 1989.

Hauser, Arnold. *Sozialgeschichte der Kunst und Literatur*. Munich: Beck, 1953.

Herf, Jeffrey. *Reactionary Modernism: Technology, Culture and Politics in Weimar and the Third Reich*. Cambridge: Cambridge University Press, 1984.

Hermand, Jost. "Das Konzept 'Avantgarde.' " In Grimm and Hermand, eds., *Faschismus*, 1–19.

Hinz, Berthold, ed. *Die Dekoration der Gewalt: Kunst und Medien im Faschismus*. Gießen: Anabas, 1979.

Hobbes, Thomas. *Leviathan*. Harmondsworth: Penguin, 1968.

Horkheimer, Max. "Authority and the Family Today." In Ruth Nanda Anshen, ed., *The Family: Its Function and Destiny*, 359–74. New York: Harper, 1949.

Howe, Irving. *Decline of the New*. New York: Harcourt, Brace and World, 1970.

Irigaray, Luce. *This Sex Which Is Not One*. Trans. Catherine Porter with Carolyn Burke. Ithaca, N.Y.: Cornell University Press, 1985.

Jameson, Fredric. *Fables of Aggression: Wyndham Lewis, the Modernist as Fascist.* Berkeley: University of California Press, 1979.

———. *The Political Unconscious: Narrative as a Socially Symbolic Act.* Ithaca, N.Y.: Cornell University Press, 1981.

———. "The Politics of Theory: Ideological Positions in the Postmodernism Debate." In *The Ideologies of Theory: Essays 1971–1986.* Vol. 2, *The Syntax of History,* 103–13. Minneapolis: University of Minnesota Press, 1988.

———. *The Prison-House of Language: A Critical Account of Structuralism and Russian Formalism.* Princeton: Princeton University Press, 1972.

Johst, Hanns. "Bekenntnis zur Bühne." *Das literarische Echo* 25 (1923): 681–83.

———. *Standpunkt und Fortschritt.* (Schriften an die Nation No. 58). Oldenburg: Stalling, 1933.

———. "Vom Geschmack des Publikums." *Das literarische Echo* 19 (1916 / 17): 417–20.

Jürgens, Martin. "Bemerkungen zur Ästhetisierung der Politik." In *Ästhetik und Gewalt,* 8–37. Gütersloh: Bertelsmann Kunstverlag, 1970.

Kant, Immanuel. *Perpetual Peace and Other Essays on Politics, History and Morals.* Trans. with introduction by Ted Humphrey. Indianapolis: Hackett, 1983.

Kaplan, Alice Yaeger. *Reproductions of Banality: (Fascism, Literature, and French Intellectual Life).* Minneapolis: University of Minnesota Press, 1986.

Kenner, Hugh. "The Making of the Modernist Canon." *Chicago Review* 34, 2 (1984): 49–61.

———. *The Pound Era.* Berkeley: University of California Press, 1971.

Koonz, Claudia. *Mothers in the Fatherland: Women, the Family, and Nazi Politics.* New York: St. Martin's Press, 1987.

Koselleck, Reinhart. *Critique and Crisis: Enlightenment and the Pathogenesis of Modern Society.* Cambridge, Mass.: MIT Press, 1988.

———. "'Neuzeit': Zur Semantik moderner Bewegungsbegriffe." In Reinhart Koselleck, ed., *Studien zum Beginn der modernen Welt,* 264–99. Stuttgart: Klett-Cotta, 1977.

Lacoue-Labarthe, Philippe. *Heidegger, Art and Politics.* Trans. Chris Turner. Oxford: Blackwell, 1990.

Lepsius, M. Rainer. "Soziologische Theoreme über die Sozialstruktur der 'Moderne' und die 'Modernisierung.'" In Koselleck, *Studien,* 10–20.

Lewis, Wyndham. "Long Live the Vortex." In Wyndham Lewis, ed., *BLAST . . . Review of the Great English Vortex* 1 (1914): 7–8. Santa Barbara: Black Sparrow, 1981.

Libby, Anthony. "Conceptual Space: The Politics of Modernism." *Chicago Review* 34, 2 (1984): 11–26.

Lindner, Burkhart. "Aufhebung der Kunst in Lebenspraxis? Über die Aktualität der Auseinandersetzung mit den historischen Avantgardebewegungen." In Lüdke, ed., *"Theorie der Avantgarde,"* 72–104.

Lista, Giovanni. "Marinetti et les anarcho-syndicalistes." In Jean-Claude Marcadé, ed., *Présence de Marinetti,* 67–85. Lausanne: L'Age d'Homme, 1982.

Littérature 39 (1980).

Lodge, David. *The Modes of Modern Writing: Metaphor, Metonymy and the Typology of Modern Literature.* Ithaca, N.Y.: Cornell University Press, 1977.

Lohner, Edgar. "Die Problematik des Begriffes der Avantgarde." In Gerald Gillespie and Edgar Lohner, eds., *Herkommen und Erneuerung: Essays für Oskar Seidlin*, 26–38. Tübingen: Max Niemayer, 1976.

Lüdke, Martin W., ed. "*Theorie der Avantgarde*": *Antworten auf Peter Bürgers Bestimmung von Kunst und bürgerlicher Gesellschaft*. Frankfurt: Suhrkamp, 1976.

Lukács, Georg. *Essays in Realism*. Ed. Rodney Livingstone, trans. David Fernbach. Cambridge, Mass.: MIT Press, 1980.

——. *Realism in Our Time: Literature and the Class Struggle*. Trans. John and Necke Mander, introduction by George Steiner. New York: Harper, 1964.

——. *Studies in European Realism*. Trans. Edith Bone, introduction by Alfred Kazin. New York: Grosset and Dunlap, 1964.

——. *Writer and Critic and Other Essays*. Trans. Arthur Kahn. London: Merlin, 1970.

Lukács, Gyorgy [Georg]. *The Destruction of Reason*. London: Merlin, 1980.

Lyotard, Jean-François. *Différend: Phrases in Dispute*. Trans. Georges van den Abbeele. Minneapolis: University of Minnesota Press, 1986.

——. *Des dispositifs pulsionnels*. Paris: Union Générale d'Editions, 1973.

——. *The Postmodern Condition: A Report on Knowledge*. Trans. Geoff Bennington and Brian Massumi. Minneapolis: University of Minnesota Press, 1984.

——. "The Sublime and the Avant-Garde." Trans. Lisa Liebmann, Geoff Bennington, and Marian Hobson. *Paragraph* 6 (October, 1985): 1–18.

Macchiochi, Maria-Antonietta. *Jungfrauen, Mütter und ein Führer: Frauen im Faschismus*. Trans. Eva Moldenhauer. Berlin: Wagenbach, 1978.

Mallarmé, Stéphane. "Crisis in Poetry." In *Selected Prose, Poems, Essays and Letters*, trans. and with introduction by Bradford Cook, 34–43. Baltimore: Johns Hopkins University Press, 1956.

Marcuse, Herbert. "The Affirmative Character of Culture." In *Negations: Essays in Critical Theory*, trans. J. Shapiro, 88–133. Boston: Beacon, 1968.

Mariani, Gaetano. *Il primo Marinetti*. Florence: Le Monnier, 1970.

Marinetti, Filippo Tommaso. *Futurismo e Fascismo*. Foligno: Campitelli, 1924.

——. *Mafarka le futuriste. Roman africain*. Paris: Sansot, 1909.

——. *Selected Writings*. Ed. and with introduction by R. W. Flint. New York: Farrar, Straus and Giroux, 1971.

——. *Teoria e Invenzione Futurista*. Preface by Aldo Palazzeschi, introduction by Luciano De Maria. Verona: Mondadori, 1968.

Marx, Karl, and Friedrich Engels. "Manifesto of the Communist Party." In *Marx-Engels Reader*, ed. Robert C. Tucker, 331–62. New York: Norton, 1972.

Mohler, Armin. *Die konservative Revolution in Deutschland, 1918–1932. Ein Handbuch*. 2d ed. Darmstadt: Wissenschaftliche Buchgesellschaft, 1972.

Müller, Michael, ed. *Autonomie der Kunst: Zur Genese und Kritik einer bürgerlichen Kategorie*. Frankfurt: Suhrkamp, 1972.

Nazzaro, Battista. *Introduzione al Futurismo*. Naples: Guida, 1973.

Perloff, Marjorie. *The Futurist Moment: Avant-Garde, Avant-Guerre, and the Language of Rupture*. Chicago: University of Chicago Press, 1986.

Peschken, Bernd. "Klassizistische und ästhetizistische Tendenzen in der Literatur der faschistischen Periode." In Horst Denkler and Karl Pruumm, eds., *Die deutsche Literatur im III. Reich: Themen—Traditionen—Wirkungen*, 207–23. Stuttgart: Reclam, 1976.

Petzold, Joachim. *Wegbereiter des deutschen Faschismus. Die Jung-Konservativen in der Weimarer Republik.* 2d ed. Cologne: Pahl-Rugenstein, 1983.

Pfanner, Helmut F. *Hanns Johst: Vom Expressionismus zum Nationalsozialismus.* The Hague: Mouton, 1970.

Poggioli, Renato. *Theory of the Avant-Garde.* Trans. Gerald Fitzgerald. Cambridge, Mass.: Belknap, 1968.

Reich, Wilhelm. *The Mass Psychology of Fascism.* 3d ed. Trans. Victor R. Carfagno. New York: Farrar, Straus and Giroux, 1970.

Ross, Kristin. *The Emergence of Social Space: Rimbaud and the Paris Commune.* Minneapolis: University of Minnesota Press, 1988.

Saint-Simon, Henri. "The Artist, the Scientist and the Industrial: Dialogue, by Saint-Simon and Léon Halévy." In *Henri Saint-Simon: 1760–1825, Selected Writings*, trans. and ed. Keith Taylor, 279–88. New York: Holmes and Meyer, 1975.

Sauer, Wolfgang. "National Socialism: Totalitarianism or Fascism?" *American Historical Review* 73, 2 (1967): 404–24.

Schäfer, Hans-Dieter. *Das gespaltene Bewußtsein: Deutsche Kultur und Lebenswirklichkeit 1933–45.* 2d ed. Munich: Carl Hanser, 1982.

Schilirò, Vincenzo. *Dall'anarchia all'accademia. Note sul Futurismo.* Palermo: La Tradizione, 1932.

Schlichting, H-B., and A. Seiverth. "Autonomie der Kunst." In *Ästhetik und Kommunikation* 12 (1973): 94 ff.

Schmitt, Carl. *Der Leviathan in der Staatslehre des Thomas Hobbes. Sinn und Fehlschlag eines politischen Symbols.* Cologne: Hohenheim, 1982.

Schmitt, Hans-Jürgen, ed. *Die Expressionismusdebatte: Materialien zu einer marxistischen Realismuskonzeption.* Frankfurt: Suhrkamp, 1973.

Schnapp, Jeffrey. "Politics and Poetics in Marinetti's *Zang Tumb Tuuum.*" *Stanford Italian Review* 5, 1 (1985): 75–92.

Schonauer, Franz. "Expressionismus und Faschismus: Eine Diskussion aus dem Jahre 1938." *Literatur und Kritik* 7 (1966): 44–53 and 8 (1966): 45–55.

Schulte-Sasse, Jochen. "Foreword: Theory of Modernism versus Theory of the Avant-Garde." In Bürger, *Theory of the Avant-Garde*, vii–xlvii.

Sontag, Susan. "Fascinating Fascism." In *Under the Sign of Saturn*, 73–105. New York: Farrar, Straus and Giroux, 1980.

Sontheimer, Kurt. *Anti-demokratisches Denken in der Weimarer Republik. Die politischen Ideen des deutschen Nationalismus zwischen 1918 und 1933.* Munich: Nymphenburger, 1962.

Stollmann, Rainer. "Fascist Politics as a Total Work of Art: Tendencies of the Aesthetization of Political Life in National Socialism." Trans. Ronald L. Smith. *New German Critique* 14 (Spring, 1978): 41–60.

Theweleit, Klaus. *Male Fantasies.* 2 vols. Trans. Stephen Conway (vol. 1), Erica Carter and Chris Turner (vol. 2). Minneapolis: University of Minnesota Press, 1987–89.

Turner, Victor. "Frame, Flow and Reflection: Ritual and Drama as Public Liminality." In Michael Benamou and Charles Caramello, eds., *Performance in Postmodern Culture*, 33–55. Madison, Wis.: Coda, 1977.

Valesio, Paolo. "The Beautiful Lie: Heroic Individuality and Fascism." In Thomas C. Heller, Morton Sosna, David E. Wellbery, Arnold I. Davidson, Ann Swidler and Ian Watt, eds., *Reconstructing Individualism: Autonomy, Individualism and the Self in Western Thought*, 163–83. Stanford: Stanford University Press, 1986.

Warneken, Bernd Jürgen. "Autonomie und Indienstnahme. Zu ihrer Beziehung in der Literatur der bürgerlichen Gesellschaft." In Joachim Goth, ed., *Rhetorik, Ästhetik, Ideologie—Aspekte einer kritischen Kulturwissenschaft*, 79–115. Stuttgart: Metzler, 1973.

Weightman, John. *The Concept of the Avant-Garde: Explorations in Modernism*. London: Alcove, 1973.

Winckler, Lutz. "Entstehung und Funktion des literarischen Marktes." In *Kulturwarenproduktion. Aufsätze zur Literatur- und Sprachsoziologie*, 12–75. Frankfurt: Suhrkamp, 1973.

Index

In this index an "f" after a number indicates a separate reference on the next page, and an "ff" indicates separate references on the next two pages. A continuous discussion over two or more pages is indicated by a span of page numbers, e.g., "57–59." *Passim* is used for a cluster of references in close but not consecutive sequence.

Library of Congress Cataloging-in-Publication Data

Hewitt, Andrew, 1961–
    Fascist modernism : aesthetics, politics, and the avant-garde /
Andrew Hewitt.
    p.   cm.
Includes bibliographical references and index.
ISBN 0-8047-2117-3 (hard)
1. Avant-garde (Aesthetics) 2. Marinetti, Filippo Tommaso,
1876–1944. 3. Futurism (Literary movement) 4. Fascism and art.
I. Title.
BH301.A94H49 1993
111′.85—dc20
92-23149   CIP

⊚ This book is printed on acid-free paper. It has been typeset by Tseng
Information Systems in 10/13 Galliard.